Practice and Problem Solving Workbook

PEARSON

Boston, Massachusetts   Chandler, Arizona   Glenview, Illinois   Upper Saddle River, New Jersey

ISBN-13: 978-0-13-368877-1
ISBN-10:   0-13-368877-1
12 13   V016   15 14 13

Contents

Chapter 4

Chapter 5

Not applicable for Foundations Series. May be used for enrichment.

Not applicable for Foundations Series. May be used for enrichment.

Chapter 12

*Not applicable for Foundations Series. May be used for enrichment.

1-1 Think About a Plan

Variables and Expressions

Volunteering Serena and Tyler are wrapping gift boxes at the same pace. Serena starts first, as shown in the diagram. Write an algebraic expression that represents the number of boxes Tyler will have wrapped when Serena has wrapped x boxes.

Think

1. Since Serena started first she will always have more boxes than Tyler. How many boxes did Serena wrap before Tyler started?

Plan

2. Examine the situation. What phrase in the situation could be rewritten as an algebraic symbol? What is the associated symbol?

Solve

3. When Serena has wrapped x boxes, how many boxes has Tyler wrapped?

4. Could this situation be expressed in another manner? Explain and give an example to prove your point.

1-1

Practice

Form G

Variables and Expressions

Write an algebraic expression for each word phrase.

1. 10 less than x

2. 5 more than d

3. 7 minus f

4. the sum of 11 and k

5. x multiplied by 6

6. a number t divided by 3

7. one fourth of a number n

8. the product of 2.5 and a number t

9. the quotient of 15 and y

10. a number q tripled

11. 3 plus the product of 2 and h

12. 3 less than the quotient of 20 and x

Write a word phrase for each algebraic expression.

13. $n + 6$

14. $5 - c$

15. $11.5 + y$

16. $\frac{x}{4} - 17$

17. $3x + 10$

18. $10x + 7z$

Write a rule in words and as an algebraic expression to model the relationship in each table.

19. The local video store charges a monthly membership fee of \$5 and \$2.25 per video.

Videos (v)	Cost (c)
1	\$7.25
2	\$9.50
3	\$11.75

1-1 Practice (continued) Form G

Variables and Expressions

20. Dorothy gets paid to walk her neighbor's dog. For every week that she walks the dog, she earns $10.

Weeks (*w*)	Pay (*p*)
4	$40.00
5	$50.00
6	$60.00

Write an algebraic expression for each word phrase.

21. 8 minus the quotient of 15 and *y*

22. a number *q* tripled plus *z* doubled

23. the product of 8 and *z* plus the product of 6.5 and *y*

24. the quotient of 5 plus *d* and 12 minus *w*

25. Error Analysis A student writes $5y \cdot 3$ to model the relationship *the sum of 5y and 3*. Explain the error.

26. Error Analysis A student writes *the difference between 15 and the product of 5 and y* to describe the expression $5y - 15$. Explain the error.

27. Jake is trying to mail a package to his grandmother. He already has *s* stamps on the package. The postal worker tells him that he's going to have to double the number of stamps on the package and then add 3 more. Write an algebraic expression that represents the number of stamps that Jake will have to put on the package.

1-1 Standardized Test Prep

Variables and Expressions

Multiple Choice

For Exercises 1–7, choose the correct letter.

1. The word *minus* corresponds to which symbol?

   A. $+$ **B.** $-$ **C.** $\div$ **D.** $\times$

2. The phrase *product* corresponds to which symbol?

   F. $\times$ **G.** $+$ **H.** $-$ **I.** $\div$

3. The word *plus* corresponds to which symbol?

   A. $-$ **B.** $+$ **C.** $<$ **D.** $\div$

4. What is an algebraic expression for the word phrase *10 more than a number f?*

   F. $10 - f$ **G.** $\dfrac{10}{f}$ **H.** $10 \times f$ **I.** $f + 10$

5. What is an algebraic expression for the word phrase *the product of 11 and a number s?*

   A. $\dfrac{11}{s}$ **B.** $11 \times s$ **C.** $11 + s$ **D.** $11 - s$

6. Hannah and Tim collect stamps. Tim is bringing his stamps to Hannah's house so that they can compare. Hannah has 60 stamps. Which expression represents the total number of stamps that they will have if *t* represents the number of stamps Tim has?

   F. $60 \times t$ **G.** $60 \div t$ **H.** $60 + t$ **I.** $60 - t$

7. Hershel's bakery sells donuts by the box. There are *d* donuts in each box. Beverly is going to buy 10 boxes for a class field trip. Which expression represents the total number of donuts that Beverly is going to get for her field trip?

   A. $10 \times d$ **B.** $10 \div d$ **C.** $10 - d$ **D.** $10 + d$

Short Response

8. There are 200 people interested in playing in a basketball league. The leaders of the league are going to divide all of the people into *n* teams. What algebraic expression represents the number of players on each team?

1-2   Think About a Plan

Order of Operations and Evaluating Expressions

Salary You earn $10 for each hour you work for a canoe rental shop. Write an expression for your salary for working h hours. Make a table to find how much you earn for working 10, 20, 30, and 40 hours.

Think

1. What word or phrase indicates the operation that should be used to help you solve this problem?

Plan

2. Using your response from Exercise 1, write an expression that will tell you how much you earn for every h hours you work.

Solve

3. Use your expression from Exercise 2 to find the amount that you will earn for working 10, 20, 30, and 40 hours.

4. Make a table summarizing your results.

1-2 Practice

Form G

Order of Operations and Evaluating Expressions

Simplify each expression.

1. 4^2

2. 5^3

3. 1^{16}

4. $\left(\frac{5}{6}\right)^2$

5. $(1 + 3)^2$

6. $(0.1)^3$

7. $5 + 3(2)$

8. $\left(\frac{16}{2}\right) - 4(5)$

9. $4^4(5) + 3(11)$

10. $17(2) - 4^2$

11. $\left(\frac{20}{5}\right)^3 - 10(3)^2$

12. $\left(\frac{27 - 12}{8 - 3}\right)^3$

13. $(4(5))^3$

14. $2^5 - 4^2 \div 2^2$

15. $\left(\frac{3(6)}{17 - 5}\right)^4$

Evaluate each expression for $s = 2$ and $t = 5$.

16. $s + 6$

17. $5 - t$

18. $11.5 + s^2$

19. $\frac{s^4}{4} - 17$

20. $3(t)^3 + 10$

21. $s^3 + t^2$

22. $-4(s)^2 + t^3 \div 5$

23. $\left(\frac{s + 2}{5t^2}\right)^2$

24. $\left(\frac{3s(3)}{11 - 5(t)}\right)^2$

25. Every weekend, Morgan buys interesting clothes at her local thrift store and then resells them on an auction website. If she brings $150.00 and spends s, write an expression for how much change she has. Evaluate your expression for $s = \$27.13$ and $s = \$55.14$.

1-2 Practice (continued) Form G

Order of Operations and Evaluating Expressions

26. A bike rider is traveling at a speed of 15 feet per second. Write an expression for the distance the rider has traveled after s seconds. Make a table that records the distance for 3.0, 5.8, 11.1, and 14.0 seconds.

Simplify each expression.

27. $4[(12 + 5) - 4^4]$

28. $3[(4 - 6)^2 + 7]^2$

29. $2.5[13 - \left(\frac{36}{6}\right)^2]$

30. $[(48 \div 8)^3 - 7]^3$

31. $\left(\frac{4(-4)(3)}{11 - 5(1)}\right)^3$

32. $4[11 - (55 - 3^5) \div 3]$

33. a. If the tax that you pay when you purchase an item is 12% of the sale price, write an expression that gives the tax on the item with a price p. Write another expression that gives the total price of the item, including tax.

b. What operations are involved in the expressions you wrote?

c. Determine the total price, including tax, of an item that costs $75.

d. Explain how the order of operations helped you solve this problem.

34. The cost to rent a hall for school functions is $60 per hour. Write an expression for the cost of renting the hall for h hours. Make a table to find how much it will cost to rent the hall for 2, 6, 8, and 10 hours.

Evaluate each expression for the given values of the variables.

35. $4(c + 5) - f^4$; $c = -1, f = 4$

36. $-3[(w - 6)^2 + x]^2$; $w = 5$, $x = 6$

37. $3.5[h^3 - \left(\frac{3j}{6}\right)^2]$; $h = 3, j = -4$

38. $x[y^2 - (55 - y^5) \div 3]$; $x = -6$, $y = 6$

1-2 Standardized Test Prep

Order of Operations and Evaluating Expressions

Gridded Response

Solve each exercise and enter your answer on the grid provided.
Round your answers to the nearest hundredth if necessary.

1. What is the simplified form of $(3.2)^4$?

2. What is the simplified form of $(6^2 + 4) - 15$?

3. What is the simplified form of $4 \times 6^2 \div 3 + 7$?

4. What is the value of $-4d^2 + 15d^2 \div 5$ for $d = 1$?

5. What is the value of $(5x^2)^3 + 16y \div 4y$ for $x = 2$ and $y = 3$?

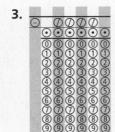 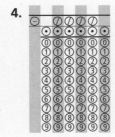

1-3

Think About a Plan

Real Numbers and the Number Line

Home Improvement If you lean a ladder against a wall, the length of the ladder should be $\sqrt{(x)^2 + (4x)^2}$ ft to be considered safe. The distance x is how far the ladder's base is from the wall. Estimate the desired length of the ladder when the base is positioned 5 ft from the wall. Round your answer to the nearest tenth.

Think

1. What does x represent in the given expression? What value is given for x?

Plan

2. What is the expression when the given value is substituted for x?

3. How do you simplify the expression under the square root symbol?

4. What is the value of the expression under the square root symbol? Is this number a perfect square?

Solve

5. What is an estimate for the desired length of the ladder? Round your answer to the nearest tenth.

1-3 Practice

Form G

Real Numbers and the Number Line

Simplify each expression.

1. $\sqrt{4}$

2. $\sqrt{36}$

3. $\sqrt{25}$

4. $\sqrt{81}$

5. $\sqrt{121}$

6. $\sqrt{169}$

7. $\sqrt{625}$

8. $\sqrt{225}$

9. $\sqrt{\frac{64}{9}}$

10. $\sqrt{\frac{25}{81}}$

11. $\sqrt{\frac{225}{169}}$

12. $\sqrt{\frac{1}{625}}$

13. $\sqrt{0.64}$

14. $\sqrt{0.81}$

15. $\sqrt{6.25}$

Estimate the square root. Round to the nearest integer.

16. $\sqrt{10}$

17. $\sqrt{15}$

18. $\sqrt{38}$

19. $\sqrt{50}$

20. $\sqrt{16.8}$

21. $\sqrt{37.5}$

22. $\sqrt{67.5}$

23. $\sqrt{81.49}$

24. $\sqrt{121.86}$

Find the approximate side length of each square figure to the nearest whole unit.

25. a rug with an area of 64 ft^2

26. an exercise mat that is 6.25 m^2

27. a plate that is 49 cm^2

1-3 Practice (continued) Form G

Real Numbers and the Number Line

Name the subset(s) of the real numbers to which each number belongs.

28. $\frac{12}{18}$ **29.** -5 **30.** π **31.** $\sqrt{2}$

32. 5564   **33.** $\sqrt{13}$ **34.** $-\frac{4}{3}$ **35.** $\sqrt{61}$

Compare the numbers in each exercise using an inequality symbol.

36. $\sqrt{25}, \sqrt{64}$ **37.** $\frac{4}{5}, \sqrt{1.3}$ **38.** $\pi, \frac{19}{6}$

39. $\sqrt{81}, -\sqrt{121}$ **40.** $\frac{27}{17}, 1.7781356$ **41.** $-\frac{14}{15}, \sqrt{0.8711}$

Order the numbers from least to greatest.

42. $1.875, \sqrt{64}, -\sqrt{121}$ **43.** $\sqrt{0.8711}, \frac{4}{5}, \sqrt{1.3}$ **44.** $8.775, \sqrt{67.4698}, \frac{64.56}{8.477}$

45. $-\frac{14}{15}, 5.587, \sqrt{81}$ **46.** $\frac{100}{22}, \sqrt{25}, \frac{27}{17}$ **47.** $\pi, \sqrt{10.5625}, -\frac{15}{5.8}$

48. Marsha, Josh, and Tyler are comparing how fast they can type. Marsha types 125 words in 7.5 minutes. Josh types 65 words in 3 minutes. Tyler types 400 words in 28 minutes. Order the students according to who can type the fastest.

1-3 Standardized Test Prep

Real Numbers and the Number Line

Multiple Choice

For Exercises 1–6, choose the correct letter.

1. To which subset of the real numbers does -18 not belong?
   A. irrational   **B.** rational   **C.** integer   **D.** negative integers

2. To which subset of the real numbers does $\sqrt{2}$ belong?
   F. irrational   **G.** rational   **H.** integer   **I.** whole

3. You can tell that π is an irrational number because it has a what?
   A. non-repeating decimal   **C.** repeating decimal
   B. non-terminating decimal   **D.** non-repeating and a non-terminating decimal

4. What is $\sqrt{324}$?
   F. 15   **G.** 18   **H.** 19   **I.** 24

5. What is $\sqrt{196}$?
   A. 14   **B.** 0   **C.** 4   **D.** 19

6. What is $\sqrt{36x^6y^4}$?
   F. $6x^6y^4$ **G.** $6x^3y^2$ **H.** $18x^3y^2$ **I.** $24x^6y^4$

Short Response

7. Why is 8.8 classified as a rational number?

1-4 Think About a Plan

Properties of Real Numbers

Travel It is 235 mi from Tulsa to Dallas. It is 390 mi from Dallas to Houston.
  a. What is the total distance of a trip from Tulsa to Dallas to Houston?
  b. What is the total distance from Houston to Dallas to Tulsa?
  c. Explain how you can tell whether the distances described in parts (a) and (b) are equal by using reasoning.

Think

1. What operation(s) will you use to solve the problem?

2. Which of the properties of real numbers involve the operations identified in part (a)?

Plan

3. Write expressions that can be simplified to solve parts (a) and (b).

4. How are the two expressions similar? How are those similarities related to the situation as described?

5. How are the expressions different? How are those differences related to the situation as described?

Solve

6. Find the total distances asked for in parts (a) and (b). What do you notice about the answers?

7. Which of the properties of real numbers best explains your results?

8. Discuss how that property explains your results.

1-4 Practice

Form G

Properties of Real Numbers

Name the property that each statement illustrates.

1. $12 + 917 = 917 + 12$

2. $74.5 \cdot 0 = 0$

3. $35 \cdot x = x \cdot 35$

4. $3 \cdot (-1 \cdot p) = 3 \cdot (-p)$

5. $m + 0 = m$

6. $53.7 \cdot 1 = 53.7$

Use mental math to simplify each expression.

7. $36 + 12 + 4$

8. $19.2 + 0.6 + 12.4 + 0.8$

9. $2 \cdot 16 \cdot 10 \cdot 5$

10. $12 \cdot 18 \cdot 0 \cdot 17$

Simplify each expression. Justify each step.

11. $6 + (8x + 12)$

12. $5(16p)$

13. $(2 + 7m) + 5$

14. $\frac{12st}{4t}$

Tell whether the expressions in each pair are equivalent.

15. $7x$ and $7x \cdot 1$

16. $4 + 6 + x$ and $4 \cdot x \cdot 6$

17. $(12 - 7) + x$ and $5x$

18. $p(4 - 4)$ and 0

19. $\frac{24xy}{2x}$ and $12y$

20. $\frac{27m}{(3 + 9 - 12)}$ and $27m$

21. You have prepared 42 mL of distilled water, 18 mL of vinegar and 47 mL of salt water for an experiment.
   a. How many milliliters of solution will you have if you first pour the distilled water, then the salt water, and finally the vinegar into your beaker?
   b. How many milliliters of solution will you have if you first pour the salt water, then the vinegar, and finally the distilled water into your beaker?
   c. Explain why the amounts described in parts (a) and (b) are equal.

1-4 Practice (continued) Form G
Properties of Real Numbers

Use deductive reasoning to tell whether each statement is *true* or *false*. If it is false, give a counterexample.

22. For all real numbers a and b, $a - b = -b + a$.

23. For all real numbers p, q and r, $p - q - r = p - r - q$.

24. For all real numbers x, y and z, $(x + y) + z = z + (x + y)$.

25. For all real numbers m and n, $\frac{m}{m} \cdot n = \frac{n}{n} \cdot m$.

26. Writing Explain why the commutative and associative properties don't hold true for subtraction and division but the identity properties do.

27. Reasoning A recipe for brownies calls for mixing one cup of sugar with two cups of flour and 4 ounces of chocolate. They are all to be mixed in a bowl before baking. Will the brownies taste different if you add the ingredients in different orders? Relate your answer to a property of real numbers.

Simplify each expression. Justify each step.

28. $(6^7)(5^3 + 2)(2 - 2)$ **29.** $(m - 16)(-7 \div -7)$

30. Open-Ended Provide examples to show the following.
  a. The associative property of addition holds true for negative integers.
  b. The commutative property of multiplication holds true for non-integers.
  c. The multiplicative property of negative one holds true regardless of the sign of the number on which the operation is performed.
  d. The commutative property of multiplication holds true if one of the factors is zero.

1-4 Standardized Test Prep

Properties of Real Numbers

Multiple Choice

For Exercises 1–5, choose the correct letter.

1. Which of the following statements is *not* always true?
   A. $a + (-b) = -b + a$
   B. $a - (-b) = (-b) - a$
   C. $(a + b) + (-c) = a + [b + (-c)]$
   D. $-(-a) = a$

2. Which pair of expressions are equivalent?
   F. $18m \cdot 0$ and 1
   G. $6 + r + 11$ and $6 \cdot r \cdot 11$
   H. $(12 - 5) + \pi$ and 7π
   I. $x(3 - 3)$ and 0

3. What property is illustrated by the equation $(8 + 2) + 7 = (2 + 8) + 7$?
   A. Commutative Property of Addition
   B. Associative Property of Addition
   C. Distributive Property
   D. Identity Property of Addition

4. Which expression is equivalent to $-a \cdot b$?
   F. $a \cdot (-b)$
   G. $b - a$
   H. $(-a)(-b)$
   I. $-a + b$

5. Which is an example of an identity property?
   A. $a \cdot 0 = 0$
   B. $x \cdot 1 = x$
   C. $(-1)x = -x$
   D. $a + b = b + a$

Short Response

6. The fact that changing the grouping of addends does not change the sum is the basis of what property of real numbers?

1-5 Think About a Plan

Adding and Subtracting Real Numbers

Meteorology Weather forecasters use a barometer to measure air pressure and make weather predictions. Suppose a standard mercury barometer reads 29.8 in. The mercury rises 0.02 in. and then falls 0.09 in. The mercury falls again 0.18 in. before rising 0.07 in. What is the final reading on the barometer?

Think

1. What operation does "rise" suggest? _____

2. What operation does "fall" suggest? _____

Plan

3. Write either *plus* or *minus* in each box so that the following represents the problem.

29.8 [   ] 0.02 [   ] 0.09 [   ] 0.18 [   ] 0.07

4. Write an expression to represent the problem.

_____

Solve

5. What is the value of the expression you wrote in Exercise 4? _____

6. What is the final reading on the barometer? _____

1-5 Practice

Form G

Adding and Subtracting Real Numbers

Use a number line to find each sum.

1. $4 + 8$

2. $-7 + 8$

3. $9 + (-4)$

4. $-6 + (-2)$

5. $-6 + 3$

6. $5 + (-10)$

7. $-7 + (-7)$

8. $9 + (-9)$

9. $-8 + 0$

Find each sum.

10. $22 + (-14)$

11. $-36 + (-13)$

12. $-15 + 17$

13. $45 + 77$

14. $19 + (-30)$

15. $-18 + (-18)$

16. $-1.5 + 6.1$

17. $-2.2 + (-16.7)$

18. $5.3 + (-7.4)$

19. $-\frac{1}{9} + \left(-\frac{5}{9}\right)$

20. $\frac{3}{4} + \left(-\frac{3}{8}\right)$

21. $-\frac{1}{5} + \frac{7}{10}$

22. Writing Explain how you would use a number line to find $6 + (-8)$.

23. Open-Ended Write an addition equation with a positive addend and a negative addend and a resulting sum of -8.

24. The Bears football team lost 7 yards and then gained 12 yards. What is the result of the two plays?

1-5

Practice (continued)   Form G

Adding and Subtracting Real Numbers

Find each difference.

25. $7 - 14$

26. $-8 - 12$

27. $-5 - (-16)$

28. $33 - (-14)$

29. $62 - 71$

30. $-25 - (-25)$

31. $1.7 - (-3.8)$

32. $-4.5 - 5.8$

33. $-3.7 - (-4.2)$

34. $-\frac{7}{8} - \left(-\frac{1}{8}\right)$

35. $\frac{2}{3} - \frac{1}{2}$

36. $\frac{4}{9} - \left(-\frac{2}{3}\right)$

Evaluate each expression for $m = -4$, $n = 5$, and $p = 1.5$.

37. $m - p$

38. $-m + n - p$

39. $n + m - p$

40. At 4:00 A.M., the temperature was $-9°$F. At noon, the temperature was $18°$F. What was the change in temperature?

41. A teacher had $57.72 in his checking account. He made a deposit of $209.54. Then he wrote a check for $72.00 and another check for $27.50. What is the new balance in his checking account?

42. A scuba diver went down 20 feet below the surface of the water. Then she dove down 3 more feet. Later, she rose 7 feet. What integer describes her depth?

43. Reasoning Without doing the calculations, determine whether $-47 - (-33)$ or $-47 + (-33)$ is greater. Explain your reasoning.

1-5 Standardized Test Prep

Adding and Subtracting Real Numbers

Multiple Choice

For Exercises 1–5, choose the correct letter.

1. Which expression is equivalent to $17 + (-15)$?

    A. $-17 + 15$ **C.** $17 - 15$

    B. $-17 - 15$ **D.** $17 + 15$

2. Which number could be placed in the square to make the equation true?

$$-5 - \square = 14$$

    F. -19 **G.** -9 **H.** 9 **I.** 19

3. Which expression has the greatest value?

    A. $-14 - (-5)$ **C.** $-14 - 5$

    B. $-5 - (-14)$ **D.** $-5 - 14$

4. The wheel was invented about 2500 BC. The gasoline automobile was invented in AD 1885. How many years passed between the invention of the wheel and the invention of the automobile?

    F. 1615 years   **H.** 1725 years

    G. 4385 years   **I.** 5385 years

5. If $r = -18$, $s = 27$, and $t = -15$, what is the value of $r - s - t$?

    A. -60 **B.** -30 **C.** -6 **D.** 6

Short Response

6. In golf, there is a number of strokes assigned to each hole, called the par for that hole. If you get the ball in the hole in fewer strokes than par, you are under par for the hole. If it takes you more strokes than the par, you are over par for the hole. On the first 9 holes of golf, Avery had a par, 1 over par, 2 under par, another par, 1 under par, 1 over par, 3 over par, 2 under par, and 1 under par.

    a. What addition expression would represent all 9 holes?

    b. What is Avery's score relative to par?

1-6

Think About a Plan

Multiplying and Dividing Real Numbers

Farmer's Market A farmer has 120 bushels of beans for sale at a farmer's market. He sells an average of $15\frac{3}{4}$ bushels each day. After 6 days, what is the change in the total number of bushels the farmer has for sale at the farmer's market?

Understanding the Problem

1. How does the number of bushels the farmer has change each day?

2. Should the change be a positive or a negative number? How do you know?

Planning the Solution

3. What expression represents the total number of bushels sold in 6 days?

Getting an Answer

4. Evaluate your expression in Exercise 3 to determine the change in the total number of bushels the farmer has for sale at the farmer's market.

5. Is your answer reasonable? Explain.

1-6 Practice

Form G

Multiplying and Dividing Real Numbers

Find each product. Simplify, if necessary.

1. $-5(-7)$

2. $8(-11)$

3. $9 \cdot 12$

4. $(-9)^2$

5. -3×12

6. $-5(-9)$

7. $-3(2.3)$

8. $(-0.6)^2$

9. $8(-2.4)$

10. $-\frac{3}{4} \cdot \frac{2}{9}$

11. $-\frac{2}{5}\left(-\frac{5}{8}\right)$

12. $\left(\frac{2}{3}\right)^2$

13. After hiking to the top of a mountain, Raul starts to descend at the rate of 350 feet per hour. What real number represents his vertical change after $1\frac{1}{2}$ hours?

14. A dolphin starts at the surface of the water. It dives down at a rate of 3 feet per second. If the water level is zero, what real number describes the dolphin's location after $3\frac{1}{2}$ seconds?

Simplify each expression.

15. $\sqrt{1600}$

16. $-\sqrt{625}$

17. $\pm\sqrt{10,000}$

18. $-\sqrt{0.81}$

19. $\pm\sqrt{1.44}$

20. $\sqrt{0.04}$

21. $\pm\sqrt{\frac{4}{9}}$

22. $-\sqrt{\frac{16}{49}}$

23. $\sqrt{\frac{100}{121}}$

1-6

Practice (continued)   Form G

Multiplying and Dividing Real Numbers

24. Writing Explain the differences among $\sqrt{25}$, $-\sqrt{25}$, and $\pm\sqrt{25}$.

25. Reasoning Can you name a real number that is represented by $\sqrt{-36}$? Explain.

Find each quotient. Simplify, if necessary.

26. $-51 \div 3$ **27.** $-250 \div (-25)$ **28.** $98 \div 2$

29. $84 \div (-4)$ **30.** $-93 \div (-3)$ **31.** $\frac{-105}{5}$

32. $14.4 \div (-3)$ **33.** $-1.7 \div (-10)$ **34.** $-8.1 \div 3$

35. $17 \div \frac{1}{3}$ **36.** $-\frac{3}{8} \div \left(-\frac{9}{10}\right)$ **37.** $-\frac{5}{6} \div \frac{1}{2}$

Evaluate each expression for $a = -\frac{1}{2}$, $b = \frac{3}{4}$, and $c = -6$.

38. $-ab$ **39.** $b \div c$ **40.** $\frac{c}{a}$

41. Writing Explain how you know that -5 and $-\frac{1}{5}$ are multiplicative inverses.

42. At 6:00 P.M., the temperature was 55°F. At 11:00 P.M. that same evening, the temperature was 40°F. What real number represents the average change in temperature per hour?

1-6 Standardized Test Prep

Multiplying and Dividing Real Numbers

Multiple Choice

For Exercises 1-5, choose the correct letter.

1. Which expression has a negative value?

   A. $(-2)^2$ **B.** $(-5)(-7)$ **C.** $(-3)^3$ **D.** $0 \times (-5)$

2. If $x = -\frac{3}{4}$ and $y = \frac{1}{6}$, what is the value of $-2xy$?

   F. $-\frac{1}{4}$ **G.** $-\frac{1}{6}$ **H.** $\frac{1}{6}$ **I.** $\frac{1}{4}$

3. Which expression has the same value as $-\frac{1}{7} \div \left(-\frac{2}{3}\right)$?

   A. $\frac{1}{7} \times \frac{3}{2}$ **B.** $-\left(\frac{1}{7} \times \frac{3}{2}\right)$ **C.** $\frac{7}{1} \times \frac{2}{3}$ **D.** $-\left(\frac{7}{1} \times \frac{2}{3}\right)$

4. ABC stock sold for $64.50. Four days later, the same stock sold for $47.10. What is the average change per day?

   F. –$4.35   **G.** –$3.48   **H.** $3.48   **I.** $4.35

5. The formula $C = \frac{5}{9}(F - 32)$ converts a temperature reading from the Fahrenheit scale F to the Celsius scale C. What is the temperature 5°F measured in Celsius?

   A. $\left(-20\frac{5}{9}\right)^{\circ}$ C   **B.** $-15°$C   **C.** $15°$C   **D.** $\left(20\frac{5}{9}\right)^{\circ}$ C

Short Response

6. A clock loses 2 minutes every 6 hours. At 3:00 P.M., the clock is set to the correct time and allowed to run without interference.
   a. What integer would describe the time loss after exactly 3 days?
   b. What would the clock read at 3:00 P.M. three days later?

1-7   Think About a Plan

The Distributive Property

Exercise The recommended heart rate for exercise, in beats per minute, is given by the expression $0.8(200 - y)$ where y is a person's age in years. Rewrite this expression using the Distributive Property. What is the recommended heart rate for a 20-year-old person? For a 50-year-old person? Use mental math.

Understanding the Problem

1. What relationship does the given expression represent? What does the variable in the expression represent?

   _____

   _____

2. What does it mean to rewrite the expression using the Distributive Property?

   _____

   _____

3. What does it mean to use mental math?

   _____

Planning the Solution

4. How do you determine the recommended heart rate for people of different ages?

   _____

   _____

Getting an Answer

5. Rewrite the expression using the Distributive Property.

   _____

6. What is the recommended heart rate for a 20-year-old person? Show your work.

   _____

   _____

7. What is the recommended heart rate for a 50-year-old person? Show your work.

   _____

   _____

1-7 Practice   Form G

The Distributive Property

Use the Distributive Property to simplify each expression.

1. $3(h - 5)$

2. $7(-5 + m)$

3. $(6 + 9v)6$

4. $(5n + 3)12$

5. $20(8 - a)$

6. $15(3y - 5)$

7. $21(2x + 4)$

8. $(7 + 6w)6$

9. $(14 - 9p)1.1$

10. $(2b - 10)3.2$

11. $\frac{1}{3}(3z + 12)$

12. $4\left(\frac{1}{2}t - 5\right)$

13. $(-5x - 14)(5.1)$

14. $1\left(-\frac{1}{2}r - \frac{5}{7}\right)$

15. $10(6.85j + 7.654)$

16. $\frac{2}{3}\left(\frac{2}{3}m - \frac{2}{3}\right)$

Write each fraction as a sum or difference.

17. $\frac{3n + 5}{7}$

18. $\frac{14 - 6x}{19}$

19. $\frac{3d + 5}{6}$

20. $\frac{9p - 6}{3}$

21. $\frac{18 + 8z}{6}$

22. $\frac{15n - 42}{14}$

23. $\frac{56 - 28w}{8}$

24. $\frac{81f + 63}{9}$

Simplify each expression.

25. $-(14 + x)$

26. $-(-8 - 6t)$

27. $-(6 + d)$

28. $-(-r + 1)$

29. $-(4m - 6n)$

30. $-(5.8a + 4.2b)$

31. $-(-x + y - 1)$

32. $-(f + 3g - 7)$

Use mental math to find each product.

33. 3.2×3

34. 5×8.2

35. 149×2

36. 6×397

37. 4.2×5

38. 4×10.1

39. 8.25×4

40. 11×4.1

41. You buy 75 candy bars at a cost of $0.49 each. What is the total cost of 75 candy bars? Use mental math.

42. The distance around a track is 400 m. If you take 14 laps around the track, what is the total distance you walk? Use mental math.

43. There are 32 classmates that are going to the fair. Each ticket costs $19. What is the total amount the classmates spend for tickets? Use mental math.

1-7 Practice (continued) Form G
The Distributive Property

Simplify each expression by combining like terms.

44. $4t + 6t$

45. $17y - 15y$

46. $-11b^2 + 4b^2$

47. $-2y - 5y$

48. $14n^2 - 7n^2$

49. $8x^2 - 10x^2$

50. $2f + 7g - 6 + 8g$

51. $8x + 3 - 5x - 9$

52. $-5k - 6k^2 - 12k + 10$

Write a word phrase for each expression. Then simplify each expression.

53. $2(n + 1)$

54. $-5(x - 7)$

55. $\frac{1}{2}(4m - 8)$

56. The tax a plumber must charge for a service call is given by the expression $0.06(35 + 25h)$ where h is the number of hours the job takes. Rewrite this expression using the Distributive Property. What is the tax for a 5 hour job and a 20 hour job? Use mental math.

Geometry Write an expression in simplified form for the area of each rectangle.

57.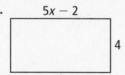

58.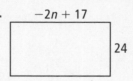

59.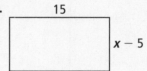

Simplify each expression.

60. $4jk - 7jk + 12jk$

61. $-17mn + 4mn - mn + 10mn$

62. $8xy^4 - 7xy^3 - 11xy^4$

63. $-2(5ab - 6)$

64. $z + \frac{2z}{5} - \frac{4z}{5}$

65. $7m^2n + 4m^2n^2 - 4m^2n - 5m^3n^2 - 5mn^2$

66. Reasoning Demonstrate why $\frac{12x - 6}{6} \neq 2x - 6$. Show your work.

Simplify each expression.

67. $4(2h + 1) + 3(4h + 7)$

68. $5(n - 8) + 6(7 - 2n)$

69. $7(3 + x) - 4(x + 1)$

70. $6(y + 5) - 3(4y + 2)$

71. $-(a - 3b + 27)$

72. $-2(5 - 4s + 6t) - 5s + t$

Prentice Hall Gold Algebra 1 • Practice and Problem Solving Workbook
28

1-7 Standardized Test Prep

The Distributive Property

Multiple Choice

For Exercises 1–6, choose the correct letter.

1. What is the simplified form of the expression $6(4x - 7)$?

   A. $10x - 1$ **B.** $24x - 7$ **C.** $24x - 42$ **D.** $24x + 42$

2. What is the simplified form of the expression $-2(-5x - 8)$?

   F. $-7x - 10$ **G.** $10x - 8$ **H.** $10x - 16$ **I.** $10x + 16$

3. What is the simplified form of the expression $14mn + 6mn^2 - 8mn - 7m^2n + 5m^2n$?

   A. $10m^2n^2$

   B. $6mn - 4m^2n$

   C. $6mn + 5m^2n - 1mn^2$

   D. $6mn - 2m^2n + 6mn^2$

4. Concert tickets cost $14.95 each. Which expression represents the total cost of 25 tickets?

   F. $25(15 - 0.05)$ **G.** $25(15 + 0.05)$ **H.** $15(25 - 10.05)$ **I.** $25(15) - 0.05$

5. Which expression represents 7 times the sum of a number and 8?

   A. $7n + 8$ **B.** $7(n + 8)$ **C.** $8(n + 7)$ **D.** $n + 56$

6. There are 297 students in a senior class. The cost of the senior trip is $150 per student. Which expression represents the total cost of the senior trip?

   F. $150(300)$ **G.** $300(150 - 3)$ **H.** $150(300 - 3)$ **I.** $150(300) - 3$

Short Response

7. The profit Samantha's company makes is given by the expression $0.1(1000 + 300m)$ where m is total number of sales. Rewrite this expression using the Distributive Property. What is the profit if her company sells 50 pieces of merchandise? Use mental math.

1-8

Think About a Plan

An Introduction to Equations

Deliveries The equation $25 + 0.25p = c$ gives the cost c in dollars that a store charges to deliver an appliance that weighs p pounds. Use the equation and a table to find the weight of an appliance that costs $55 to deliver.

Understanding the Problem

1. What information are you given about the situation? What is the relationship between the delivery charge and the weight of an appliance?

   _____

   _____

2. What are you being asked to determine?

   _____

Planning the Solution

3. How can you determine the cost to deliver an appliance that weighs 50 pounds?

   _____

   _____

4. Make a table that shows the delivery charge for appliances of various weights. Your table should include the weight of an appliance that produces the desired delivery cost.

Getting an Answer

5. What is the weight of an appliance that costs $55 to deliver?

   _____

1-8 Practice   Form G
An Introduction to Equations

Tell whether each equation is true, false, or open. Explain.

1. $45 \div x - 14 = 22$

2. $-42 - 10 = -52$

3. $3(-6) + 5 = 26 - 3$

4. $(12 + 8) \div (-10) = -12 \div 6$

5. $-14n - 7 = 7$

6. $7k - 8k = -15$

7. $10 + (-15) - 5 = -5$

8. $32 \div (-4) + 6 = -72 \div 8 + 7$

Tell whether the given number is a solution of each equation.

9. $3b - 8 = 13; -7$

10. $-4x + 7 = 15; -2$

11. $12 = 14 - 2f; -1$

12. $-6 = 14 - 11n; 2$

13. $7c - (-5) = 26; 3$

14. $25 - 10z = 15; -1$

15. $-8a - 12 = -4; 1$

16. $20 = \frac{1}{2}t + 25; -10$

17. $\frac{2}{3}m + 2 = \frac{7}{3}; \frac{1}{2}$

Write an equation for each sentence.

18. The difference of a number and 7 is 8.

19. 6 times the sum of a number and 5 is 16.

20. A computer programmer works 40 hours per week. What is an equation that relates the number of weeks w that the programmer works and the number of hours h that the programmer spends working?

21. Josie is 11 years older than Macy. What is an equation that relates the age of Josie J and the age of Macy M?

Use mental math to find the solution of each equation.

22. $t - 7 = 10$

23. $12 = 5 - h$

24. $22 + p = 30$

25. $6 - g = 12$

26. $\frac{x}{4} = 3$

27. $\frac{v}{8} = -6$

28. $4x = 36$

29. $12b = 60$

1-8 Practice (continued) Form G

An Introduction to Equations

Use a table to find the solution of each equation.

30. $4m - 5 = 11$ **31.** $-3d + 10 = 43$ **32.** $2 = 3a + 8$ **33.** $5h - 13 = 12$

34. $-8 = 3y - 2$ **35.** $8n + 16 = 24$ **36.** $35 = 7z - 7$ **37.** $\frac{1}{4}p + 6 = 8$

Use a table to find two consecutive integers between which the solution lies.

38. $7t - 20 = 33$ **39.** $7.5 = 3.2 - 2.1n$ **40.** $37d + 48 = 368$

41. The population of a particular village can be modeled by the equation $y = 110x + 56$, where x is the number of years since 1990. In what year were there 1706 people living in the village?

42. Open-Ended Write four equations that all have a solution of -10. The equations should consist of one multiplication, one division, one addition, and one subtraction equation.

43. There are 68 members of the marching band. The vans the band uses to travel to games each carry 15 passengers. How many vans does the band need to reserve for each away game?

Find the solution of each equation using mental math or a table. If the solution lies between two consecutive integers, identify those integers.

44. $d + 8 = 10$ **45.** $3p - 14 = 9$ **46.** $8.3 = 4k - 2.5$ **47.** $c - 8 = -12$

48. $6y - 13 = -13$ **49.** $15 = 8 + (-a)$ **50.** $-3 = -\frac{1}{3}h - 10$ **51.** $21 = 7x + 8$

52. Writing Explain the difference between an expression and an equation.

1-8 Standardized Test Prep

An Introduction to Equations

Multiple Choice

For Exercises 1–5, choose the correct letter.

1. Which equation is true?

A. $25 - (-18) = 7$

B. $\frac{1}{3}(-9) - 6 = -9$

C. $25(-2) + 7 = -39 + 4$

D. $-19 + 8(-2) = -7(-5)$

2. Which equation has a solution of -6?

F. $15x - 20 = 70$ **G.** $14 = 6x - 22$ **H.** $3x - 8 = -10$ **I.** $\frac{1}{2}x - 8 = -11$

3. Which equation has a solution of $\frac{1}{2}$?

A. $13x - 12 = 14$ **B.** $9x + 15 = 20$ **C.** $-6x - 18 = -21$ **D.** $-11x = 12x + 12$

4. The money a company received from sales of their product is represented by the equation $y = 45x - 120$, where y is the money in dollars and x is the number of products sold. How many products does the company need to sell in order to receive $3705?

F. 42   **G.** 85   **H.** 105   **I.** 166,605

5. Mrs. Decker walks for 30 minutes each day as often as possible. What is an equation that relates the number of days d that Mrs. Decker walks and the number of minutes m that she spends walking?

A. $m = 30d$ **B.** $d = 30m$ **C.** $d = m + 30$ **D.** $m = d + 30$

Short Response

6. There are 450 people travelling to watch a playoff football game. Each bus can seat up to 55 people. Write an equation that represents the number of buses it will take to transport the fans. Use a table to find a solution.

1-9

Think About a Plan

Patterns, Equations, and Graphs

Air Travel Use the table below. How long will the jet take to travel 5390 miles?

Passenger Jet Travel				
Hours, h	1	2	3	4
Miles, m	490	980	1470	1960

Understanding the Problem

1. What does the information in the table represent?

_____

_____

2. What is the pattern in each row of numbers?

_____

Planning the Solution

3. What is a general equation that represents the relationship between hours and miles?

_____

4. How can you determine the number of hours it will take for the jet to travel 5390 miles?

_____

_____

Getting an Answer

5. How long will the jet take to travel 5390 miles? Show your work.

_____

_____

6. Besides the distance the jet travels and the time it is in flight, what else could be determined from the information in the table?

_____

_____

1-9 Practice

Form G

Patterns, Equations, and Graphs

Tell whether the given equation has the ordered pair as a solution.

1. $y = x - 4; (5, 1)$

2. $y = x + 8; (8, 0)$

3. $y = -x - 2; (2, -4)$

4. $y = -3x; (2, -6)$

5. $y = x + 1; (1, 0)$

6. $y = -x; (-7, 7)$

7. $y = x + \frac{1}{2}; (1, \frac{1}{2})$

8. $y = x - \frac{2}{5}; (-2, -2\frac{2}{5})$

9. $\frac{x}{-3} = y; (2, -6)$

Use a table, an equation, and a graph to represent each relationship.

10. Petra earns $22 per hour.

11. The calling plan costs $0.10 per minute.

Use the table to draw a graph and answer the question.

12. The table shows the height in feet of a stack of medium sized moving boxes. What is the height of a stack of 14 boxes?

Boxes	Height (ft)
2	4.5
3	6.75
5	11.25
7	15.75
8	18

13. The table shows the number of pages Dustin read in terms of hours. How many pages will Dustin read in 12 hours?

Hours	Pages
1	23
2	46
3	69
4	92
5	115

1-9 Practice (continued) Form G
Patterns, Equations, and Graphs

Use the table to write an equation and answer the question.

14. The table shows the amount earned for washing cars. How much is earned for washing 25 cars?

Cars	Money Earned ($)
3	13.50
6	27
9	40.50
12	54

15. The table shows the distance in terms of hours Jerry and Michelle have traveled on the way to visit their family. They take turns driving for 12 hours. What distance will they travel in that time?

Hours	Miles
1	67
2	134
3	201
4	268
5	335

16. A worker finds that it takes 9 tiles to cover one square foot of floor. Make a table and draw a graph to show the relationship between the number of tiles and the number of square feet of floor covered. How many square feet of floor will be covered by 261 tiles?

Tell whether the given equation has the ordered pair as a solution.

17. $y = 3x - 2; (-1, -5)$ **18.** $y = -5x + 7; (1, -2)$ **19.** $y = -4x - 3; (1, 1)$

20. $y = 13 + 6x; (-1, 7)$ **21.** $-\frac{2}{3}x - 5 = y; (9, -11)$ **22.** $y = 10 - \frac{x}{2}; (5, \frac{15}{2})$

23. Writing Explain what inductive reasoning is. Include in your explanation what inductive reasoning can be used for.

1-9 Standardized Test Prep

Patterns, Equations, and Graphs

Multiple Choice

For Exercises 1–5, choose the correct letter.

1. If $x = -3$ and $y = -5$, what does $3x - 2y$ equal?

   A. -19 **B.** -1 **C.** 1 **D.** 19

2. Which ordered pair is a solution of $y = 6x - 1$?

   F. $(-3, -17)$ **G.** $(-1, 7)$ **H.** $(1, 7)$ **I.** $(3, 17)$

3. Which ordered pair is a solution of $-x = y$?

   A. $(-1, -1)$ **B.** $(1, -1)$ **C.** $(1, 1)$ **D.** $(-1, -2)$

4. Which equation represents the table shown?

   F. $y = 8.5x$

   G. $y = 8.5x + 12.50$

   H. $y = 15x$

   I. $y = 15x + 12.50$

Hours	Money ($)
15	127.50
25	212.50
35	297.50

5. Sally is 3 years younger than Ralph. Which equation represents this relationship?

   A. $R = 3S$ **B.** $R = S - 3$ **C.** $S = R + 3$ **D.** $S = R - 3$

Extended Response

6. Justin earns $19.50 per hour working as a store manager.

   a. Use a table to represent this relationship.

   b. Use an equation to represent this relationship.

   c. Use a graph to represent this relationship.

   d. What will Justin earn for working 40 hours?

2-1 Think About a Plan

Solving One-Step Equations

Volleyball In volleyball, players serve the ball to the opposing team. If the opposing team fails to hit the ball, the service is called an ace. A player's ace average is the number of aces served divided by the number of games played. A certain player has an ace average of 0.3 and has played in 70 games this season. How many aces has the player served?

Understanding the Problem

1. What values are you given?

_____

_____

Planning the Solution

2. Write an expression, using words, to represent the relationship between ace average, number of aces, and the number of games played.

$$\text{Ace Average} = \frac{\boxed{}}{\boxed{}}$$

3. Use the expression to write an equation, where A = number of aces.

$$\boxed{} = \frac{\boxed{}}{\boxed{}}$$

Getting an Answer

4. Solve the equation you wrote in Step 3.

5. Explain what this solution represents.

_____

_____

6. Is your answer reasonable? Explain.

_____

_____

2-1 Practice

Solving One-Step Equations

Form G

Solve each equation using addition or subtraction. Check your answer.

1. $8 = a - 2$

2. $x + 7 = 11$

3. $r - 2 = -6$

4. $-18 = m + 12$

5. $f + 10 = -10$

6. $-1 = n + 5$

Solve each equation using multiplication or division. Check your answer.

7. $-3p = -48$

8. $-98 = 7t$

9. $-4.4 = -4y$

10. $2.8c = 4.2$

11. $\dfrac{k}{6} = 8$

12. $16 = \dfrac{w}{8}$

13. $-9 = \dfrac{y}{-3}$

14. $\dfrac{h}{10} = \dfrac{-22}{5}$

Solve each equation. Check your answer.

15. $\dfrac{3}{5}n = 12$

16. $-4 = \dfrac{2}{3}b$

17. $\dfrac{5}{8}x = -15$

18. $\dfrac{1}{4}z = \dfrac{2}{5}$

19. Jeremy mowed several lawns to earn money for camp. After he paid $17 for gas, he had $75 leftover to pay towards camp. Write and solve an equation to find how much money Jeremy earned mowing lawns.

2-1 **Practice** (continued) Form G

Solving One-Step Equations

Define a variable and write an equation for each situation. Then solve.

20. Susan's cell phone plan allows her to use 950 minutes per month with no additional charge. She has 188 minutes left for this month. How many minutes has she already used this month?

21. In the fifth year of operation, the profit of a company was 3 times the profit it earned in the first year of operation. If its profit was $114,000 in the fifth year of operation, what was the profit in the first year?

Solve each equation. Check your answer.

22. $-9x = 48$

23. $-\frac{7}{8} = \frac{2}{3} + n$

24. $a + 1\frac{1}{4} = 2\frac{7}{10}$

25. $-7t = 5.6$

26. $2.3 = -7.9 + y$

27. $\frac{5}{3}p = \frac{8}{3}$

28. $\frac{g}{8} = -\frac{3}{4}$

29. $\frac{m}{8} = 8\frac{1}{3}$

30. A community center is serving a free meal to senior citizens. The center plans to feed 700 people in 4 hours.
   a. Write and solve an equation to find the average number of people the center is planning to feed each hour.

   b. During the first hour and a half, the center fed 270 people. Write and solve an equation to find the number of people that remain to be fed.

2-1

Standardized Test Prep

Solving One-Step Equations

Multiple Choice

For Exercises 1–6, choose the correct letter.

1. What is the solution of $-3 = x + 5$?

   A. -15 **B.** -8 **C.** 2   **D.** 8

2. What operation should you use to solve $-6x = -24$?

   F. addition   **G.** subtraction   **H.** multiplication   **I.** division

3. Which of the following solutions is true for $\frac{x}{3} = \frac{1}{4}$?

   A. $-2\frac{3}{4}$ **B.** $\frac{1}{12}$ **C.** $\frac{3}{4}$ **D.** $3\frac{1}{4}$

4. There are 37 more cats c than dogs d in an animal shelter. If there are 78 cats at the shelter, which equation represents the relationship between the number of cats and dogs?

   F. $d + 37 = 78$ **G.** $d - 37 = 78$ **H.** $c + 37 = 78$ **I.** $c - 37 = 78$

5. Which property of equality should you use to solve $6x = 48$?

   A. Addition Property of Equality
   B. Subtraction Property of Equality
   C. Multiplication Property of Equality
   D. Division Property of Equality

6. Shelly completed 10 problems of her homework in study hall. This is $\frac{2}{7}$ of the total assignment. How many problems does she have left to complete?

   F. 20   **G.** 25   **H.** 30   **I.** 35

Short Response

7. A high school marching band has 55 male members. It is determined that five-eighths of the band members are male.
   a. What equation represents the total number of members in the band?
   b. How many members are in the band?

2-2 Think About a Plan

Solving Two-Step Equations

Earth Science The temperature beneath Earth's surface increases by 10°C per kilometer. The surface temperature and the temperature at the bottom of a mine are shown. How many kilometers below Earth's surface is the bottom of the mine?

Surface: 18°C

Bottom of mine: 38°C

Understanding the Problem

1. What happens to the temperature as the distance below Earth's surface increases?

_____

2. What do you need to determine?

_____

3. What is the change in temperature from Earth's surface to the bottom of the mine?

_____

Planning the Solution

4. Write an expression for how much the temperature increases x kilometers below the surface.

_____

5. Write an equation that relates the change in temperature, from 18°C at Earth's surface to 38°C at the bottom of the mine, to the expression for how much the temperature increases x kilometers below the surface.

_____

Getting an Answer

6. Solve the equation.

7. Is your answer reasonable? Explain.

_____

_____

2-2 Practice   Form G

Solving Two-Step Equations

Solve each equation. Check your answer.

1. $6 + 3b = -18$

2. $-3 + 5x = 12$

3. $7n + 12 = -23$

4. $\dfrac{t}{6} - 3 = 8$

5. $-12 = 8 + \dfrac{f}{2}$

6. $13 = 8 - 5d$

7. $\dfrac{k}{4} + 6 = -2$

8. $-22 = -8 + 7y$

9. $16 - 3p = 34$

10. $15 + \dfrac{q}{6} = -21$

11. $-19 + \dfrac{c}{3} = 8$

12. $-18 - 11r = 26$

13. $-9 = \dfrac{y}{-3} - 6$

14. $14 + \dfrac{m}{10} = 24$

Define a variable and write an equation for each situation. Then solve.

15. Chip earns a base salary of $500 per month as a salesman. In addition to the salary, he earns $90 per product that he sells. If his goal is to earn $5000 per month, how many products does he need to sell?

16. A pizza shop charges $9 for a large cheese pizza. Additional toppings cost $1.25 per topping. Heather paid $15.25 for her large pizza. How many toppings did she order?

2-2 Practice (continued)   Form G

Solving Two-Step Equations

Solve each equation. Check your answer.

17. $\dfrac{z + 6}{3} = 8$ **18.** $\dfrac{n - 7}{2} = -11$

19. $\dfrac{j + 18}{-4} = 8$ **20.** $\dfrac{1}{3}a - 6 = -15$

21. $\dfrac{1}{4} = \dfrac{1}{4}h + 4$ **22.** $6.42 - 10d = 2.5$

23. The selling price of a television in a retail store is $66 less than 3 times the wholesale price. If the selling price of a television is $899, write and solve an equation to find the wholesale price of the television.

24. The fare for a taxicab is $5 per trip plus $0.50 per mile. The fare for the trip from the airport to the convention center was $11.50. Write and solve an equation to find how many miles the trip is from the airport to the convention center.

25. An online movie club offers a membership for $5 per month. Members can rent movies for $1.50 per rental. A member was billed $15.50 one month. Write and solve an equation to find how many movies the member rented.

26. Writing Describe, using words, how to solve the equation $6 - 4x = 18$. List any properties utilized in the solution.

27. a. Solve $-8 = \dfrac{x + 2}{4}$

    b. Write the right side of the equation in part (a) as the sum of two fractions. Solve the equation.

    c. Did you find the equation in part (a) or the rewritten equation easier to solve? Why?

2-2 Standardized Test Prep

Solving Two-Step Equations

Gridded Response

Solve each exercise and enter your answer on the grid provided.

1. What is the solution of $-28 = 22 - 5x$?

2. What is the solution of $\frac{m}{4} - 3 = 7$?

3. The amount of money that Pamela p has and Julie j has are related by the equation $3p + 5 = j$. If Julie has \$83, how much money does Pamela have?

4. An ice cream sundae costs \$1.75 plus an additional \$0.35 for each topping. If the total cost is \$2.80, how many toppings did the sundae have?

5. The cost of a gallon of gasoline g is \$3.25 less than 2 times the cost of a gallon of diesel d. If a gallon of gasoline costs \$3.95, what is the cost of a gallon of diesel?

1. 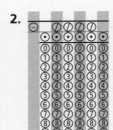 2. 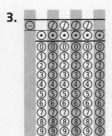 3. 4. 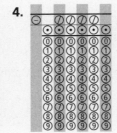 5.

2-3 Think About a Plan

Solving Multi-Step Equations

Online Video Games Angie and Kenny play online video games. Angie buys 1 software package and 3 months of game play. Kenny buys 1 software package and 2 months of game play. Each software package costs $20. If their total cost is $115, what is the cost of one month of game play?

Know

1. What values are you given?

_____

_____

Need

2. What do you need to find?

_____

Plan

3. What equation can you use to solve the problem?

_____

4. Solve the equation. Show your work and justify each step.

_____

_____

_____

_____

_____

_____

5. Check your answer.

_____

_____

_____

6. Is your answer reasonable? Explain.

_____

_____

_____

2-3 Practice   *Form G*

Solving Multi-Step Equations

Solve each equation. Check your answer.

1. $19 - h - h = -13$

2. $14 + 6a - 8 = 18$

3. $25 = 7 + 3k - 12$

4. $5n - 16 - 8n = -10$

5. $-34 = v + 42 - 5v$

6. $x - 1 + 5x = 23$

7. $42j + 18 - 19j = -28$

8. $-49 = 6c - 13 - 4c$

9. $-28 + 15 - 22z = 31$

Write an equation to model each situation. Then solve the equation.

10. General admission tickets to the fair cost $3.50 per person. Ride passes cost an additional $5.50 per person. Parking costs $6 for the family. The total costs for ride passes and parking was $51. How many people in the family attended the fair?

11. Five times a number decreased by 18 minus 4 times the same number is -36. What is the number?

Solve each equation. Check your answer.

12. $6(3m + 5) = 66$

13. $3(4y - 8) = 12$

14. $-5(x - 3) = -25$

15. $42 = 3(2 - 3h)$

16. $-10 = 5(2w - 4)$

17. $3p - 4 = 31$

18. $-3 = -3(2t - 1)$

19. $x - 2(x + 10) = 12$

20. $-15 = 5(3q - 10) - 5q$

21. Angela ate at the same restaurant four times. Each time she ordered a salad and left a $5 tip. She spent a total of $54. Write and solve an equation to find the cost of each salad.

2-3 · Practice (continued) · Form G
Solving Multi-Step Equations

Solve each equation. Choose the method you prefer to use. Check your answer.

22. $\frac{a}{7} + \frac{5}{7} = \frac{2}{7}$

23. $6v - \frac{5}{8} = \frac{7}{8}$

24. $\frac{j}{6} - 9 = \frac{5}{6}$

25. $\frac{x}{3} - \frac{1}{2} = \frac{3}{4}$

26. $\frac{g}{5} + \frac{5}{6} = 6$

27. $\frac{b}{9} - \frac{1}{2} = \frac{5}{18}$

28. $0.52y + 2.5 = 5.1$

29. $4n + 0.24 = 15.76$

30. $2.45 - 3.1t = 21.05$

31. $-4.2 = 9.1x + 23.1$

32. $11.3 - 7.2f = -3.82$

33. $14.2 = -6.8 + 4.2d$

34. Reasoning Suppose you want to solve $-5 = 6x + 3 + 7x$. What would you do as your first step? Explain.

35. Writing Describe two different ways to solve $-10 = \frac{1}{4}(8y - 12)$.

Solve each equation. Round to the nearest hundredth if necessary.

36. $5 + \frac{2a}{-3} = \frac{5}{11}$

37. $\frac{3}{5}(p - 3) = -4$

38. $11m - (6m - 5) = 25$

39. The sum of three integers is 228. The second integer is 1 more than the first, and the third integer is 2 more than the first. Write an equation to determine the integers. Solve your equation. Show your work.

40. Can you solve the equation $\frac{2}{3}(4x - 5) = 8$ by using the Division Property of Equality? Explain.

2-3 Standardized Test Prep

Solving Multi-Step Equations

Multiple Choice

For Exercises 1–5, choose the correct letter.

1. What is the solution of $-17 = -2n + 13 - 8n$?

   A. -3 **B.** $-\frac{2}{3}$ **C.** 3 **D.** 5

2. What is the solution of $-4(-3m - 2) = 32$?

   F. -2 **G.** 2 **H.** 4 **I.** 6

3. What is the solution of $\frac{x}{3} + \frac{3}{5} = -\frac{1}{15}$?

   A. -2 **B.** $\frac{8}{5}$ **C.** 2 **D.** $\frac{16}{3}$

4. When the sum of a number and 7 is multiplied by 4, the result is 16. What is the original number?

   F. -12 **G.** -3 **H.** 3 **I.** 11

5. A merchant is selling wind chimes from a booth at a flea market. He rents his space for $125 per day. The profit from each wind chime sold is $12. His goal is to make $3500 in a five day work week. Which equation represents how many chimes he needs to sell in a week to meet his goal?

   A. $12c - 625 = 3500$

   B. $5(12c) - 125 = 3500$

   C. $5(12c + 125) = 3500$

   D. $5(12c - 125) = 3500$

Short Response

6. Four friends are planning to play 18 holes of golf. Two of them need to rent clubs at $5 per set. Total cart rental is $10. The total cost of the golf outing, including green fees, is $92.

   a. Write an equation to represent the total cost of the golf outing.

   b. How much did the friends pay in green fees?

2-4 Think About a Plan

Solving Equations With Variables on Both Sides

Skiing A skier is trying to decide whether or not to buy a season ski pass. A daily pass costs $67. A season ski pass costs $350. The skier would have to rent skis with either pass for $25 per day. How many days would the skier have to go skiing in order to make the season pass less expensive than daily passes?

Understanding the Problem

1. What do you know about the costs associated with buying a daily pass?

_____

2. What do you know about the costs associated with buying a season pass?

_____

Planning the Solution

3. Write an expression using words to represent the cost of a daily pass. Write the algebraic expression.

_____

_____

4. Write an expression using words to represent the cost of a season pass. Write the algebraic expression.

_____

_____

5. How can you compare the cost of a daily pass with the cost of a season pass algebraically? What is the equation?

_____

_____

Getting an Answer

6. Solve the equation you wrote in Step 5. Show your work.

_____

_____

7. Explain what this solution means.

_____

2-4 **Practice**   *Form G*

Solving Equations With Variables on Both Sides

Solve each equation. Check your answer.

1. $3n + 2 = -2n - 8$ **2.** $8b - 7 = 7b - 2$ **3.** $-12 + 5k = 15 - 4k$

4. $-q - 11 = 2q + 4$ **5.** $4t + 9 = -8t - 13$ **6.** $22p + 11 = 4p - 7$

7. $17 - 9y = -3 + 16y$ **8.** $15m + 22 = -7m + 18$ **9.** $3x + 7 = 14 + 3x$

Write and solve an equation for each situation. Check your solution.

10. Shirley is going to have the exterior of her home painted. Tim's Painting charges $250 plus $14 per hour. Colorful Paints charges $22 per hour. How many hours would the job need to take for Tim's Painting to be the better deal?

11. Tracey is looking at two different travel agencies to plan her vacation. ABC Travel offers a plane ticket for $295 and a rental car for $39 per day. M & N Travel offers a plane ticket for $350 and a rental car for $33 per day. What is the minimum number of days that Shirley's vacation should be for M & N Travel to have the better deal?

Solve each equation. Check your answer.

12. $7(h + 3) = 6(h - 3)$ **13.** $-(5a + 6) = 2(3a + 8)$

14. $-2(2f - 4) = -4(-f + 2)$ **15.** $3w - 6 + 2w = -2 + w$

16. $-8x - (3x + 6) = 4 - x$ **17.** $14 + 3n = 8n - 3(n - 4)$

Determine whether each equation is an *identity* or whether it has *no solution*.

18. $4(3m + 4) = 2(6m + 8)$ **19.** $5x + 2x - 3 = -3x + 10x$

20. $-(3z + 4) = 6z - 3(3z + 2)$ **21.** $-2(j - 3) = -2j + 6$

2-4 Practice (continued) Form G

Solving Equations With Variables on Both Sides

Solve each equation. If the equation is an identity, write *identity*. If it has no solution, write *no solution*.

22. $6.8 - 4.2b = 5.6b - 3$

23. $\frac{1}{3} + \frac{2}{3}m = \frac{2}{3}m - \frac{2}{3}$

24. $-2(5.25 + 6.2x) = 4(-3.1x + 2.68)$

25. $\frac{1}{2}r + 6 = 3 - 2r$

26. $0.5t + 0.25(t + 16) = 4 + 0.75t$

27. $2.5(2z + 5) = 5(z + 2.5)$

28. $-6(-p + 8) = -6p + 12$

29. $\frac{3}{8}f + \frac{1}{2} = 6(\frac{1}{16}f - 3)$

30. Three times the sum of a number and 4 is 8 less than one-half the number. Write and solve an equation to find the number.

31. A square and a rectangle have the same perimeters. The length of a side of the square is $4x - 1$. The length of the rectangle is $2x + 1$ and the width is $x + 2$. Write and solve an equation to find x.

32. A movie club charges a one-time membership fee of $25 which allows members to purchase movies for $7 each. Another club does not charge a membership fee and sells movies for $12 each. How many movies must a member purchase for the cost of the two clubs to be equal?

33. Writing Describe the difference between an equation that is defined as an identity and an equation that has no solution. Provide an example of each and explain why each example is an identity or has no solution.

2-4 Standardized Test Prep
Solving Equations With Variables on Both Sides

Multiple Choice

For Exercises 1–5, choose the correct letter.

1. What is the solution of $-8x - 5 + 3x = 7 + 4x - 9$?

   A. -3 **B.** $-\frac{1}{3}$ **C.** $\frac{1}{3}$ **D.** 3

2. What is the solution of $-(-5 - 6x) = 4(5x + 3)$?

   F. -2 **G.** $-\frac{1}{2}$ **H.** $\frac{1}{2}$ **I.** 2

3. What is the solution of $2n - 3(4n + 5) = -6(n - 3) - 1$?

   A. -8 **B.** -6 **C.** $-\frac{1}{2}$ **D.** 4

4. Negative one times the sum of twice a number and 3 is equal to two times the difference of -4 times the number and 3. What is the number?

   F. -4 **G.** -2 **H.** $-\frac{1}{2}$ **I.** 2

5. Jacob is saving for a new bicycle which costs $175. He has already saved $35. His goal is to have enough money saved in six weeks to pay for the bicycle. Which equation represents how much money he needs to save each week to meet his goal?

   A. $35 + 6d = 175$
   B. $35 + 12d = 175$
   C. $6(35 + 2d) = 175$
   D. $2(35 + 6d) = 175$

Short Response

6. Admission for a water park is $17.50 per day. A season pass costs $125. A locker rental costs $3.50 per day.
   a. What is an equation that represents the relationship between the cost of a daily pass and the cost of a season pass?
   b. How many days would you have to go to the water park for the season pass to save you money?

2-5 | Think About a Plan

Literal Equations and Formulas

Density The density of an object is calculated using the formula $D = \frac{m}{V}$, where m is the object's mass and V is its volume. Gold has a density of 19.3 g/cm^3. What is the volume of an amount of gold that has a mass of 96.5 g?

KNOW

1. What is the formula you are given for the density of an object?

_____

2. What values are you given in the problem?

_____

_____

NEED

3. What measurement are you asked to determine?

_____

4. Solve $D = \frac{m}{V}$ for the variable V. Show your work.

_____

_____

_____

PLAN

5. Write your new formula. Substitute the values you are given into the formula.

_____

6. What is the volume of 96.5 g of gold?

_____

7. In what units is your answer? Do these units make sense? Explain.

_____

_____

_____

2-5 Practice

Form G

Literal Equations and Formulas

Solve each equation for m. Then find the value of m for each value of n.

1. $m + 3n = 7; n = -2, 0, 1$

2. $3m - 9n = 24; n = -1, 1, 3$

3. $-5n = 4m + 8; n = -1, 0, 1$

4. $2m = -6n - 5; n = 1, 2, 3$

5. $8n = -3m + 1; n = -2, 2, 4$

6. $4n - 6m = -2; n = -2, 0, 2$

7. $-5n = 13 - 3m; n = -3, 0, 3$

8. $10m + 6n = 12; n = -2, -1, 0$

Solve each equation for x.

9. $fx - gx = h$

10. $qx + x = r$

11. $m = \dfrac{x + n}{p}$

12. $d = f + fx$

13. $-3(x + n) = x$

14. $\dfrac{x - 4}{y + 2} = 5$

Solve each problem. Round to the nearest tenth, if necessary. Use 3.14 for pi.

15. What is the width of a rectangle with length 14 cm and area 161 cm^2?

16. What is the radius of a circle with circumference 13 ft?

17. A rectangle has perimeter 182 in. and length 52 in. What is the width?

18. A triangle has base 7 m and area 17.5 m^2. What is the height?

2-5

Practice (continued)   Form G

Literal Equations and Formulas

Solve each problem. Round to the nearest tenth, if necessary.

19. To find the average number of points per game a player scores, use the formula Points Per Game $= \frac{\text{Total Points}}{\text{Games}}$. Find the number of games a player has played if she has scored a total of 221 points and is averaging 17 points per game.

20. Joan drives 333.5 miles before she has to buy gas. Her car gets 29 miles per gallon. How many gallons of gas did the car start out with?

21. Stan is purchasing sub-flooring for a kitchen he is remodeling. The area of the floor is 180 ft^2 and the width of the kitchen is 12 ft. What is the length of the sub-floor?

Solve each equation for the given variable.

22. $4k + mn = n - 3; n$

23. $\frac{c}{d} + 2 = \frac{f}{g}; c$

24. $3ab - 2bc = 12; c$

25. $z = \left(\frac{x + y}{3}\right)w; y$

26. $-3(m - 2n) = 5m; m$

27. $A = \frac{1}{2}bcd + bc; d$

28. A room with width w, length l, and height h with four walls needs to be painted.

   a. Write a formula for the area that needs to be painted not accounting for doors or windows.

   b. Rewrite the formula to find h in terms of A, l, and w.

   c. If l is 18 ft, w is 14 ft and A is 512 ft^2, what is the height of the room?

   d. **Reasoning** Suppose l is equal to w. Write a formula for A in terms of w and h.

2-5 Standardized Test Prep

Literal Equations and Formulas

Multiple Choice

For Exercises 1–5, choose the correct letter.

1. What is the value of the expression $-2(3x - 2) + x + 9$ when $x = -3$?

   A. -16 **B.** -2 **C.** 28 **D.** 34

2. What is the value of the expression $6m + m - 4(-2m + 1 - m)$ when $m = -8$?

   F. -156 **G.** -92 **H.** -44 **I.** 36

3. What is the solution of $2d = \dfrac{a - b}{b - c}$ when you solve for a?

   A. $2d - b + c + b$

   B. $\dfrac{2d + b}{b - c}$

   C. $\dfrac{2d}{b - c} + b$

   D. $2d(b - c) + b$

4. A triangle has area 49.5 cm^2. If the base of the triangle is 9 cm, what is the height of the triangle?

   F. 5.5 cm   **G.** 11 cm   **H.** 222.75 cm   **I.** 445.5 cm

5. A circle has circumference 10.99 yd. What is the radius of the circle? Round to the nearest tenth if necessary. (Use 3.14 for π.)

   A. 1.8 yd   **B.** 3.5 yd   **C.** 7 yd   **D.** 34.5 yd

Short Response

6. The formula for the circumference of a circle is $C = 2\pi r$, where r is the radius of the circle.

   a. What is the formula when solved for r?

   b. What is the radius of a circle with a circumference of 37.7 m? Round to the nearest tenth if necessary.

2-6 Think About a Plan

Ratios, Rates, and Conversions

Reasoning A traveler changed $300 to euros for a trip to Germany, but the trip was canceled. Three months later, the traveler changed the euros back to dollars. Would you expect that the traveler got exactly $300 back? Explain.

Know

1. What facts do you know about the situation?

   _____

   _____

2. What circumstances would affect whether or not the traveler would receive exactly $300 back?

   _____

   _____

Need

3. What would you need to know to determine the amount of dollars the traveler would receive after three months?

   _____

   _____

4. How do you convert the amount in euros to dollars?

   _____

Plan

5. Once you have the information you need to answer the question, explain how you would determine the amount of dollars the traveler would receive in exchange for the euros.

   _____

   _____

   _____

6. Would this process change over time? Explain.

   _____

   _____

2-6 Practice

Form G

Ratios, Rates, and Conversions

Convert the given amount to the given unit.

1. 15 days; hours

2. 60 ft; yd

3. 100 meters; cm

4. 5 hr; min

5. 12 meters; ft

6. 16 in.; cm

7. 5 liters; qt

8. 2076 cm; yd

9. 15 pounds; grams

10. 25 km; cm

11. 3 mi; ft

12. 60 min; s

13. The builder measures the perimeter of the foundation to be 425 ft. He must order steel beams to install around the perimeter of the foundation. Steel must be ordered in meters. How many meters of steel should the builder order?

14. Mrs. Jacobsen purchased a 5-pound package of ground beef for $12.40. She decided to use 8 ounces each day for dinner recipes. What was the cost of ground beef per meal?

15. Car 1 drove 408 miles in 6 hours and Car 2 drove 365 miles in 5 hours during the cross-country road race. Who had the fastest average speed?

Copy and complete each statement.

16. 25 mi/hr = ___ m/min

17. 32 mi/gal = ___ km/L

18. 10 m/s = ___ ft/s

19. 14 gal/s = ___ qt/min

20. 3.5 days = ___ min

21. 100 yd = ___ m

22. 15 dollars/hr = ___ cents/min

23. 5 L/s = ___ kL/min

24. 62 in. = ___ m

25. 7 days = ___ s

2-6 Practice (continued)   Form G
Ratios, Rates, and Conversions

26. Which weighs more, 500 pounds or 200 kilograms?

27. Which is longer, 4000 ft or 1 kilometer?

28. Which is the better buy, 7 pounds for $8.47 or 9 pounds for $11.07? Explain.

29. A runner is running 10 miles per hour.
  a. What conversion factors should be used to convert 10 mi/hr to ft/s?

  b. How many feet per second is the runner running?

Determine if each rate is a unit rate. Explain.

30. $1.99 per pound   **31.** 100 feet per 2 seconds   **32.** 22 miles per gallon

Find each unit rate.

33. 4 pounds of green peppers cost $7.56.

34. Rahul travelled 348 miles in 6 hours.

35. Cheryl assembled 128 chairs in 16 hours.

36. Writing Suppose you want to convert feet per second to miles per hour. What conversion factors would you use? How did you determine which unit should go in the numerator and which unit should go in the denominator of the conversion factors?

37. The volume of a box is 1344 cubic inches or in^3.
  a. How many cubic inches are in one cubic foot? Justify your answer.

  b. What is the volume of the box in cubic feet? Justify your answer.

2-6 Standardized Test Prep

Ratios, Rates, and Conversions

Multiple Choice

For Exercises 1–6, choose the correct letter.

1. Which of the following rates is a unit rate?
   - **A.** $\dfrac{24 \text{ in.}}{1 \text{ yd}}$
   - **B.** $\dfrac{24 \text{ in.}}{2 \text{ ft}}$
   - **C.** $\dfrac{3 \text{ ft}}{1 \text{ yd}}$
   - **D.** $\dfrac{1 \text{ ft}}{12 \text{ in.}}$

2. How many centimeters are in 1 kilometer?
   - **F.** 0.000001
   - **G.** 0.00001
   - **H.** 10,000
   - **I.** 100,000

3. How many inches are in 3 yd 2 ft?
   - **A.** 60
   - **B.** 72
   - **C.** 132
   - **D.** 180

4. To convert miles per hour to feet per second, which conversion factor would not be used?
   - **F.** $\dfrac{1 \text{ hr}}{60 \text{ min}}$
   - **G.** $\dfrac{1 \text{ min}}{60 \text{ sec}}$
   - **H.** $\dfrac{5280 \text{ ft}}{1 \text{ mi}}$
   - **I.** $\dfrac{1 \text{ mi}}{5280 \text{ ft}}$

5. A healthy, adult cheetah can run 110 feet per second. How fast can a cheetah run in miles per hour?
   - **A.** 55
   - **B.** 75
   - **C.** 87
   - **D.** 161.3

6. Emmanuel was speaking with a friend from another country. His friend told him that the speed limit on most highways is 100 kilometers per hour in her country. This speed sounded fast to Emmanuel. Approximately what speed is this in miles per hour?
   - **F.** 62 mph
   - **G.** 65 mph
   - **H.** 70 mph
   - **I.** 100 mph

Short Response

7. Samantha earns $22 per hour as a plumbing apprentice. How much does she earn per minute in cents?
   a. What conversion factors would she use?

   b. What amount does she earn per minute in cents?

2-7   Think About a Plan

Solving Proportions

Video Downloads A particular computer takes 15 min to download a 45-min TV show. How long will it take the computer to download a 2-hour movie?

Understanding the Problem

1. What facts do you know about the situation?

   _____

   _____

   _____

2. Are the units given in such a way that the numerators and the denominators of the proportion have the same units? If so, what are the units? If not, which units need to be converted?

   _____

   _____

   _____

Planning the Solution

3. If unit conversions are necessary, use conversion factors to convert the units. Show your work.

   _____

   _____

4. Write a proportion that can be used to determine the length of time necessary for the computer to download the movie.

   _____

   _____

Getting an Answer

5. Solve the proportion you wrote in Step 4 to find how long it will take the computer to download the movie.

2-7 Practice

Form G

Solving Proportions

Solve each proportion using the Multiplication Property of Equality.

1. $\frac{3}{2} = \frac{n}{6}$

2. $\frac{1}{5} = \frac{t}{3}$

3. $\frac{g}{3} = \frac{10}{9}$

4. $\frac{m}{4} = \frac{6}{5}$

5. $\frac{7}{6} = \frac{b}{2}$

6. $\frac{2}{9} = \frac{j}{18}$

7. $\frac{z}{3} = \frac{5}{4}$

8. $\frac{11}{12} = \frac{w}{15}$

9. $\frac{19}{10} = \frac{c}{23}$

Solve each proportion using the Cross Products Property.

10. $\frac{1}{4} = \frac{x}{10}$

11. $\frac{3}{n} = \frac{2}{3}$

12. $\frac{r}{12} = \frac{3}{4}$

13. $\frac{5}{y} = \frac{-3}{5}$

14. $\frac{-3}{4} = \frac{k}{16}$

15. $\frac{22}{a} = \frac{-6}{5}$

16. $\frac{15}{9} = \frac{8}{z}$

17. $\frac{11}{5} = \frac{q}{-6}$

18. $\frac{f}{-18} = \frac{6}{-12}$

19. The windows on a building are proportional to the size of the building. The height of each window is 18 in., and the width is 11 in. If the height of the building is 108 ft, what is the width of the building?

20. Eric is planning to bake approximately 305 cookies. If 3 pounds of cookie dough make 96 cookies, how many pounds of cookie dough should he make?

21. On a map, the distance between Sheila's house and Shardae's house is 6.75 inches. According to the scale, 1.5 inches represents 5 miles. How far apart are the houses?

2-7 **Practice** (continued)

Solving Proportions

Solve each proportion using any method.

22. $\dfrac{n+4}{-6} = \dfrac{8}{2}$

23. $\dfrac{10}{4} = \dfrac{z-8}{16}$

24. $\dfrac{3}{t+7} = \dfrac{5}{-8}$

25. $\dfrac{x-3}{3} = \dfrac{x+4}{4}$

26. $\dfrac{3}{n+1} = \dfrac{4}{n+4}$

27. $\dfrac{4d+1}{d+9} = \dfrac{-3}{-2}$

28. Sixty-two students, out of 100 surveyed, chose pizza as their favorite lunch item. If the school has 1250 students, how many students would likely say that pizza is their favorite if the survey is a fair representation of the student body?

29. The senior class is taking a trip to an amusement park. They received a special deal where for every 3 tickets they purchased they received one free ticket. 3 tickets cost $53.25. The total purchase of tickets cost $1384.50. How many tickets did they receive?

Solve each proportion.

30. $\dfrac{x-1}{2} = \dfrac{x-2}{3}$

31. $\dfrac{2n+1}{n+2} = \dfrac{5}{4}$

32. $\dfrac{3}{2b-1} = \dfrac{2}{b+2}$

33. Open-Ended Give one example of a proportion. Describe the means and the extremes of the proportion. Explain how you know it is a proportion. Give one non-example of a proportion. Explain how you know it is not a proportion.

2-7 Standardized Test Prep

Solving Proportions

Multiple Choice

For Exercises 1–5, choose the correct letter.

1. What is the solution to the proportion $\frac{3}{5} = \frac{x}{10}$?

   A. $\frac{10}{3}$ **B.** 6   **C.** 10   **D.** 150

2. What is the solution to the proportion $\frac{x-1}{x} = \frac{2}{3}$?

   F. -2 **G.** 0   **H.** 2   **I.** 3

3. There are 105 members of the high school marching band. For every 3 boys there are 4 girls. Which proportion represents how many boys are in the marching band?

   A. $\frac{3}{7} = \frac{b}{105}$ **B.** $\frac{3}{4} = \frac{b}{105}$ **C.** $\frac{4}{7} = \frac{b}{105}$ **D.** $\frac{7}{3} = \frac{b}{105}$

4. A baker is making bread dough. He uses 3 cups of flour for every 8 ounces of water. How many cups of flour will he use if he uses 96 ounces of water?

   F. 4   **G.** 12   **H.** 32   **I.** 36

5. Mr. Carter offered to stay after school for an extra help session, and $\frac{2}{11}$ of his students stayed for the session. If there were 24 students that stayed for the help session, how many students does Mr. Carter teach throughout the day?

   A. 100   **B.** 121   **C.** 132   **D.** 144

Extended Response

6. Elisabeth goes on a 5 mile run each Saturday. Her run typically takes her 45 minutes. She wants to increase this distance to 7 miles. Determine the proportion you use to find the time it would take her to run 7 miles. Solve the proportion. What proportion can be used to determine the time it takes for her to run a marathon, which is approximately 26 miles? What is her time?

2-8   Think About a Plan

Proportions and Similar Figures

Trucks A model of a trailer is shaped like a rectangular prism and has a width of 2 in., a length of 9 in., and a height of 4 in. The scale of the model is 1 : 34. How many times the volume of the model of the trailer is the volume of the actual trailer?

Understanding the Problem

1. What is the formula you use to find the volume of a rectangular prism?

_____

2. Using the scale, how can we find the dimensions of the actual trailer?

_____

_____

Planning the Solution

3. What is the volume of the model?

_____

_____

4. Write three proportions that can be used to determine the actual length, height, and width of the trailer. Solve the proportions.

_____

_____

_____

_____

5. What is the volume of the actual trailer?

_____

_____

Getting an Answer

6. How many times the volume of the model of the trailer is the volume of the actual trailer?

_____

_____

Prentice Hall Algebra 1 • Practice and Problem Solving Workbook

2-8   Practice

Proportions and Similar Figures

Form G

The figures in each pair are similar. Identify the corresponding sides and angles.

1. $\triangle ABC \sim \triangle DEF$

2. $QRST \sim UVWX$

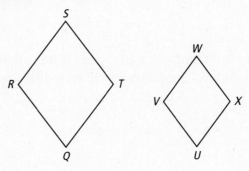

The figures in each pair are similar. Find the missing length.

3.

4.

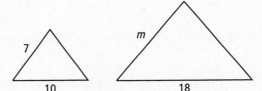

5.

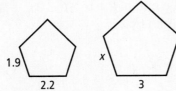

6.

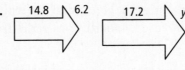

The scale of a map is 0.5 in. : 20 mi. Find the actual distance corresponding to each map distance.

7. 2 in.   **8.** 3.5 in.   **9.** 4.75 in.

10. A museum has a wax sculpture of a historical village. The scale is 1.5 : 8. If the height of a hut in the sculpture is 5 feet, how tall was the original hut to the nearest whole foot?

11. On a map, the length of a river is 4.75 in. The actual length of the river is 247 miles. What is the scale of the map?

2-8   **Practice** (continued)   *Form G*

Proportions and Similar Figures

12. Sammy is constructing a model bridge out of sticks. The actual bridge is 1320 ft long. He wants the scale of his bridge to be 1 : 400. How long should the model be?

13. The Finish-Line Company is drawing up plans for a room addition shown below. The addition will include a large bedroom with a bathroom as shown.

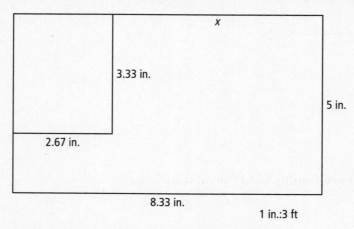

8.33 in.

1 in.:3 ft

a. What are the actual dimensions of the room addition?

b. What are the actual dimensions of the bathroom?

c. What is the actual length of the exterior wall between the end of the room addition and the bathroom wall? This length is represented by *x*.

14. Writing Are all right triangles similar? Explain your answer.

15. Writing A pizza shop sells small 6 in. pizzas and medium 12 in. pizzas. Should the medium pizzas cost twice as much as the small pizzas because they are twice the size? Explain.

2-8 Standardized Test Prep

Proportions and Similar Figures

Multiple Choice

For Exercises 1–4, choose the correct letter.

1. The distance between Capeton and Jonesville is 80 miles. The scale on the map is 0.75 in. : 10 miles. How far apart are the cities on the map?

   A. 6 in.   **B.** 60 in.   **C.** 600 in.   **D.** 1067 in.

2. The floor plan of a room has a scale of 2.5 in.: 35 ft. In the drawing, the length of the room is 8 in. and the width of the room is 6 in. What is the perimeter of the actual room?

   F. 84 ft   **G.** 112 ft   **H.** 196 ft   **I.** 392 ft

3. The figures are similar. What is the missing length?

   A. 9.33 cm
   B. 5.4 cm
   C. 6 cm
   D. 21 cm

   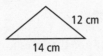
   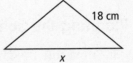

4. A model car is constructed with a scale of 1 : 15. If the actual car is 12 feet long, which proportion represents the length x of the model car?

   F. $\frac{1}{15} = \frac{x}{12}$ **G.** $\frac{1}{15} = \frac{12}{x}$ **H.** $\frac{12}{15} = \frac{1}{x}$ **I.** $\frac{1}{12} = \frac{15}{x}$

Short Response

5. The scale of a map is 0.5 in. : 25 mi. The actual distance between two cities is 725 mi. Write a proportion that represents the relationship. How far apart will the cities be on the map?

2-9 Think About a Plan

Percents

Finance A savings account earns simple interest at a rate of 6% per year. Last year the account earned $10.86 in interest. What was the balance in the account at the beginning of last year?

Understanding the Problem

1. What is the formula for finding simple interest?

   _____

2. What values are given in terms of the formula you wrote in Step 1?

   _____

   _____

Planning the Solution

3. Substitute the given values into the formula for simple interest.

   _____

Getting an Answer

4. Solve for the unknown value.

   _____

   _____

5. Is your answer reasonable? Explain.

   _____

   _____

6. What does your solution mean?

   _____

   _____

2-9 **Practice**

Percents

Find each percent.

1. What percent of 42 is 28?

2. What percent of 48 is 18?

3. What percent of 150 is 350?

4. What percent of 99 is 72?

5. What percent of 15 is 12?

6. What percent of 120 is 200?

Find each part.

7. What is 75% of 180?

8. What is 40% of 720?

9. What is 125% of 62?

10. What is 50% of 821?

11. What is 2.75% of 20?

12. What is 16.5% of 33?

13. A set of golf clubs that costs $600 are on sale for 40% off the regular price. What is the sale price of the clubs?

14. A discount store marks up the merchandise it sells by 55%. If the wholesale price of a particular item is $25, what should the retail price be set at?

15. A used car lot runs sales at the end of the year to reduce inventory. This year the sale price is 15% less than the regular price. If the regular price of a car is $12,000, what is the sale price of the car?

2-9

Practice (continued)

Percents

Form G

Find each base.

16. 60% of what number is 75?

17. 115% of what number is 120?

18. 15% of what number is 6.75?

19. 5% of what number is 4.1?

20. 68% of what number is 64.6?

21. 65% of what number is 577.2?

22. If you deposit $800 in a savings account that earns simple interest at a rate of 1.5% per year, how much interest will you have earned after 5 years?

23. When Marty was born, his parents deposited $5000 in a college savings account that earns simple interest at a rate of 7.25% per year. How much interest will the money have earned after 18 years?

24. You have $10,000 to deposit in a savings account that earns simple interest at a rate of 4.5% per year. How much interest will be in the account after 2 years?

Tell whether you are finding a *percent*, a *part*, or a *base*. Then solve.

25. What is 25% of 50?

26. What percent of 18 is 63?

27. What is 133% of 90?

28. What is 44% of 88?

29. What percent of 67 is 26.8?

30. 42 is 14% of what number?

2-9 Standardized Test Prep

Percents

Multiple Choice

For Exercises 1–5, choose the correct letter.

1. What percent of 92 is 23?
   A. 0.25%　　　　**B.** 4%　　　　　　**C.** 25%　　　　　　**D.** 400%

2. 60% of a number is 66. Which proportion best represents this relationship?
   F. $\frac{66}{b} = \frac{60}{100}$　　　**G.** $\frac{a}{66} = \frac{60}{100}$　　　**H.** $\frac{60}{b} = \frac{66}{100}$　　　**I.** $\frac{60}{66} = \frac{b}{100}$

3. A store is having a clearance sale where merchandise on the sales racks is reduced by 80% from the original price. If a jacket was originally priced at $76, what is the sale price?
   A. $15.20　　　**B.** $24.20　　　　**C.** $60.80　　　　**D.** $72.40

4. If you deposit $3000 in a savings account that earns simple interest at a rate of 2.5% per year, how much interest will you have earned after 4 years?
   F. $30　　　　**G.** $300　　　　**H.** $3000　　　　**I.** $30,000

5. Five years ago you deposited a sum of money into a savings account which has earned $150 in interest. The interest rate for the account is 3% simple interest per year. How much money was originally deposited in the account?
   A. $22.50　　　**B.** $100　　　　**C.** $1000　　　　**D.** $10,000

Short Response

6. There are 3200 students at Martinsville High School. There are 575 students involved in athletics during the spring athletic seasons. What proportion represents the percent of students not involved in athletics during the spring season? What percent of students is not involved in athletics?

2-10   Think About a Plan

Change Expressed as a Percent

Student Discounts You show your student identification at a local restaurant in order to receive a 5% discount. You spend $12 for your meal at the restaurant. How much would your meal cost without the discount?

Understanding the Problem

1. What information are you given in the problem? What are you looking to find?

_____

_____

2. Does this question represent an amount of increase or an amount of decrease? In general, how is the amount of increase or decrease determined?

_____

_____

Planning the Solution

3. What formula can you use to determine the solution?

_____

4. Substitute values from the problem into your formula using x for the unknown value.

_____

Getting an Answer

5. Solve for the unknown value.

_____

_____

6. Check your answer.

_____

_____

7. Is your answer reasonable? Explain.

_____

_____

2-10 Practice

Form G

Change Expressed as a Percent

Tell whether each percent change is an increase or decrease. Then find the percent change. Round to the nearest percent.

1. Original amount: 10
   New amount: 12

2. Original amount: 72
   New amount: 67

3. Original amount: 36
   New amount: 68

4. Original amount: 23
   New amount: 25

5. Original amount: 83
   New amount: 41

6. Original amount: 19
   New amount: 30

7. Original amount: 38
   New amount: 45

8. Original amount: 16
   New amount: 11

9. Original amount: 177
   New amount: 151

10. The price of the truck was advertised as $19,900. After talking with the salesperson, Jack agreed to pay $18,200 for the truck. What is the percent decrease to the nearest percent?

11. The Ragnier's purchased a house for $357,000. They sold their home for $475,000. What was the percent increase to the nearest percent?

12. The original price for a gallon of milk is $4.19. The sale price this week for a gallon of milk is $2.99. What is the percent decrease to the nearest percent?

Find the percent error in each estimation. Round to the nearest percent.

13. You estimate that a building is 20 m tall. It is actually 23 m tall.

14. You estimate the salesman is 45 years old. He is actually 38 years old.

15. You estimate the volume of the storage room is 800 ft^3. The room's volume is actually 810 ft^3.

2-10

Practice (continued)

Change Expressed as a Percent

Form G

A measurement is given. Find the minimum and maximum possible measurements.

16. A nurse measures a newborn baby to be 22 in. long to the nearest in.

17. A bag of apples weighs 4 lbs to the nearest lb.

18. Fencing sections come in lengths of 8 ft to the nearest foot.

Find the percent change. Round to the nearest percent.

19. 16 m to $11\frac{1}{4}$ m

20. 76 ft to $58\frac{1}{2}$ ft

21. $215\frac{1}{2}$ lb to $133\frac{1}{4}$ lb

22. $42.75 to $39.99

23. $315.99 to $499.89

24. $5762.76 to $4999.99

The measured dimensions of a rectangle are given to the nearest whole unit. Find the minimum and maximum possible areas of each rectangle.

25. 4 cm by 7 cm

26. 16 ft by 15 ft

27. 5 m by 12 m

The measured dimensions of a shape or a solid are given to the nearest whole unit. Find the greatest percent error of each shape or solid.

28. The perimeter of a rectangle with length 127 ft and width 211 ft.

29. The area of a rectangle with length 14 in. and width 11 in.

30. The volume of a rectangular prism with length 22 cm, width 36 cm, and height 19 cm.

2-10 Standardized Test Prep

Change Expressed as a Percent

Multiple Choice

For Exercises 1–5, choose the correct letter.

1. Sam ran 3.5 miles on Saturday. On Wednesday, he ran 5.2 miles. What was his percent increase to the nearest percent?
   A. 33% **B.** 42% **C.** 49% **D.** 67%

2. A department store purchases sweaters wholesale for $16. The sweaters sell retail for $35. What is the percent increase to the nearest percent?
   F. 19% **G.** 46% **H.** 54% **I.** 119%

3. Josephine measured the room to be 125 ft wide and 225 ft long. What is the maximum possible area of the room?
   A. 700 ft^2 **B.** 27,950.25 ft^2 **C.** 28,125 ft^2 **D.** 28,300.25 ft^2

4. You estimate the height of the flagpole to be 16 ft tall. The actual height of the flagpole is 18 ft. Which equation can be used to determine your percent error in the estimated height?
   F. $\dfrac{16 - 18}{18}$ **G.** $\dfrac{|16 - 18|}{18}$ **H.** $\dfrac{|16 - 18|}{16}$ **I.** $\dfrac{16 - 18}{16}$

5. You estimate that a box can hold 1152 in^3. The box is actually 10.5 in. long, 10.5 in. wide, and 8 in. tall. What is the percent error in your estimation? Round to the nearest percent.
   A. 23% **B.** 31% **C.** 42% **D.** 77%

Short Response

6. You measure a tub shaped as a rectangular prism to be 3 ft wide, 4 ft long, and 2.5 feet tall to the nearest half foot. What are the minimum and maximum volumes of the tub? What is the greatest possible percent error in calculating the volume of the tub?

3-1   Think About a Plan

Inequalities and Their Graphs

Class Party You are making muffins for a class party. You need 2 cups of flour to make a pan of 12 muffins. You have a 5-lb bag of flour, which contains 20 cups. Write an inequality that represents the possible numbers of muffins you can make.

What do you know?

1. [＿＿＿＿] cups make [＿＿＿＿] muffins.

2. The maximum number of cups in a 5-lb bag of flour is [＿＿＿＿] cups.

What do you need to solve the problem?

3. What is the greatest number of muffins you can make with a 5-lb bag of flour?

How do you solve the problem?

4. What inequality can you use to describe n, the possible number of muffins you can make with 2 cups of flour?

5. What inequality can you use to show the possible number of muffins you can make with 20 cups of flour?

6. What are two solutions to the inequality for 20 cups?

7. What is the greatest possible solution?

8. Are the solutions you wrote in Exercise 6 reasonable? Explain.

_____

_____

_____

3-1 Practice   Form G
Inequalities and Their Graphs

Write an inequality that represents each verbal expression.

1. v is greater 10.

2. b is less than or equal to -1.

3. the product of g and 2 is less than or equal to 6.

4. 2 more than k is greater than -3.

Determine whether each number is a solution of the given inequality.

5. $3y + 5 < 20$ **a.** 2   **b.** 0   **c.** 5

6. $2m - 4 \geq 10$ **a.** -1 **b.** 8   **c.** 10

7. $4x + 3 > -9$ **a.** 0   **b.** -2 **c.** -4

8. $\frac{3 - n}{2} \leq 4$ **a.** 3   **b.** 2   **c.** -10

Graph each inequality.

9. $y < -2$ 10. $t \geq 4$

11. $z > -3$ 12. $v \leq 15$

13. $-3 \geq f$ 14. $-\frac{5}{3} < c$

3-1 Practice (continued) Form G
Inequalities and Their Graphs

Write an inequality for each graph.

15.

16.

17.

18.

Define a variable and write an inequality to model each situation.

19. The school auditorium can seat at most 1200 people.

20. For a certain swim meet, a competitor must swim faster than 23 seconds to qualify.

21. For a touch-typing test, a student must type at least 65 wpm to receive an "A."

Write each inequality in words.

22. $n < 3$ 23. $b > 0$ 24. $-5 \le x$

25. $z \ge 3.14$ 26. $-4 < q$ 27. $18 \ge m$

28. A local pizzeria offered a special. Two pizzas cost $14.99. A group of students spent less than $75. They purchased three pitchers of soda for $12.99. How many pizzas could the group purchase?

29. A student needs at least seven hours of sleep each night. The student goes to bed at 11:00 P.M. and wakes up before 6:30 A.M. Is the student getting enough sleep? Write an inequality for the number of hours of sleep the student gets each night.

3-1 Standardized Test Prep

Inequalities and Their Graphs

Multiple Choice

For Exercises 1–6, choose the correct letter.

1. A student will study French for at least 3 years. Which inequality describes the situation?

   A. $y < 3$ **B.** $y \le 3$ **C.** $y > 3$ **D.** $y \ge 3$

2. All employees of a company work less than 40 hours. Which inequality describes the situation?

   F. $h < 40$ **G.** $h \le 40$ **H.** $h > 40$ **I.** $h \ge 40$

3. Which inequality has the same solutions as $d < -5$?

   A. $d < 5$ **B.** $-5 > d$ **C.** $-d < -5$ **D.** $-d < 5$

4. Which value of n makes the inequality $-3 + (-n) \le n$ false?

   F. -3 **G.** -1 **H.** 0 **I.** 1

5. Which number is a solution of the inequality $7x - 5 \ge -2$?

   A. -3 **B.** -1 **C.** 0 **D.** 1

6. Which inequality represents the graph shown below?

   F. $x < -2$ **G.** $x \le -2$ **H.** $x > -2$ **I.** $x \ge -2$

Short Response

7. The chess club is seeking to raise at least $150 in a fundraiser.

   a. What inequality represents this situation?

   b. What is the graph of the inequality?

3-2   Think About a Plan

Solving Inequalities Using Addition or Subtraction

Government The U.S. Senate is composed of 2 senators from each of the 50 states. In order for a treaty to be ratified, at least two thirds of the senators present must approve the treaty. Suppose all senators are present and 48 of them have voted in favor of a treaty. What are the possible numbers of additional senators who must vote in favor of the treaty in order to ratify it?

What do you know?

1. How many senators make up the U.S. Senate? _____

2. How many senators already have voted in favor of a treaty? _____

3. What words make you think of an inequality? _____

What do you need to solve the problem?

4. What inequality can you use to describe the possible numbers of senators needed to ratify a treaty?

   _____

5. What inequality can you use to find the possible numbers of senators needed to ratify a treaty, if 48 of them already approve?

   _____

6. Does the value of the variable need to be a whole number? Why?

   _____

   _____

How do you solve the problem?

7. What inequality gives the possible numbers of additional senators needed?

3-2 **Practice**   *Form G*

Solving Inequalities Using Addition or Subtraction

State what number you would add to or subtract from each side of the inequality to solve the inequality.

1. $x - 4 < 0$ **2.** $3 > -\frac{7}{5} + s$ **3.** $6.8 \leq m - 4.2$

4. $x + 3 \geq 0$ **5.** $2 \leq \frac{5}{4} + s$ **6.** $-3.8 > m + 4.2$

Solve each inequality. Graph and check your solutions.

7. $y - 2 < -7$ **8.** $v + 6 > 5$

9. $12 \geq c - 2$ **10.** $8 \leq f + 4$

11. $-4.3 \geq 2.4 + s$ **12.** $22.5 < n - 0.9$

13. $c + \frac{4}{7} \leq \frac{6}{7}$ **14.** $p + 1\frac{1}{2} \geq 1\frac{1}{2}$

3-2

Practice (continued)   Form G

Solving Inequalities Using Addition or Subtraction

Solve each inequality. Justify each step.

15. $-y - 4 + 2y > 11$

16. $\frac{1}{7} + d < 1\frac{2}{7}$

17. $\frac{2}{3} + v - \frac{7}{9} \le 0$

18. $-2p - 4 + 3p > 10$

19. $4y + 2 - 3y \le 8$

20. $5m - 4m + 4 > 12$

21. The goal of a toy drive is to donate more than 1000 toys. The toy drive already has collected 300 toys. How many more toys does the toy drive need to meet its goal? Write and solve an inequality to find the number of toys needed.

22. A family earns $1800 a month. The family's expenses are at least $1250. Write and solve an inequality to find the possible amounts the family can save each month.

23. To go to the next level in a certain video game, you must score at least 50 points. You currently have 40 points. You fall into a trap and lose 5 points. What inequality shows the points you must earn to go to the next level?

3-2

Standardized Test Prep

Solving Inequalities Using Addition or Subtraction

Multiple Choice

For Exercises 1–6, choose the correct letter.

1. What is the solution of $p - 12 > -18$?

   A. $p < -30$ **B.** $p < -6$ **C.** $p > -6$ **D.** $p > -30$

2. What is the solution of $x + 5 \le 29$?

   F. $x < 24$ **G.** $x \le 24$ **H.** $x > 24$ **I.** $x \ge 24$

3. Which graph represents all of the solutions of $z - 7 \le -3$?

   A.   **C.**

   B.   **D.**

   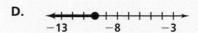

4. Which graph represents all of the solutions of $n - 2 > 0$?

   F.   **H.**

   G.   **I.**

   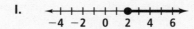

5. Which inequality is equivalent to $-1 \ge m + 4$?

   A. $m < -5$ **B.** $m \le -5$ **C.** $m \ge -5$ **D.** $m \le 3$

6. Your goal in training for the race is to run more than 50 miles per week. So far this week you have run 32 miles. Which inequality represents the situation?

   F. $d \ge 18$ **G.** $d - 32 > 50$ **H.** $d + 32 \ge 50$ **I.** $d + 32 > 50$

Short Response

7. In order to earn an A in a class, your test scores must average at least 92%. On the first 6 tests, you have an average of 91%. What score do you need to get on the last test to earn an A? Show your work.

3-3

Think About a Plan

Solving Inequalities Using Multiplication or Division

Lunch You have $30 and would like to buy a sandwich and a drink for yourself and two friends from the menu at the right. What is the least number of snacks you can afford? What is the greatest number of snacks? Explain.

Drinks   Sandwiches
Sm $ 1   Veggie $ 4
Med $ 1.50   Chicken $ 5
Lg $ 2   Roast Beef $ 7
              Snacks
Pretzels $ 1   Ice cream $ 2
          Brownie $ 3

What do you know?

1. What combinations of one sandwich and one drink can you buy?

_____

_____

_____

_____

How do you plan to solve the problem?

2. What is the most money you can spend on three sandwiches? _____

3. What is the least money you can spend on three sandwiches? _____

4. What is the most money you can spend on three drinks? _____

5. What is the least money you can spend on three drinks? _____

6. How can you have the most money to buy snacks? _____

How do you solve the problem?

7. What is the least number of snacks you can afford? Explain.

_____

_____

8. What is the greatest number of snacks you can afford? Explain.

_____

_____

3-3 Practice

Form G

Solving Inequalities Using Multiplication or Division

Solve each inequality. Graph and check your solution.

1. $\frac{x}{3} > -1$

2. $\frac{w}{4} < 1$

3. $4 \le -\frac{p}{2}$

4. $1 \ge -\frac{2}{3}y$

5. $-6 \ge \frac{2}{3}x$

6. $-1 \le \frac{2}{3}k$

7. $3m > 6$

8. $3t < -12$

9. $-18 \ge -6c$

10. $-3w < 21$

11. $9z > -36$

12. $108 \ge -9d$

3-3 **Practice** (continued)   Form G

Solving Inequalities Using Multiplication or Division

Solve each inequality. Graph and check your solution.

13. $-2.5 > 5p$

14. $-1 < \frac{t}{6}$

15. $\frac{2}{3}n \le 4$

16. $-27u \ge 3$

17. Writing On a certain marathon course, a runner reaches a big hill that is at least 10 miles into the race. If a total marathon is 26.2 miles, how can you find the number of miles the runner still has to go?

18. You wonder if you can save money by using your cell phone for all long distance calls. Long distance calls cost $.05 per minute on your cell phone. The basic plan for your cell phone is $29.99 each month. The cost of regular phone service with unlimited long distance is $39.99. Define a variable and write an inequality that will help you find the number of long-distance call minutes you may make and still save money.

19. The unit cost for a piece of fabric is $4.99 per yard. You have $30 to spend on material. How many feet of material could you buy? Define a variable and write an inequality to solve this problem.

3-3 Standardized Test Prep

Solving Inequalities Using Multiplication or Division

Multiple Choice

For Exercises 1–5, choose the correct letter.

1. What is the solution of $\frac{a}{10} < -2$?

   A. $a < -20$ **B.** $a > -20$ **C.** $a < -5$ **D.** $a > -5$

2. What is the solution of $-3 \geq -\frac{2}{3}z$?

   F. $z \leq -\frac{9}{2}$ **G.** $z \leq \frac{9}{2}$ **H.** $z \geq -\frac{9}{2}$ **I.** $z \geq \frac{9}{2}$

3. What is the solution of $48 < -6h$?

   A. $h < -8$ **B.** $h > -8$ **C.** $h \geq -8$ **D.** $h \leq -8$

4. You have budgeted to spend no more than $108 on gasoline for your vehicle this month. It typically takes $27 to fill up your tank. Which inequality represents how many times you can fill your tank this month?

   F. $27f = 108$ **G.** $27f > 108$ **H.** $27f \leq 108$ **I.** $27f < 108$

5. Which graph represents all of the solutions of $-15b \leq 45$?

   A.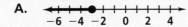

   C.

   B.

   D.

Short Response

6. In a town, there are 170 teenagers that own portable media players. This is at least $\frac{2}{3}$ of all the teenagers in the town. What is the maximum number of teenagers who live in the town? Show your work.

3-4

Think About a Plan

Solving Multi-Step Inequalities

Commission A sales associate in a shoe store earns $325 each week, plus a commission equal to 4% of her sales. This week her goal is to earn at least $475. At least how many dollars' worth of shoes must the associate sell in order to reach her goal?

What do you know?

1. Write an expression to represent how much a sales associate earns each week. Let s = total sales.

   _____

2. How much does she want to earn this week?

   _____

How do you plan to solve the problem?

3. Should you use an equation or an inequality to compare the amount the sales associate earns and her goal? Explain.

   _____

How do you solve the problem?

4. What inequality can you use to find how many dollars' worth of shoes she must sell this week to reach her goal?

   _____

5. Solve the inequality. Show your work.

3-4 Practice
Form G

Solving Multi-Step Inequalities

Solve each inequality. Check your solutions.

1. $3f + 9 < 21$

2. $4n - 3 \geq 105$

3. $33y - 3 \leq 8$

4. $2 + 2p > -17$

5. $12 > 60 - 6r$

6. $-5 \leq 11 + 4j$

Solve each inequality.

7. $2(k + 4) - 3k \leq 14$

8. $3(4c - 5) - 2c > 0$

9. $15(j - 3) + 3j < 45$

10. $22 \geq 5(2y + 3) - 3y$

11. $-53 > -3(3z + 3) + 3z$

12. $20(d - 4) + 4d \leq 8$

13. $-x + 2 < 3x - 6$

14. $3v - 12 > 5v + 10$

Solve each inequality, if possible. If the inequality has no solution, write
***no solution*. If the solutions are all real numbers, write *all real numbers*.**

15. $6w + 5 > 2(3w + 3)$

16. $-5r + 15 \geq -5(r - 2)$

17. $-2(6 + s) < -16 + 2s$

18. $9 - 2x < 7 + 2(x - 3)$

19. $2(n - 3) \leq -13 + 2n$

20. $-3(w + 3) < 9 - 3w$

3-4

Practice (continued)   *Form G*

Solving Multi-Step Inequalities

21. A grandmother says her grandson is two years older than her granddaughter and that together, they are at least 12 years old. How old are her grandson and granddaughter?

22. A family decides to rent a boat for the day while on vacation. The boat's rental rate is $500 for the first two hours and $50 for each additional half hour. Suppose the family can spend $700 for the boat. What inequality represents the number of hours for which they can rent the boat?

23. Writing Suppose a friend is having difficulty solving $-1.75(q - 5) > 3(q + 2.5)$. Explain how to solve the inequality, showing all the necessary steps and identifying the properties you would use.

24. Open-Ended Write two different inequalities that you can solve by adding 2 to each side and then dividing each side by -12. Solve each inequality.

25. Reasoning a. Solve $3v - 5 \le 2v + 10$ by gathering the variable terms on the left side and the constant terms on the right side of the inequality.

b. Solve $3v - 5 \le 2v + 10$ by gathering the constant terms on the left side and the variable terms on the right side of the inequality.

c. Compare the results of parts (a) and (b).

d. Which method do you prefer? Explain.

3-4

Standardized Test Prep

Solving Multi-Step Inequalities

Multiple Choice

For Exercises 1–6, choose the correct letter.

1. What is the solution of $6w - 8 \geq 22$?

   A. $w > \frac{7}{3}$ **B.** $w \geq \frac{7}{3}$ **C.** $w > 5$ **D.** $w \geq 5$

2. What is the solution of $2(y + 5) + 7y \leq 19$?

   F. $y < 1$ **G.** $y \leq 1$ **H.** $y > 1$ **I.** $y \geq 1$

3. What is the solution of $25 > -3(4n - 3)$?

   A. $n < -\frac{4}{3}$ **B.** $n < \frac{4}{3}$ **C.** $n > -\frac{4}{3}$ **D.** $n > \frac{4}{3}$

4. Which graph represents all of the solutions of $-12 > -k - (3k + 4)$?

   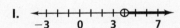

5. You have already saved $55. You earn $9 per hour at your job. You are saving for a bicycle that costs $199. What inequality represents the possible numbers of hours you need to work to buy the bicycle?

   A. $h < 16$ **B.** $h \leq 16$ **C.** $h \geq 16$ **D.** $h > 16$

6. Admission to the fair costs $7.75. Each ride costs you $.50. You have $15 to spend at the fair including admission. Which inequality represents the possible numbers of rides you can ride?

   F. $r > 14$ **G.** $r < 14$ **H.** $r \leq 14$ **I.** $r \leq 15$

Short Response

7. The perimeter of a rectangle is at least 32 cm. The length of the rectangle is 9 cm. What are the possible widths of the rectangle? Show your work.

3-5

Think About a Plan

Working With Sets

Universal set U = {planets in Earth's solar system} and set P = {planets that are farther from the sun than Earth}. What is the complement of set P? Write your answer in roster form.

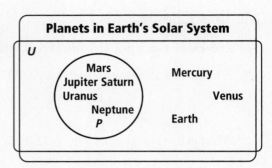

Planets in Earth's Solar System

U

Mars
Jupiter Saturn
Uranus
Neptune
P

Mercury

Venus

Earth

1. What does complement mean?

_____

_____

2. Where is the complement of set P on the Venn diagram?

_____

_____

3. What planets belong to the complement of set P?

_____

_____

4. How do you write your answer in roster form?

_____

_____

3-5

Practice

Working With Sets

Form G

Write each set in roster form and in set-builder notation.

1. M is the set of integers that are greater than -5.

2. N is the set of even numbers that are less than 2.5.

3. P is the set of natural numbers that are factors of 25.

4. R is the set of odd natural numbers that are less than 12.

Write each set in set-builder notation.

5. $B = \{-3, -2, -1, 0, 1, \ldots\}$

6. $M = \{2, 4, 6, 8, 10\}$

7. $S = \{1, 2, 3, 6, 9, 18\}$

8. $G = \{\ldots, -5, -3, -1, 1, 3, 5, \ldots\}$

Write the solutions of each inequality in set-builder notation.

9. $2y + 5 < 21$

10. $3r + 3 > 63$

11. $12 - 8m \geq 60$

12. $-(3x + 5) \leq -13$

13. $-2(x - 7) > -10 - 6x$

14. $-2(x + 7) \leq -14 + 2x$

15. $-3(2x + 4) + 1 > -13$

16. $-3(2x - 4) - 1 < -25 + 6x$

17. $-(x - 1) + 5 \geq -10 - 3x$

3-5

Practice (continued)   Form G
Working With Sets

List all the subsets of each set.

18. {a, b, c, d}   **19.** {0, 3, 6, 9}   **20.** {car, bus, truck}

21. {−5, 5}   **22.** {0}   **23.** {red, blue, yellow}

24. Suppose $U = \{0, 2, 4, 6, 8, 10\}$ is the universal set and $A = \{2, 4, 6\}$. What is A'?

25. Suppose $U = \{\ldots, -5, -3, -1, 1, 3, 5, \ldots\}$ is the universal set and $R = \{1, 3, 5, \ldots\}$. What is R'?

26. Suppose $U = \{x \,|\, x$ is a multiple of 3, $x \geq 18\}$ is the universal set and $C = \{21, 24, 27, 30\}$. What is C'?

27. Suppose $U = \{x \,|\, x$ is a real number, $x < -3\}$ is the universal set and $T = \{x \,|\, x$ is a real number, $x < -10\}$. What is T'?

Suppose $U = \{1, 2, 4, 7, 11, 15\}$, $A = \{2, 4, 7\}$, and $B = \{1, 2, 4\}$. Tell whether each statement is *true* or *false*. Explain your reasoning.

28. $A \subseteq U$ **29.** $U \subseteq B$ **30.** $B \subseteq A$ **31.** $\emptyset \subseteq B$

32. Let the universal set U and set B be as defined below. What are the elements of the complement of B? Write your answer in roster form and in set-builder notation.

   $U = \{$all the months in a calendar year$\}$

   $B = \{$all months that have 31 days$\}$

3-5 Standardized Test Prep

Working With Sets

Multiple Choice

For Exercises 1–6, choose the correct letter.

1. What is the solution of $-(3n - 7) \geq 4$ written in set-builder notation?

   A. $n \leq 1$ **B.** $\{1\}$ **C.** $\{n \mid n \geq 1\}$ **D.** $\{n \mid n \leq 1\}$

2. What set represents the solution of $15 < -9j - 3$?

   F. $j < -2$ **G.** $\{-2\}$ **H.** $\{j \mid j > -2\}$ **I.** $\{j \mid j < -2\}$

3. Which of the following sets is not a subset of $\{-1, 1, 3\}$?

   A. $\{\}$ **B.** $\{0\}$ **C.** $\{-1, 3\}$ **D.** $\{-1, 1, 3\}$

4. Given the universal set $U = \{$dog, cat, fish, gerbil, snake$\}$ and set L is the set of pets in U that have legs, what is the complement of set L?

   F. $\{$dog, cat, fish, gerbil, snake$\}$

   G. $\{$fish, snake$\}$

   H. $\{$dog, cat, gerbil$\}$

   I. $\emptyset$

5. Suppose the universal set U is the set of all real numbers and M is the set of all real numbers greater than or equal to 8. Which number is not in M'?

   A. -8 **B.** 0   **C.** 5   **D.** 8

6. Suppose $U = \{-2, 0, 2, 4\}$ is the universal set and $A = \{-2, 2\}$. What is A'?

   F. $\emptyset$ **G.** $\{-2, 2\}$ **H.** $\{0, 4\}$ **I.** $\{-2, 0, 2, 4\}$

Short Response

7. The width of a soccer field must be between 55 yd and 80 yd.

   a. What compound inequality represents the width of a soccer field?

   b. List the possible values for the field's width if the width is a multiple of 5.

3-6

Think About a Plan

Compound Inequalities

Physics The force exerted on a spring is proportional to the distance the spring is stretched from its relaxed position. Suppose you stretch a spring a distance of d inches by applying a force of F pounds. For your spring, $\frac{d}{F} = 0.8$. You apply forces between 25 and 40 lb, inclusive. What inequality describes the distances the spring is stretched? Write the inequality in interval notation.

What do you know?

1. What inequality would you use to describe the forces that are applied to the spring?

   _____

2. How would you rewrite the proportion $\frac{d}{F} = 0.8$ to solve for d?

   _____

What do you need to solve the problem?

3. What variable will be in the inequality that solves the problem?

   _____

4. By what factor will you multiply each part of the compound inequality?

   _____

How do you solve the problem?

5. How do you write the inequality you found in interval notation?

   _____

3-6 Practice   Form G
Compound Inequalities

Write a compound inequality that represents each phrase. Graph the solutions.

1. all real numbers that are less than -3 or greater than or equal to 5

2. The time a cake must bake is between 25 minutes and 30 minutes, inclusive.

Solve each compound inequality. Graph your solutions.

3. $5 < k - 2 < 11$

4. $-4 > y + 2 > -10$

5. $6b - 1 \leq 41$ or $2b + 1 \geq 11$

6. $5 - m < 4$ or $7m > 35$

7. $3 < 2p - 3 \leq 12$

8. $3 > \frac{11 + k}{4} \geq -3$

9. $3d + 3 \leq -1$ or $5d + 2 \geq 12$

10. $9 - c < 2$ or $-3c > 15$

11. $4 \leq y + 2 \leq -3(y - 2) + 24$

12. $5z + 3 < -7$ or $-2z - 6 > -8$

Write each interval as an inequality. Then graph the solutions.

13. $(-1, 10]$

14. $[-3, 3]$

15. $(-\infty, 0]$ or $(5, \infty)$

16. $[3, \infty)$

17. $(-\infty, 4)$

18. $[25, 50)$

3-6

Practice (continued)   Form G

Compound Inequalities

Write each inequality or set in interval notation. Then graph the interval.

19. $x < -2$

20. $x > 0$

21. $x < -2$ or $x \geq 1$

22. $-3 \leq x < 4$

Write a compound inequality that each graph could represent.

23.

24.

25.

26.

Solve each compound inequality. Justify each step.

27. $3r + 2 < 5$ or $7r - 10 > 60$

28. $3 > -0.25v > -2.5$

29. $\dfrac{y - 2}{2} - 5 \leq 3$ or $\dfrac{1 + 2y}{3} \geq 41$

30. $-\dfrac{3}{2} \leq \dfrac{5}{6}w - \dfrac{3}{4} \leq 2$

31. The absorbency of a certain towel is considered normal if the towel is able to hold between six and eight mL. The first checks for materials result in absorbency measures of 6.2 mL and 7.2 mL. What possible values for the third reading m will make the average absorbency normal?

32. A family is comparing different car seats. One car seat is designed for a child up to and including 30 lb. Another car seat is designed for a child between 15 lb and 40 lb. A third car seat is designed for a child between 30 lb and 85 lb, inclusive. Model these ranges on a number line. Represent each range of weight using interval notation. Which car seats are appropriate for a 32-lb child?

3-6 Standardized Test Prep

Compound Inequalities

Multiple Choice

For Exercises 1–5, choose the correct letter.

1. Which inequality represents the phrase all real numbers that are greater than -7 and less than -4?

    A. $n > -7$ **B.** $n < -4$ **C.** $-7 < n < -4$ **D.** $n > -7$ or $n < -4$

2. What are the solutions of $8 \leq x + 2 < 12$?

    F. $x \geq 6$ **G.** $6 \leq x < 10$ **H.** $10 \leq x < 14$ **I.** $x < 10$

3. What are the solutions of $3d - 4 < -10$ or $2d + 7 \geq 9$?

    A. $d > -2$ **B.** $d \leq 1$ **C.** $-2 < d \leq 1$ **D.** $d < -2$ or $d \geq 1$

4. Which compound inequality represents the graph shown below?

    F. $7d + 1 > 0$ **H.** $1 < 7d + 1 \leq 15$

    G. $7d + 1 < 1$ or $7d + 1 \geq 15$ **I.** $1 \leq 7d + 1 < 15$

5. A teacher knows that 80% of her students will score no more than 5 points above or below the class average, 85%, on the test. Which inequality represents the test scores of 80% of her students?

    A. $75 < A < 85$ **C.** $80 < A < 90$

    B. $85 \leq A \leq 90$ **D.** $80 \leq A \leq 90$

Extended Response

6. **a.** Solve the compound inequality $-4 \leq 3p - 7 < 5$. Show your work.

    b. Graph your solution.

3-7 Think About a Plan

Absolute Value Equations and Inequalities

Banking The official mass of a nickel is 5 g, but the actual mass can vary from this amount by up to 0.194 gram. Suppose a bank measures the mass of a roll of 40 nickels. The wrapper has a mass of 1.5 g.
- **a.** What is the range of possible masses for the roll of nickels?
- **b. Reasoning** If all of the nickels in the roll each have the official mass, then the roll's mass is $40(5) + 1.5 = 201.5$ g. Is it possible for a roll to have a mass of 201.5 g and contain nickels that do not have the official mass? Explain.

What do you know?

1. What inequality describes the possible mass range of a single nickel?

_____

What do you need to solve the problem?

2. What inequality would you use to describe the possible mass range of a roll of nickels?

_____

3. Is the mass 201.5 g within the interval you found above? _____

How do you solve the problem?

4. Is it possible for a roll to have a mass of 201.5 g and contain nickels that do not have the official mass? Explain.

_____

_____

3-7 Practice   Form G
Absolute Value Equations and Inequalities

Solve each equation. Graph and check your solutions.

1. $|b| = \frac{2}{3}$ **2.** $10 = |y|$

3. $|n| + 2 = 5$ **4.** $4 = |s| - 3$

5. $|x| - 5 = -1$ **6.** $7|d| = 49$

Solve each equation. If there is no solution, write *no solution*.

7. $|r - 9| = -3$ **8.** $|c + 3| = 15$ **9.** $1 = |g + 3|$

10. $2 = \left| m + \frac{2}{3} \right|$ **11.** $-2|3d| = 4$ **12.** $-3|2w| = -6$

13. $4|v - 5| = 16$ **14.** $3|d - 4| = 12$ **15.** $|3f + 0.5| - 1 = 7$

Solve and graph each inequality.

16. $|x| > 1$ **17.** $|x| < 2$

18. $|x + 3| < 10$ **19.** $|y + 4| > 12$

20. $|y - 1| \leq 8$ **21.** $|p - 6| \geq 5$

22. $|3c - 4| > 12$ **23.** $\left| 2t + \frac{2}{3} \right| \leq 4$

3-7 Practice (continued) Form G
Absolute Value Equations and Inequalities

Solve each equation or inequality. If there is no solution, write *no solution*.

24. $|d| + 3 = 33$

25. $1.5|3p| = 4.5$

26. $\left|d + \frac{2}{3}\right| + \frac{3}{4} = 0$

27. $|f| - \frac{1}{5} = \frac{3}{15}$

28. $7|3y - 4| - 8 \le 48$

29. $|t| - 1.2 = 3.8$

30. $-1|c + 4| = -3.6$

31. $\frac{|y|}{4} < 3$

32. $|9d| > 6.3$

Write an absolute value inequality that represents each set of numbers.

33. all real numbers less than 3 units from 0

34. all real numbers at most 6 units from 0

35. all real numbers more than 4 units from 6

36. all real numbers at least 3 units from −2

37. A child takes a nap averaging three hours and gets an average of 12 hours of sleep at night. Nap time and night time sleep can each vary by 30 minutes. What are the possible time lengths for the child's nap and night time sleep?

38. In a sports poll, 53% of those surveyed believe their high school football team will win the state championship. The poll shows a margin of error of ±5 percentage points. Write and solve an absolute value inequality to find the least and the greatest percent of people that think their team will win the state championship.

3-7 Standardized Test Prep

Absolute Value Equations and Inequalities

Multiple Choice

For Exercises 1–5, choose the correct letter.

1. What are the solutions of $|4a| \geq 32$?

    A. $a \geq 8$

    B. $a \leq -8$ or $a \geq 8$

    C. $-8 \leq a \leq 8$

    D. $\emptyset$

2. What are the solution(s) of $|n| - 4 = 14$?

    F. $n = 10$ **G.** $n = -18$ or $n = 18$ **H.** $n = 10$ or $n = 18$ **I.** $\emptyset$

3. What are the solution(s) of $4|2x| + 1 = -3$?

    A. $z = -\frac{1}{2}$ **B.** $z = \frac{1}{2}$ **C.** $z = -\frac{1}{2}$ or $z = \frac{1}{2}$ **D.** $\emptyset$

4. Some people are guessing the number of jelly beans in a jar. Each person who guesses within 15 of the correct number will win a prize. The correct number of jelly beans is 389. What values of n represent the numbers that will win a prize?

    F. $n = 389$ or $n = 404$

    G. $n = 389$ and $n = 404$

    H. $389 \leq n \leq 404$

    I. $374 \leq n \leq 404$

5. A carpenter is cutting a 2 by 4 for the framing of a roof. The length needs to be 5 feet. He allows 0.1 foot possible variation for the length of the cut. What values of l represent the acceptable lengths for the board, in feet?

    A. $l = 5$

    B. $l \leq 5.1$

    C. $l \geq 4.9$

    D. $4.9 \leq l \leq 5.1$

Short Response

6. A student reads an average of 34 pages per day. The number of pages she reads per day varies from the average by up to 8 pages.

    a. Write an absolute value inequality that represents the range of the number of pages she reads per day.

    b. Solve your inequality.

3-8   Think About a Plan

Unions and Intersections of Sets

In a survey of students about favorite sports, the results include 22 who like tennis, 25 who like football, 9 who like tennis and football, 17 who like tennis and baseball, 20 who like football and baseball, 6 who like all three sports, and 4 who like none of the sports. How many students like only tennis and football? How many students like only tennis and baseball? How many students like only baseball and football?

1. How can a Venn diagram help you solve the problem?

_____

_____

2. How many circles will you need in your diagram? _____

3. What strategies can you use to complete the Venn diagram?

_____

_____

    a. Which parts of the Venn diagram can you complete? _____

    b. Where will you place the students who like all 3 sports? _____

    c. Where will you place the students who like none of the sports? _____

4. How many students like only tennis
   and football?

5. How many students like only tennis
   and baseball?

6. How many students like only baseball
   and football?

3-8 Practice   Form G

Unions and Intersections of Sets

Find each union or intersection. Let $A = \{1, 3, 5, 7, 9\}$, $B = \{x \mid x$ **is a positive odd integer less than** $10\}$, $C = \{1, 2, 4, 7\}$, **and** $D = \{x \mid x$ **is a negative integer between** -5 **and** $-1\}$.

1. $A \cup B$ **2.** $A \cap C$ **3.** $A \cap D$

4. $B \cup C$ **5.** $B \cap D$ **6.** $C \cup D$

7. $A \cap B$ **8.** $A \cup C$ **9.** $A \cup D$

10. $A \cap B \cap C$ **11.** $D \cup C \cup B$ **12.** $A \cap C \cap D$

13. $A \cap B \cap D$ **14.** $A \cup C \cup D$ **15.** $B \cap C \cap D$

Draw a Venn diagram to represent the union and intersection of these sets.

16. Let $V = \{p, m, b, a, d, e\}$, $W = \{i, t, b, p\}$, and $X = \{g, e, r, z, p\}$.

17. Let $L = \{$all negative odd integers$\}$, $M = \{$all negative integers greater than or equal to $-5\}$, and $N = \{-3, -1, 0, 3, 1\}$.

3-8

Practice (continued)   Form G
Unions and Intersections of Sets

18. Each student at a particular school participates in at least one type of activity–sports or music. Fifty students participate in both sports and music. Two hundred students participate in sports. Fifty students participate in music only. There are a total of 250 students at the school. How many students only participate in sports?

19. A local parks department asked 300 people if they should build new basketball courts and/or new skateboard ramps. They were not allowed to answer "neither." If 233 people said they want new basketball courts and 94 people said they want both new basketball courts and skateboard ramps, how many people said they wanted new skateboard ramps?

Solve each inequality. Write the solutions as either the union or intersection of two sets.

20. $|2x - 3| \le 11$

21. $50 > 7n + 8 > 22$

22. $|2w - 5| \ge 0$

23. $12 > |4d + 16|$

24. $-5 < -n + 3 < 10$

25. $|1.5t - 0.75| < 4$

26. A salon offers three services–manicures, massages, and hair styling. Five clients come in for all three services. Forty clients come in for both hair styling and manicures. Thirty-five clients come in for both manicures and massages. Fifteen clients come in for both hair styling and massages. Ten clients come in only for massages. Five clients only come in for hair styling and only two clients come in for just manicures. How many total clients are represented by the data?

Prentice Hall Gold Algebra 1 • Practice and Problem Solving Workbook
Copyright © by Pearson Education, Inc., or its affiliates. All Rights Reserved.

3-8

Standardized Test Prep

Unions and Intersections of Sets

Gridded Response

Solve each exercise and enter your answer on the grid provided.

1. Let $A = \{1, 3, 5\}$ and $B = \{x \mid x$ is an integer less than 2$\}$. Find $A \cap B$.

2. Let $C = \{1, 2, 3, 4, 5\}$ and $D = \{x \mid x$ is a positive, even integer less than 7$\}$. How many elements are in $C \cup D$?

3. Let $X = \{8, 10, 12\}$, $Y = \{6, 7, 8\}$, and $Z = \{-4, 4, 8\}$. Find $X \cap Y \cap Z$.

4. Let $M = \{1, 3, 5, 7\}$, $N = \{x \mid x$ is an even whole number less than 12$\}$, and $P = \{x \mid x$ is an odd whole number less than 4$\}$. How many elements are in $(M \cup N) \cap P$?

5. Let $F = \{-1, 0, 1, 2, 3\}$, $G = \{1, 3, 5, 7\}$, and $H = \{2, 4, 6, 8\}$. What is the difference of the number of elements of $G \cup H$ and the number of elements of $F \cap G$?

1. 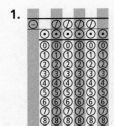 **2.** 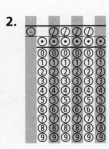 **3.** 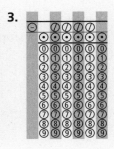 **4.** 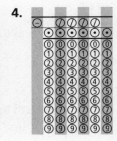 **5.**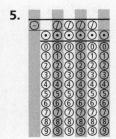

4-1 Think About a Plan

Using Graphs to Relate Two Quantities

Skiing Sketch a graph of each situation. Are the graphs the same? Explain.
a. your speed as you travel from the bottom of a ski slope to the top
b. your speed as you travel from the top of a ski slope to the bottom

Understanding the Problem

1. What is likely to be true about your speed as you go from the bottom of the ski slope to the top?

   _____

   _____

2. What is likely to be true about your speed as you go from the top of the ski slope to the bottom?

   _____

   _____

Planning the Solution

3. What will the graph tend to look like relating to your speed as you go up the ski slope?

   _____

4. What will the graph tend to look like relating to your speed as you go down the ski slope?

   _____

Getting an Answer

5. Sketch the graph as you travel to the top of the slope.

6. Sketch the graph as you travel to the bottom of the slope.

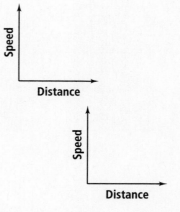

7. Are the graphs the same? Explain.

   _____

   _____

4-1

Practice

Form G

Using Graphs to Relate Two Quantities

What are the variables in each graph? Describe how the variables are related at various points on the graph.

1. **Volume of Pool Water**

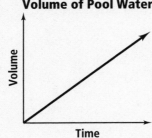

2. **Temperature of Water**

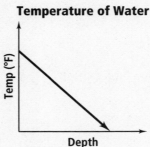

3. **Plant Height**

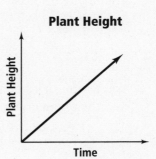

Match each graph with its related table. Explain your answers.

4.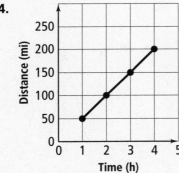

5.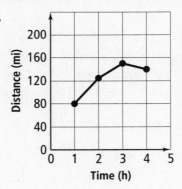

6.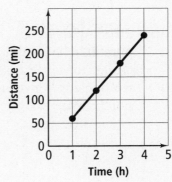

A.

Time (h)	Distance (mi)
1	60
2	120
3	180
4	240

B.

Time (h)	Distance (mi)
1	80
2	125
3	150
4	140

C.

Time (h)	Distance (mi)
1	50
2	100
3	150
4	200

Prentice Hall Gold Algebra 1 • Practice and Problem Solving Workbook

4-1 Practice (continued)   Form G

Using Graphs to Relate Two Quantities

Sketch a graph to represent the situation. Label each section.

7. You buy two shirts. The third one is free.

8. You warm up for gym class, play basketball, and then cool down.

9. The temperature warms up during the day and then decreases at night.

10. Error Analysis DVDs cost $19.99 each for the first 2 purchased. After that, they cost $5.99 each. Describe and correct the error in sketching a graph to represent the relationship between the total cost and the number of DVDs purchased.

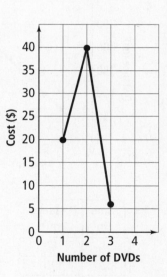

11. Sketch a graph of each situation. Are the graphs the same? Explain.
   a. your distance from school as you leave your house and walk to school
   b. your distance from school as you leave school and walk to your house

4-1

Standardized Test Prep

Using Graphs to Relate Two Quantities

Multiple Choice

For Exercises 1–3, choose the correct letter.

1. The graph shows your distance from the practice field as you go home after practice. You received a ride from a friend back to his house where you ate supper. You then walked home from there. Which point represents a time when you are walking home?

   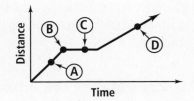

   A. A **B.** B **C.** C **D.** D

2. Which table is related to the graph at the right?

   F.

Time (h)	Temp. (°F)
1	68
2	73
3	78
4	85

   H.

Time (h)	Temp. (°F)
68	1
73	2
78	3
85	4

   G.

Temp. (°F)	Time (h)
1	85
2	78
3	73
4	68

   I.

Temp. (°F)	Time (h)
85	1
78	2
73	3
68	4

3. How are the variables related on the graph?

   A. as speed decreases, height stay constant
   B. as speed decreases, height increases
   C. as speed increases, height decreases
   D. as speed increases, height increases

   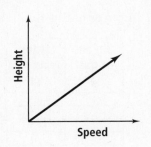

Short Response

4. For the race you swim 1 mile, run 10 miles, and bike 25 miles. Sketch a graph to represent the relationship. Label the axes with the related variables. What are the important points on the graph?

4-2 Think About a Plan

Patterns and Linear Functions

Electric Car An automaker produces a car that can travel 40 mi on its charged battery before it begins to use gas. Then the car travels 50 mi for each gallon of gas used. Represent the relationship between the amount of gas used and the distance traveled using a table, an equation, and a graph. Is total distance traveled a function of the gas used? What are the independent and dependent variables? Explain.

Understanding the Problem

1. Describe the miles that the car can travel on the different types of fuel.

   _____

Planning the Solution

2. Give a verbal description of the relationship between the miles the car travels and gallons of gas it uses.

   _____

   _____

Getting an Answer

3. Represent this relationship with an equation.

   _____

4. Represent this relationship with a table.

Gallons of gas, g	Miles Traveled, m

5. Represent this relationship with a graph.

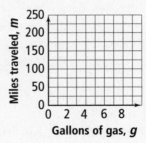

6. Is total distance traveled a function of the gas used? What are the independent and dependent variables? Explain.

   _____

   _____

4-2 Practice
Patterns and Linear Functions

Form G

For each diagram, find the relationship between the number of shapes and the perimeter of the figure they form. Represent this relationship using a table, words, an equation, and a graph.

1.

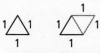

1 triangle 2 triangles 3 triangles 4 triangles

Triangles	1	2	3	4	5	6		n
Perimeter	3	4	5				12	

2.

1 square   2 squares   3 squares

Squares	1	2	3	4	5	6		n
Perimeter	4	6	8				22	

For each table, determine whether the relationship is a function. Then represent the relationship using words, an equation, and a graph.

3.

x	y
0	1
1	3
2	5
3	7

4.

x	y
0	6
1	7
2	8
3	9

4-2

Practice (continued)   Form G

Patterns and Linear Functions

For each table, determine whether the relationship is a function. Then represent the relationship using words, an equation, and a graph.

5.   **Distance Traveled**

Time (h)	Distance (mi)
0	0
1	55
2	110
3	165

6.   **Calories Burned**

Minutes (min)	Calories (C)
0	0
10	50
20	100
30	150

7. **Reasoning** Graph the set of ordered pairs (0, 2), (1, 4), (2, 6), (3, 8). Determine whether the relationship is a linear function. Explain how you know.

8. You can make a bubble solution by mixing 1 cup of liquid soap with 4 cups of water. Represent the relationship between the cups of liquid soap and the cups of bubble solution made using a table, an equation, and a graph. Is the amount of bubble solution made a function of the amount of liquid soap used? Explain.

4-2 Standardized Test Prep

Patterns and Linear Functions

Multiple Choice

For Exercises 1–4, choose the correct letter.

1. Which equation represents the relationship shown in the table at the right?

   A. $y = -x - 3$ **C.** $y = 2x - 3$

   B. $y = x - 3$ **D.** $y = -2x + 3$

x	y
0	−3
1	−1
2	1
3	3

2. In a relationship between variables, what is the variable called that changes in response to another variable?

   F. function   **H.** independent variable

   G. input function   **I.** dependent variable

3. A lawn care company charges a $10 trip fee plus $0.15 per square foot of x square feet of lawn for fertilization. Which equation represents the relationship?

   A. $x = 0.10y + 15$ **B.** $y = 0.15x + 10$ **C.** $y = 10x + 0.15$ **D.** $x = 10y + 0.15$

4. Which equation represents the relationship shown in the graph?

   F. $y = -2x$ **H.** $y = -\frac{1}{2}x$

   G. $y = 2x$ **I.** $y = \frac{1}{2}x$

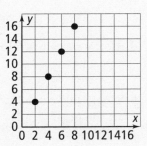

Short Response

5. The table below shows the relationship between the number of teachers and the number of students going on a field trip. How can the relationship be described using words, an equation, and a graph?

Field Trip					
Teachers	2	3	4	5	6
Students	34	51	68	85	102

4-3

Think About a Plan

Patterns and Nonlinear Functions

Fountain A designer wants to make a circular fountain inside a square of grass as shown at the right. What is a rule for the area A of the grass as a function of r?

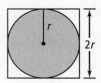

Understanding the Problem

1. What shapes are involved in the areas of grass and the fountain?

_____

2. What are the formulas for the areas of these shapes?

_____

Planning the Solution

3. Using r as shown in the drawing, what is a rule for the area of the square?

_____

4. Using r as shown in the drawing, what is a rule for the area of the circle?

_____

5. How will you find the area of the remaining grass after the fountain is placed in the grass?

_____

_____

Getting an Answer

6. What is a rule for the area A of the grass as a function of r after the fountain is placed in the grass?

_____

_____

4-3 Practice

Form G

Patterns and Nonlinear Functions

1. A student's earnings E, in dollars, is a function of the number h of hours worked. Graph the function shown by the table. Tell whether the function is *linear* or *nonlinear*.

Hours, h	2	4	6	8	10
Earnings (\$), E	18	36	54	72	90

Graph the function shown by each table. Tell whether the function is *linear* or *nonlinear*.

2.

x	y
0	3
1	5
2	7
3	9

3.

x	y
0	0
1	2
2	−4
3	7

4-3

Practice (continued)

Form G

Patterns and Nonlinear Functions

Each set of ordered pairs represents a function. Write a rule that represents the function.

4. $(0, 1), (1, 3), (2, 9), (3, 27), (4, 81)$

5. $(0, 0), (1, 1), (2, 4), (3, 9), (4, 16)$

6. $(0, 1), (1, 0.5), (2, 0.25), (3, 0.125), (4, 0.0625)$

7. $(0, 0), (1, 1), (2, 8), (3, 27), (4, 64)$

8. Reasoning A certain function fits the following description: *As the value of x increases by 1 each time, the value of y decreases by the square of x.* Is this function *linear* or *nonlinear*? Explain your reasoning.

9. Writing The rule $C = 6.3r$ gives the approximate circumference C of a circle as a function of its radius r. Identify the independent and dependent variables in this relationship. Explain your reasoning.

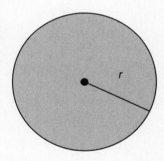

10. Open-Ended What is a rule for the function represented by $(0, -2), (1, -1), (2, 2), (3, 7)$? Explain your reasoning.

11. A landscape architect wants to make a triangular garden inside a square of land as shown at the right. What is a rule for the area A of the garden as a function of s?

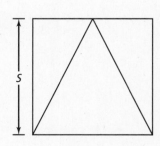

4-3 Standardized Test Prep

Patterns and Nonlinear Functions

Multiple Choice

For Exercises 1–5, choose the correct letter.

1. Which ordered pair represents a linear function?
   A. $(-2, -15), (-1, -9), (0, -3), (1, 3)$, and $(2, 9)$
   B. $(-2, 4), (-1, 1), (0, 0), (1, 1)$, and $(2, 4)$
   C. $(-2, -1), (-1, -4), (0, -5), (1, -4)$ and $(2, -1)$
   D. $(-2, -8), (-1, -1), (0, 0), (1, 1)$, and $(2, 8)$

2. The following ordered pairs represent a function: $(-2, 10), (-1, 7), (0, 6), (1, 7)$, and $(2, 10)$. Which equation could represent the function?
   F. $y = -4x + 2$ **G.** $y = x^2 - 6$ **H.** $y = 5x$ **I.** $y = x^2 + 6$

3. Which rule could represent the function shown by the table at the right?
   A. $y = -x^3$
   B. $y = x^2 + 1$
   C. $y = -x^2 + 1$
   D. $y = -x - 1$

x	y
−2	−3
−1	0
0	1
1	0
2	−3

4. The ordered pairs $(-1, 1), (0, 2), (1, 1), (2, -2)$, and $(3, -7)$ represent a function. Which rule could represent the function?
   F. $y = -x^2 - 2$ **G.** $y = -x^2 + 2$ **H.** $y = x^2 - 2$ **I.** $y = x^2 + 2$

5. Which ordered pair represents a nonlinear function?
   A. $(0, 0), (1, 1), (2, 2), (3, 3)$, and $(4, 4)$ **C.** $(0, -1), (1, 0), (2, 1), (3, 2)$, and $(4, 3)$
   B. $(0, 0), (1, -1), (2, -2)$, and $(4, -4)$ **D.** $(0, 0), (1, 1), (2, 8), (3, 27)$, and $(4, 64)$

Short Response

6. Graph the function shown in the table below. Is the function *linear* or *nonlinear*?

x	1	2	3	4
y	−9	−8	−5	0

4-4

Think About a Plan

Graphing a Function Rule

Falling Objects The height h, in feet, of an acorn that falls from a branch 100 ft above the ground depends on the time t, in seconds, since it has fallen. This is represented by the rule $h = 100 - 16t^2$. About how much time does it take for the acorn to hit the ground? Use a graph and estimate your answer between two consecutive whole-number values of t.

Understanding the Problem

1. What do the variables represent in the situation?

_____

2. What does h equal when the acorn hits the ground?

_____

_____

Planning the Solution

3. How can you determine how much time has elapsed when the acorn hits the ground algebraically?

_____

4. How will you use a graph to estimate the time?

_____

_____

Getting an Answer

5. Graph the function on the grid shown at the right.

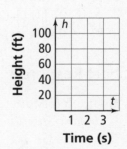

6. What two whole-number values is the answer between? What is your estimate? What does this answer mean?

_____

_____

7. Check your answer algebraically. Show your work.

4-4

Practice

Form G

Graphing a Function Rule

Graph each function rule.

1. $y = 2 - x$

2. $y = \frac{1}{2}x$

3. $y = 3x + 1$

Graph each function rule. Tell whether the graph is *continuous* or *discrete*.

4. The cost C, in dollars, for a health club membership depends on the number m of whole months you join. This situation is represented by the function rule $C = 49 + 20m$.

5. The cost C, in dollars, for bananas depends on the weight w, in pounds, of the bananas. This situation is represented by the function rule $C = 0.5w$.

4-4

Practice (continued)   *Form G*

Graphing a Function Rule

Graph each function rule.

6. $y = |x| + 1$ **7.** $y = x^3$ **8.** $y = |x| - 2$

9. $y = |x - 1| + 2$ **10.** $y = -x^2$ **11.** $y = x^3 - 3$

12. Open-Ended Sketch a graph of a quadratic function that has x-intercepts at 0 and 4.

13. Writing Describe the general shape of the graphs of functions of the form $y = ax^3$.

4-4

Standardized Test Prep
Graphing a Function Rule

Multiple Choice

For Exercises 1–4, choose the correct letter.

1. Which table of values can be used to graph the function $y = -4x + 3$?

A.

x	y
−1	−1
0	3
1	7
2	11

C.

x	y
0	3
1	−1
2	−5
3	−9

B.

x	y
−3	−9
−1	−1
1	7
3	15

D.

x	y
0	3
1	7
2	11
3	15

2. Which term best describes a function whose graph is composed of isolated points?
   F. continuous   **G.** linear   **H.** discrete   **I.** nonlinear

3. Which relationship is continuous?
   A. the number of cows a farmer has owned over the years
   B. the number of cookies Stan baked for the party
   C. the number of people attending the assembly
   D. the distance a runner ran during training

4. The total cost c a painter charges to paint a house depends on the number h of hours
   it takes to paint the house. This situation can be represented by the function rule
   $c = 15h + 245$. What is the total cost if the painter works for 30.25 hours?
   F. $245   **G.** $453.75   **H.** $572.75   **I.** $698.75

Short Response

5. The profit y on the number x of items a store
   sells is represented by the rule $y = 2x - 1$.
   What does a table of values for the function
   rule and the graph of the function look like?

4-5

Think About a Plan

Writing a Function Rule

Projectors You consult your new projector's instruction manual before mounting it to the ceiling. The manual says *multiply the desired image width by 1.8 to find the correct distance of the projector lens from the wall.*

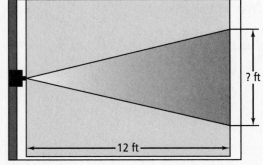

a. Write a rule to describe the distance of the lens from the wall as a function of desired image width.

b. The diagram shows the room in which the projector will be installed. Will you be able to project an image 7 ft wide? Explain.

c. What is the maximum image width you can project in the room?

1. What represents the desired image width in the drawing?

_____

2. What variables will you use in writing the rule and what do they represent?

_____

3. Write a rule to describe the distance of the lens from the wall as a function of desired image width.

_____

4. How can you determine if the room is large enough to project an image that is 7 ft wide?

_____

5. Is the room large enough to project an image that is 7 ft wide? Explain.

_____

_____

6. How can you determine the maximum image width that can be projected in this room?

_____

7. What is the maximum image width you can project in the room? Show your work.

_____

_____

4-5 Practice
Writing a Function Rule

Form G

Write a function rule that represents each sentence.

1. 5 less than one fourth of x is y.

2. 7 more than the quotient of a number n and 4 is 9.

3. P is 9 more than half of q.

4. 8 more than 5 times a number is -27.

5. 1.5 more than the quotient of a and 4 is b.

For Exercises 6–10, write a function rule that represents each situation.

6. The price p of an ice cream is $3.95 plus $0.85 for each topping t on the ice cream.

7. A babysitter's earnings e are a function of the number of hours n worked at a rate of $7.25 per hour.

8. The price p of a club's membership is $30 for an enrollment fee and $12 per week w to be a member.

9. A plumber's fees f are $75 for a house call and $60 per hour h for each hour worked.

10. A hot dog d costs $1 more than one-half the cost of a hamburger h.

11. José is 3 years younger than 3 times his brother's age. Write a rule that represents José's age j as a function of his brother's age b. How old is José if his brother is 5?

12. A taxicab charges $4.25 for the first mile and $1.50 for each additional mile. Write a rule for describing the total rate r as a function of the total miles m. What is the taxi rate for 12 miles?

4-5 **Practice** (continued)   Form G

Writing a Function Rule

13. Write a function rule for the area of a rectangle whose length is 4 in. more than its width. What is the area of the rectangle when its width is 8 in.?

14. Write a function rule for the area of a rectangle with a length 3 ft more than two times its width. What is the area of the rectangle when its width is 4 ft?

15. Write a function rule for the area of a triangle with a base 2 m less than 4 times its height. What is the area of the triangle when its height is 8 m?

16. Reasoning Write a rule that is an example of a nonlinear function that fits the following description.

When b is 49, a is 7, and a is a function of b.

17. Open-Ended Describe a real-world situation that represents a nonlinear function.

18. Writing Explain whether or not the relationship between inches and feet represents a function.

19. Multiple Representations Use the table shown at the right.

  a. Graph the ordered pairs on a coordinate plane.

  b. Write an equation that can be used to find
     y for any x value.

  c. Is the equation a function? Explain.

x	y
1	6
2	8
3	10
4	12

4-5 Standardized Test Prep

Writing a Function Rule

Multiple Choice

For Exercises 1–5, choose the correct letter.

1. Jill earns $45 per hour. Using p for her pay and h for the hours she works, what function rule represents the situation?

   A. $h = 45p$ **B.** $p = 45h$ **C.** $h = p + 45$ **D.** $p = h + 45$

2. What is a function rule for the perimeter P of a building with a rectangular base if the width w is two times the length l?

   F. $P = 2l$ **G.** $P = 2w$ **H.** $P = 6l$ **I.** $P = 6w$

3. Which function rule can be used to represent the area of a triangle with a base b 8 in. longer than twice the height h in terms of the height?

   A. $A = \frac{1}{2}bh$ **C.** $A = h^2 + 4h$

   B. $A = \frac{1}{2}h(h + 8)$ **D.** $A = \frac{1}{2}(2h)(h + 8)$

4. Which equation represents the sentence "d is 17 less than the quotient of n and 4"?

   F. $d = \frac{n}{4} - 17$ **H.** $d = 4n - 17$

   G. $d = \frac{n}{4} + 17$ **I.** $d - 17 = \frac{n}{4}$

5. The function rule for the profit a company expects to earn is $P = 1500m + 2700$, where P represents profit and m represents the number of months the company has been in business. How much profit should the company earn after 12 months in business?

   A. $15,700   **B.** $17,700   **C.** $18,000   **D.** $20,700

Extended Response

6. A plane was flying at an altitude of 30,000 feet when it began the descent toward the airport. The airplane descends at a rate of 850 feet per minute.

   a. What is the function rule that describes this situation?

   b. What is the altitude of the plane after it has descended for 8 minutes? Show your work.

   c. Use the function in part a to determine how long it takes for the plane to land if it descends at a continuous rate.

4-6 Think About a Plan

Formalizing Relations and Functions

Car Wash A theater group is having a carwash fundraiser. The liquid soap costs $34 and is enough to wash 40 cars. Each car is charged $5.

a. If c is the total number of cars washed and p is the profit, which is the independent variable and which is the dependent variable?

b. Is the relationship between c and p a function? Explain.

c. Write an equation that shows this relationship.

d. Find a reasonable domain and range for the situation.

Understanding the Problem

1. What are the expenses associated with the car wash?

_____

2. If c is the total number of cars washed and p is the profit, which is the independent variable and which is the dependent variable? Explain.

_____

Planning the Solution

3. How do you know if a relation is a function?

_____

4. How are a reasonable domain and range determined for a function?

_____

5. What limitations does the domain of this function have?

_____

Getting an Answer

6. Is the relationship between c and p a function? Explain.

_____

7. Write an equation that shows this relationship.

_____

8. Describe a reasonable domain and range for the situation.

_____

4-6

Practice

Formalizing Relations and Functions

Identify the domain and range of each relation. Use a mapping diagram to determine whether the relation is a function.

1. {(3, 6), (5, 7), (7, 7) (8, 9)}

2. {(0, 0.4), (1, 0.8), (2, 1.2), (3, 1.6)}

3. {(5, −4), (3, −5), (4, −3), (6, 4)}

4. {(0.3, 0.6), (0.4, 0.8), (0.3, 0.7), (0.5, 0.5)}

Use the vertical line test to determine whether the relation is a function.

5.

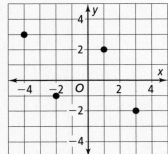

6.

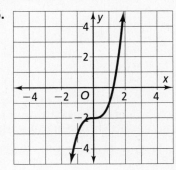

7. The function $w(x) = 60x$ represents the number of words $w(x)$ you can type in x minutes. How many words can you type in 9 minutes?

8. Sound travels about 343 meters per second. The function $d(t) = 343t$ gives the distance $d(t)$ in meters that sound travels in t seconds. How far does sound travel in 8 seconds?

4-6

Practice (continued)   Form G

Formalizing Relations and Functions

Find the range of each function for the given domain.

9. $f(x) = -3x + 2; \{-2, -1, 0, 1, 2\}$

10. $f(x) = x^3; \{-1, -0.5, 0, 0.5, 1\}$

11. $f(x) = 4x + 1; \{-4, -2, 0, 2, 4\}$

12. $f(x) = x^2 + 2; \{0, \frac{1}{4}, \frac{1}{2}, \frac{3}{4}, 1\}$

Find a reasonable domain and range for each function. Then graph the function.

13. A high school is having a pancake breakfast fundraiser. They have 3 packages of pancake mix that each feed 90 people. The function $N(p) = 90p$ represents the number of people $N(p)$ that p packages of pancake mix feed.

14. A charter boat travels at a maximum rate of 25 miles per hour. The function $d(x) = 25x$ represents the distance $d(x)$, in miles, that the boat can travel in x hours. The charter boat travels a maximum distance of 75 miles from the shore.

15. **Reasoning** If $f(x) = x^2 - 3$ and $f(a) = 46$, what is the value of a? Explain.

16. **Open-Ended** What is a value of x that makes the relation $\{(2, 4), (3, 6), (8, x)\}$ a function?

4-6 Standardized Test Prep

Formalizing Relations and Functions

Gridded Response

Solve each exercise and enter your answer on the grid provided.

1. What is $f(-3)$ for the function $f(x) = -5x - 7$?

2. You have returned some merchandise to a store and received a store credit of $23. In the same store, you are purchasing picture frames that cost $9 each. The function $f(x) = 9x - 23$ represents your total cost $f(x)$ if you purchase x picture frames. How many dollars will you pay if you purchase 7 picture frames?

3. If $f(x) = 12x + 14$, what is the range value for the domain value 3?

4. When Jerome travels on the highway, he sets his cruise control at 65 mi/h. The function $f(x) = 65x$ represents his total distance $f(x)$ when he has traveled x hours. How many miles will he have travelled after 3.5 hours of driving on the highway?

5. For what value of x is the value of $f(x) = 4x - 2$ equal to 18?

1. 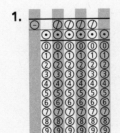 2. 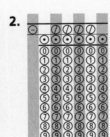 3. 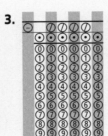 4. 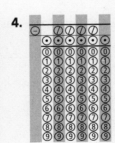 5.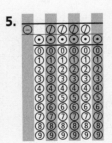

4-7 Think About a Plan

Sequences and Functions

Transportation Buses on your route run every 9 minutes from 6:00 A.M. to 10:00 A.M. You get to the bus stop at 7:16 A.M. How long will you wait for a bus?

Understanding the Problem

1. What is the maximum amount of time you should have to wait for a bus?

   _____

2. How many minutes after the buses begin running at 6:00 A.M. do you arrive at the bus stop?

   _____

3. What time does the first bus of the day arrive at your bus stop?

   _____

Planning the Solution

4. Fill in the table at the right showing the times a bus will stop at your stop.

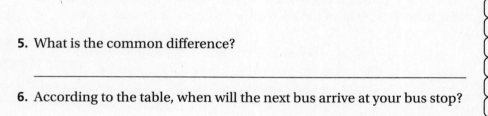

5. What is the common difference?

   _____

6. According to the table, when will the next bus arrive at your bus stop?

   _____

Getting an Answer

7. How long will you wait for a bus?

   _____

   _____

4-7 Practice

Form G

Sequences and Functions

Describe the pattern in each sequence. Then find the next two terms of the sequence.

1. 3, 6, 12, 24, …

2. 9, 15, 21, 27, …

3. 1.5, 2.25, 3, 3.75, …

4. 9.9, 8.8, 7.7, 6.6, …

5. 1.5, 4.5, 13.5, 40.5, …

6. 40, 20, 10, 5, …

7. 7, 11, 15, 19, …

8. 67, 60, 53, 46, …

9. 12, 7, 2, −3, …

Tell whether the sequence is arithmetic. If it is, identify the common difference.

10. 4, 8, 12, 16, …

11. −11, 5, 0, 6, …

12. 4, 8, 16, 32, …

13. 12, 23, 34, 45, …

14. 2, 4, 7, 9, …

15. 1, 3, 9, 27, …

16. −16, −11, −6, −1, …

17. −9, −4.5, −0.5, 4, …

18. −7, −14, −21, −28, …

19. 0, $\frac{1}{3}$, $\frac{2}{3}$, 1, …

20. 5, 10, 15, 20, …

21. 2, 20, 200, 2000, …

22. You have a gift card for a coffee shop worth $90. Each day you use the card to get a coffee for $4.10. Write a rule to represent the amount of money left on the card as an arithmetic sequence. What is the value of the card after buying 8 coffees?

23. You start a savings account with $200 and save $30 each month. Write a rule to represent the amount of money you invest into your savings account as an arithmetic sequence. How much money will you have invested after 12 months?

4-7 **Practice** (continued)

Sequences and Functions

Form G

Find the third, fifth, and tenth terms of the sequence described by each rule.

24. $A(n) = 4 + (n - 1)(-5)$

25. $A(n) = 2 + (n - 1)(6)$

26. $A(n) = -5.5 + (n - 1)(2)$

27. $A(n) = 3 + (n - 1)(1.5)$

28. $A(n) = -2 + (n - 1)(5)$

29. $A(n) = 1.4 + (n - 1)(3)$

30. $A(n) = 9 + (n - 1)(8)$

31. $A(n) = 2.5 + (n - 1)(2.5)$

Tell whether each sequence is arithmetic. Justify your answer. If the sequence is arithmetic, write a function rule to represent it.

32. 1.6, 0.8, 0, −0.8, ...

33. 5, 10, 20, 40, ...

34. 5, 13, 21, 29, ...

35. 51, 47, 43, 39, ...

36. 0.2, 0.5, 0.8, 1.1, ...

37. 7, 14, 28, 56, ...

38. Open-Ended Write an arithmetic sequence whose common difference is −2.5.

39. Error Analysis Your friend writes $A(8) = 3 + (8)(5)$ as a rule for finding the eighth term of the arithmetic sequence 3, 8, 13, 18, ... Describe and correct your friend's error.

40. The local traffic update is given on a radio channel every 12 minutes from 4:00 P.M. to 6:30 P.M. You turn the radio on at 4:16 P.M. How long will you wait for the local traffic update?

4-7 Standardized Test Prep

Sequences and Functions

Multiple Choice

For Exercises 1–5, choose the correct letter.

1. What are the next two terms of the following sequence? $-3, 1, 5, 9, \ldots$

  A. $-7, -11$ **B.** $10, 11$ **C.** $12, 15$ **D.** $13, 17$

2. What are the next two terms of the following sequence? $-2, 4, -8, 16, \ldots$

  F. $-32, -64$ **G.** $32, -64$ **H.** $-32, 64$ **I.** $32, 64$

3. What is the common difference of the following arithmetic sequence?
$13, -7, -27, -47, \ldots$

  A. -20 **B.** -6 **C.** -4 **D.** 20

4. What is the ninth term of the arithmetic sequence defined by the rule
$A(n) = -14 + (n - 1)(2)$?

  F. -32 **G.** -30 **H.** 2 **I.** 4

5. Each time a touchdown is scored in a football game, 6 points are added to the score of the scoring team. A team already has 12 points. What rule represents the number of points as an arithmetic sequence?

  A. $A(n) = 12 + 6n$ **C.** $A(n) = 12 + (n - 1)(6)$

  B. $A(n) = 12 - (n - 1)(6)$ **D.** $A(n) = 12 + (n - 6)$

Short Response

6. A friend opens a savings account by depositing $1000. He deposits an additional $75 into the account each month.

  a. What is a rule that represents the amount of money in the account as an arithmetic sequence?

  b. How much money is in the account after 18 months? Show your work.

5-1

Think About a Plan

Rate of Change and Slope

Profit John's business made $4500 in January and $8600 in March. What is the rate of change in his profit for this time period?

Understanding the Problem

1. What is the formula for finding rate of change?

   _____

2. What are the two changing quantities that affect rate of change in this problem? What are the units of each quantity?

   _____

   _____

3. Will the rate of change be positive or negative? Explain.

   _____

   _____

Planning the Solution

4. Which quantity is the dependent variable? Which quantity is the independent variable? Explain.

   _____

   _____

5. What is the general equation that represents the rate of change?

   _____

Getting an Answer

6. Substitute values into your general equation and simplify. Show your work.

   _____

   _____

7. If you were to graph this relationship, what would the rate of change be in relation to your graph?

   _____

   _____

5-1

Practice

Rate of Change and Slope

Determine whether each rate of change is constant. If it is, find the rate of change and explain what it represents.

1. Hockey Team's Offense

Games	Goals
1	2
2	4
3	6

2. Miles Per Gallon

Gallons	Miles
1	28
3	84
5	140
7	196

3. Cars Washed

Hours	Cars
1	4
2	8
3	12
4	16

Find the slope of each line.

4.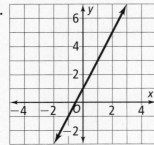

5.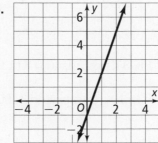

6.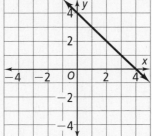

Find the slope of the line that passes through each pair of points.

7. $(2, 1), (0, 0)$

8. $(4, 5), (6, 2)$

9. $(3, 8), (7, 3)$

10. $(1, 0), (-4, 2)$

11. $(8, -4), (-6, -3)$

12. $(-2, -3), (6, 5)$

Find the slope of each line.

13.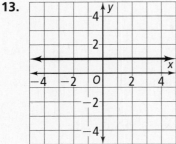

14.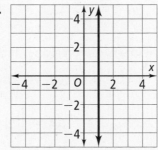

15.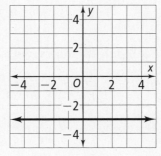

Prentice Hall Gold Algebra 1 • Practice and Problem Solving Workbook

5-1 Practice (continued)

Rate of Change and Slope

Form G

Without graphing, tell whether the slope of a line that models each situation is
positive, *negative*, *zero*, or *undefined*. **Then find the slope.**

16. The cost of tickets to the amusement park is $19.50 for 1 ticket and $78 for 4 tickets.

17. The late fee is $2 regardless of the number of days the movie is late.

18. On the trip, Jerry had his cruise control set at 60 mi/h for 4 hours.

19. The contract states that every day past the agreed upon completion date the project is not finished, the price is reduced by $25.

State the independent variable and the dependent variable in each situation. Then find the rate of change for each situation.

20. Shelly delivered 12 newspapers after 20 minutes and 36 papers after 60 minutes.

21. Two pounds of apples cost $3.98. Six pounds cost $11.94.

22. An airplane ascended 3000 feet in 10 minutes and 4500 feet in 15 minutes.

Find the slope of the line that passes through each pair of points.

23. $(-5, 0), (-5, 5)$

24. $(-2, -4), (-1.5, -1.5)$

25. $(4.75, -3.575), (2.25, 1.425)$

26. $\left(-\frac{1}{4}, \frac{3}{4}\right), \left(\frac{1}{2}, -\frac{3}{4}\right)$

27. $\left(\frac{2}{5}, \frac{3}{7}\right), \left(\frac{1}{5}, \frac{4}{7}\right)$

28. $(-3.35, 6.5), (5.65, -3.5)$

29. Writing Explain why the slope of a horizontal line is always zero.

30. Writing Describe how to draw a line that passes through the origin and has a slope of $-\frac{2}{3}$.

Each pair of points lies on a line with the given slope. Find x or y.

31. $(7, 4), (3, y)$; slope $= \frac{1}{4}$

32. $(5, y), (6, 4)$; slope $= 0$

33. $(x, 5), (-3, 6)$; slope $= -1$

34. $(-12, 9), (x, -2)$; slope $= -\frac{1}{2}$

5-1 Standardized Test Prep
Rate of Change and Slope

Multiple Choice

For Exercises 1–5, choose the correct letter.

1. What is the slope of the line that passes through the points $(-2, 5)$ and $(1, 4)$?

   A. -3 B. -1 C. $-\frac{1}{3}$ D. $\frac{1}{3}$

2. A line has slope $-\frac{5}{3}$. Through which two points could this line pass?

   F. $(12, 13), (17, 10)$ H. $(0, 7), (3, 10)$

   G. $(16, 15), (13, 10)$ I. $(11, 13), (8, 18)$

3. The pair of points $(6, y)$ and $(10, -1)$ lie on a line with slope $\frac{1}{4}$. What is the value of y?

   A. -5 B. -2 C. 2 D. 5

4. What is the slope of a vertical line?

   F. -1 G. 0 H. 1 I. undefined

5. Shawn needs to read a book that is 374 pages long. The graph shown at the right shows his progress over the first 8 hours of reading. If he continues to read at the same rate, how many hours total will it take for Shawn to read the entire book?

   A. 15 hours   C. 19 hours

   B. 17 hours   D. 21 hours

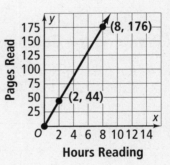

Short Response

6. Robi has run the first 4 miles of a race in 30 minutes. She reached the 6 mile point after 45 minutes. Without graphing, is the slope of the line that represents this situation positive, negative, zero, or undefined? What is the slope?

5-2 Think About a Plan

Direct Variation

Electricity Ohm's Law $V = I \times R$ relates the voltage, current, and resistance of a circuit. V is the voltage measured in volts. I is the current measured in amperes. R is the resistance measured in ohms.

a. Find the voltage of a circuit with a current of 24 amperes and a resistance of 2 ohms.

b. Find the resistance of a circuit with a current of 24 amperes and a voltage of 18 volts.

Understanding the Problem

1. Does Ohm's Law represent a direct variation? Explain.

   _____

   _____

2. If the formula is rearranged to solve for R or I, is it still a direct variation? Explain.

   _____

   _____

Planning the Solution

3. For part (a), does Ohm's Law need to be rearranged to answer the question? Explain. If it does, how should the formula be rearranged?

   _____

   _____

4. For part (b), does Ohm's Law need to be rearranged to answer the question? Explain. If it does, how should the formula be rearranged?

   _____

   _____

Getting an Answer

5. For part (a), substitute the given values into the formula and simplify.

   _____

6. For part (b), substitute the given values into the formula and simplify.

   _____

5-2 Practice

Form G

Direct Variation

Determine whether each equation represents a direct variation. If it does, find the constant of variation.

1. $-8y = 2x$

2. $3x + 4y = -5$

3. $12x = -36y$

4. $-7 + 9y + 7 = 2x$

5. $y - 12 = 12x$

6. $5x + 12.5y = 0$

Suppose y varies directly with x. Write a direct variation equation that relates x and y. Then find the value of y when $x = 8$.

7. $y = 10$ when $x = 2$.

8. $y = 6$ when $x = 18$.

9. $y = 2$ when $x = 5$.

10. $y = 9.92$ when $x = 12.8$.

11. $y = 1.85$ when $x = 0.925$.

12. $y = 1\frac{2}{9}$ when $x = 3\frac{2}{3}$.

Graph each direct variation equation.

13. $y = 5x$

14. $y = -\frac{2}{5}x$

15. $y = \frac{3}{4}x$

16. An equilateral triangle is a triangle with three equal sides. The perimeter of an equilateral triangle varies directly with the length of one side. What is an equation that relates the perimeter p and length l of a side? What is the graph of the equation?

17. The amount a you fill a tub varies directly with the amount of time t you fill it. Suppose you fill 25 gallons in 5 minutes. What is an equation that relates a and t? What is the graph of the equation?

5-2 Practice (continued) Form G

Direct Variation

For the data in each table, tell whether y varies directly with x. If it does, write an equation for the direct variation.

18.

x	y
2	−2.5
−7	8.75
5	−6.25

19.

x	y
9	10.8
12	14.4
−3	3.6

20.

x	y
−6.5	−19.5
−5.2	−15.6
4.8	14.4

Suppose y varies directly with x. Write and graph a direct variation equation that relates x and y.

21. $y = -6$ when $x = 3$.   **22.** $y = -\frac{4}{3}$ when $x = -4$.   **23.** $y = \frac{5}{8}$ when $x = \frac{1}{2}$.

Tell whether the two quantities vary directly. Explain your reasoning.

24. the total number of miles run and the number of miles you run per day when training for a race

25. Jackson's age and Dylan's age

26. a recipe that calls for 2 cups of sugar for each cup of flour

27. Writing In a direct variation equation, describe how the slope of the graph of the line is related to the constant of variation.

28. Janine gets paid $16.75 per hour at her job. Write a direct variation equation where h represents the number of hours she works and d represents the amount of money she earns. Graph the equation.

5-2 Standardized Test Prep

Direct Variation

Gridded Response

Solve each exercise and enter your answer on the grid provided.

1. Suppose y varies directly with x and $y = 14$ when $x = -4$. What is the value of y when $x = -6$?

2. Suppose y varies directly with x and $y = 25$ when $x = 140$. What is the value of x when $y = 36$?

3. The point $(12, 9)$ is included in a direct variation. What is the constant of variation?

4. The equation of the line on the graph at the right is a direct variation equation. What is the constant of variation?

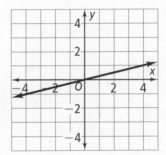

5. The distance d a train travels varies directly with the amount of time t that has elapsed since departure. If the train travels 475 miles in 9.5 hours, how many miles did the train travel after 4 hours?

1. 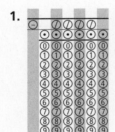 2. 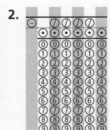 3. 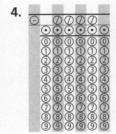 4. 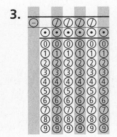 5.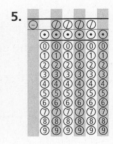

5-3

Think About a Plan

Slope-Intercept Form

Hobbies Suppose you are doing a 5000-piece puzzle. You have already placed 175 pieces. Every minute you place 10 more pieces.

a. Write an equation in slope-intercept form to model the number of pieces placed. Graph the equation.

b. After 50 more minutes, how many pieces will you have placed?

Understanding the Problem

1. Is this relationship linear? How do you know?

_____

_____

Planning the Solution

2. How many pieces have you already placed? What does this represent in the slope-intercept form?

_____

_____

3. What two quantities are used to find the rate of change or slope? What is the slope of this relationship?

_____

_____

Getting an Answer

4. Use your answers in Steps 2 and 3 to write an equation in slope-intercept form to model the number of pieces placed.

_____

5. Graph the equation on a coordinate grid.

6. How many pieces will you have placed after 50 more minutes?

_____

5-3 Practice

Slope-Intercept Form

Form G

Find the slope and y-intercept of the graph of each equation.

1. $y = 3x - 5$

2. $y = -5x + 13$

3. $y = -x - 1$

4. $y = -11x + 6$

5. $y = -5$

6. $y = \frac{1}{2}x + 6$

7. $y = -6.75x + 8.54$

8. $y = -\frac{2}{3}x - \frac{1}{9}$

9. $y = 2.25$

Write an equation of a line with the given slope m and y-intercept b.

10. $m = -1, b = 3$

11. $m = 4, b = -2$

12. $m = -5, b = -8$

13. $m = 0.25, b = 6$

14. $m = 0, b = -11$

15. $m = 1, b = \frac{3}{8}$

Write an equation in slope-intercept form of each line.

16.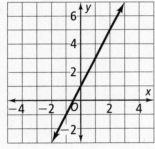

17.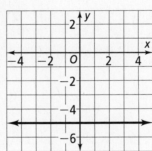

18.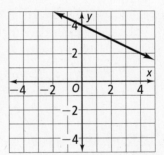

Write an equation in slope-intercept form of the line that passes through the given points.

19. $(3, 5)$ and $(0, 4)$

20. $(2, 6)$ and $(-4, -2)$

21. $(-1, 3)$ and $(-3, 1)$

22. $(-7, 5)$ and $(3, 0)$

23. $(10, 2)$ and $(-2, -2)$

24. $(0, -1)$ and $(5, 6)$

25. $(3, 2)$ and $(-1, 6)$

26. $(-4, -3)$ and $(3, 4)$

27. $(2, 8)$ and $(-3, 6)$

5-3 **Practice** (continued)   Form G
Slope-Intercept Form

Graph each equation.

28. $y = x + 3$

29. $y = 4x - 1$

30. $y = -x + 6$

31. $y = 3x - 2$

32. $y = -5x + 1$

33. $y = -7x - 4$

34. Hudson is already 40 miles away from home on his drive back to college. He is driving 65 mi/h. Write an equation that models the total distance d travelled after h hours. What is the graph of the equation?

35. When Phil started his new job, he owed the company \$65 for his uniforms. He is earning \$13 per hour. The cost of his uniforms is withheld from his earnings. Write an equation that models the total money he has m after h hours of work. What is the graph of the equation?

Find the slope and the y-intercept of the graph of each equation.

36. $y + 4 = -6x$

37. $y + \frac{1}{2}x = -4$

38. $3y - 12x + 6 = 0$

39. $y - 5 = \frac{1}{3}(x - 9)$

40. $y - \frac{2}{5}x = 0$

41. $2y + 6a - 4x = 0$

5-3 Standardized Test Prep

Slope-Intercept Form

Multiple Choice

For Exercises 1–5, choose the correct letter.

1. What is an equation of the line shown in the graph at the right?

   A. $y = -\frac{3}{2}x + 4$ **C.** $y = -\frac{2}{3}x + 4$

   B. $y = \frac{2}{3}x + 4$ **D.** $y = -\frac{2}{3}x + 6$

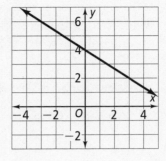

2. What is an equation of the line that has slope -4 and passes through the point $(-2, -5)$?

   F. $y = -4x - 8$ **G.** $y = -4x - 13$ **H.** $y = -4x - 5$ **I.** $y = -4x + 3$

3. What is an equation of the line that passes through the points $(-4, 3)$ and $(-1, 6)$?

   A. $y = -x - 7$ **B.** $y = -x - 1$ **C.** $y = 7x + 1$ **D.** $y = x + 7$

4. The data shown in the table is linear. Which equation models the data?

   F. $y = \frac{1}{2}x + 12$ **H.** $y = 2x + 9$

   G. $y = \frac{1}{2}x + 6$ **I.** $y = 2x - 3$

x	y
2	13
6	15
10	17

5. Karissa earns $200 per week plus $25 per item she sells. Which equation models the relationship between her pay p per week and the number of items n she sells?

   A. $p = 200n + 25$ **C.** $n = 25p + 200$

   B. $p = 25n + 200$ **D.** $n = 200p + 25$

Short Response

6. What is an equation of the line that passes through $(-8, 2)$ and has slope $-\frac{3}{4}$? What is the graph of the equation?

5-4 | Think About a Plan

Point-Slope Form

Boiling Point The relationship between altitude and the boiling point of water is linear. When the altitude is 8000 ft, water boils at 197.6°F. When the altitude is 4500 ft, water boils at 203.9°F. Write an equation giving the boiling point b of water (in degrees Fahrenheit) in terms of the altitude a (in feet). What is the boiling point of water at 2500 ft?

Understanding the Problem

1. What are you given?

_____

2. In general, how can this information be used to answer the question?

_____

Planning the Solution

3. What is the slope formula?

_____

4. Substitute given values into the slope formula and simplify. Show your work.

_____

5. Which point can be used to write the point-slope form of the equation?

_____

6. What strategy can you use to solve this problem?

_____

7. How can you determine the boiling point of water at 2500 ft?

_____

Getting an Answer

8. Write an equation giving the boiling point b of water (in degrees Fahrenheit) in terms of the altitude a.

_____

9. What is the boiling point of water at 2500 ft? Show your work.

_____

_____

5-4 Practice
Form G

Point-Slope Form

Write an equation of the line in point-slope form through the given point and with the given slope *m*.

1. $(2, 1); m = 3$

2. $(-3, -5); m = -2$

3. $(-4, 11); m = \frac{3}{4}$

4. $(0, -3); m = -\frac{2}{3}$

Graph each equation.

5. $y - 2 = 2(x + 3)$

6. $y + 3 = -2(x + 1)$

7. $y + 1 = -\frac{3}{5}(x + 5)$

Write an equation in point-slope form for each line.

8.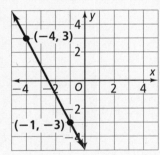

9.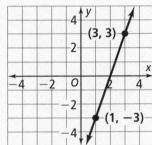

10.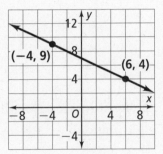

Write an equation in point-slope form of the line through the given points. Then write the equation in slope-intercept form.

11. $(4, 0), (-2, 1)$

12. $(-3, -2), (5, 3)$

13. $(-5, 1), (3, 4)$

14. **Open-Ended** Write an equation of a line that has a slope of $-\frac{1}{2}$ in each form.

   a. point-slope form

   b. slope-intercept form

5-4   **Practice** (continued)   *Form G*

Point-Slope Form

Model the data in each table with a linear equation in slope-intercept form. What do the slope and *y*-intercept represent?

15.

Time Washing (hr)	Cars washed
3	18
5	30
6	36
8	48

16.

Time Flying (hr)	Distance from Airport (mi)
2	3600
4	2700
6	1800
8	900

Graph the line that passes through the given point and has the given slope *m*.

17. $(-3, -4)$; $m = 6$ **18.** $(-2, 1)$, $m = -3$ **19.** $(-4, -2)$; $m = \frac{1}{2}$

20. Writing Describe what you know about the graph of a line represented by the equation $y - 3 = -\frac{2}{3}(x + 4)$.

21. Writing Describe how you would use the point-slope form to write the equation of a line that passes through the points $(-1, 4)$ and $(-3, -5)$ in slope-intercept form.

22. Writing Describe how linear data given in a table can help you write an equation of a line in slope-intercept form.

23. A sign says that 3 tickets cost $22.50 and that 7 tickets cost $52.50. Write an equation in point-slope form that represents the cost of tickets. What is the graph of the equation?

5-4 Standardized Test Prep

Point-Slope Form

Multiple Choice

For Exercises 1–5, choose the correct letter.

1. Which equation is equivalent to $y - 6 = -12(x + 4)$?
   - **A.** $y = -6x - 48$
   - **B.** $y = 6x - 48$
   - **C.** $y = -12x - 42$
   - **D.** $y = -12x - 54$

2. Which point is located on the line represented by the equation $y + 4 = -5(x - 3)$?
   - **F.** $(-4, -5)$
   - **G.** $(-5, -4)$
   - **H.** $(3, -4)$
   - **I.** $(-3, 4)$

3. Which equation represents the line that passes through the points $(6, -3)$ and $(-4, -9)$?
   - **A.** $y + 4 = -\frac{3}{5}(x + 9)$
   - **B.** $y + 4 = \frac{5}{3}(x + 9)$
   - **C.** $y - 3 = \frac{3}{5}(x + 6)$
   - **D.** $y + 3 = \frac{3}{5}(x - 6)$

4. Which equation represents the line shown in the graph?
   - **F.** $y = -3x - 2$
   - **G.** $y = 3x + 2$
   - **H.** $y + 4 = -3(x - 2)$
   - **I.** $y + 8 = -3(x - 2)$

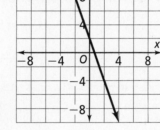

5. The population of a city increases by 4000 people each year. In 2025, the population is projected to be 450,000 people. What is an equation that gives the city's population p (in thousands of people) x years after 2010?
   - **A.** $p = 4x + 450$
   - **B.** $p - 450 = 4(x - 15)$
   - **C.** $p - 15 = 4(x - 450)$
   - **D.** $p = 4x + 15$

Short Response

6. The table shows the cost of a large cheese pizza with additional toppings on it.
   - **a.** What is an equation in point-slope form that represents the relationship between the number of toppings and the cost of the pizza?
   - **b.** What is the graph of the equation?

Toppings	Cost ($)
2	10.50
3	11.75
5	14.25

5-5

Think About a Plan

Standard Form

Sports A football team scores 63 points. All of the points come from field goals worth 3 points and touchdowns (with successful extra-point attempts) worth 7 points. Write and graph a linear equation that represents this situation. List every possible combination of field goals and touchdowns the team could have scored.

Understanding the Problem

1. What are you given?

   _____

2. How can touchdowns and field goals be represented? How can these be written as terms to represent the point value of each?

   _____

Planning the Solution

3. What is the equation in standard form that models the situation?

   _____

4. How can you find the y-intercept?

   _____

5. How can you find the x-intercept?

   _____

6. How can you use the intercepts to graph the line?

   _____

Getting an Answer

7. Graph the relation on a coordinate grid.

8. Use the graph to determine and list all of the combinations.

   _____

5-5 Practice

Form G

Standard Form

Find the *x*- and *y*-intercepts of the graph of each equation.

1. $x + y = 7$

2. $x - 3y = 9$

3. $2x + 3y = -6$

4. $-4x - 2y = -8$

5. $5x - 4y = -12$

6. $-2x + 7y = 11$

Draw a line with the given intercepts.

7. *x*-intercept: 4
   y-intercept: 5

8. *x*-intercept: −3
   y-intercept: 1

9. *x*-intercept: −6
   y-intercept: −8

Graph each equation using *x*- and *y*-intercepts.

10. $-5x + y = -10$

11. $-3x - 6y = 12$

12. $4x - 12y = -24$

For each equation, tell whether its graph is a *horizontal* or a *vertical* line.

13. $y = -2$

14. $x = 0$

15. $y = -0.25$

16. $x = -\frac{3}{5}$

Graph each equation.

17. $y = 6$

18. $x = -2$

19. $y = -7$

20. $x = 3$

Prentice Hall Gold Algebra 1 • Practice and Problem Solving Workbook
155

5-5

Practice (continued)

Standard Form

Form G

Write each equation in standard form using integers.

21. $y = x - 4$

22. $y - 4 = 5(x - 8)$

23. $y + 6 = -3(x + 1)$

24. $y = -\frac{3}{5}x + 2$

25. $y = \frac{1}{2}x - 10$

26. $y - 3 = -\frac{7}{9}(x + 4)$

27. You have only nickels and dimes in your piggy bank. When you ran the coins through a change counter, it indicated you have 595 cents. Write and graph an equation that represents this situation. What are three combinations of nickels and dimes you could have?

For each graph, find the *x*- and *y*-intercepts. Then write an equation in standard form using integers.

28.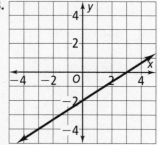

29.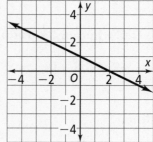

Find the *x*- and *y*-intercepts of the line that passes through the given points.

30. $(4, -2), (5, -4)$

31. $(1, 1), (-5, 7)$

32. $(-3, 2), (-4, 10)$

5-5

Standardized Test Prep

Standard Form

Multiple Choice

For Exercises 1–4, choose the correct letter.

1. What is $y = -\frac{5}{3}x - 6$ written in standard form using integers?

   A. $\frac{5}{3}x + y = -6$ **B.** $5x + 3y = -6$ **C.** $5x + 3y = -18$ **D.** $-5x + 3y = 6$

2. Which of the following is an equation of a vertical line?

   F. $4x + 5y = 0$ **G.** $-4 = 16x$ **H.** $3y = -9$ **I.** $4x + 5y = -1$

3. What are the x- and y-intercepts of the graph of $-7x + 4y = -14$

   A. x-intercept: -7
      y-intercept: 4

   B. x-intercept: 7
      y-intercept: -4

   C. x-intercept: -2
      y-intercept: 3.5

   D. x-intercept: 2
      y-intercept: -3.5

4. Cheryl is planning to spend $75 on a Christmas gift for her father. He needs new socks and ties. A store has socks s and ties t on sale for $4 and $11, respectively. Which equation models this situation?

   F. $4s + 11t = 75$ **H.** $s = 15t + 75$

   G. $11s + 4t = 75$ **I.** $t = 4s - 11$

Extended Response

5. The grocery store is selling eggs for $2 per dozen and bacon for $5 per pound. You plan to spend $50 in food for the benefit breakfast. Write and graph an equation that represents this situation. What are three combinations of dozens of eggs and pounds of bacon you can purchase?

5-6 Think About a Plan

Parallel and Perpendicular Lines

Agriculture Two farmers use combines to harvest corn from their fields. One farmer has 600 acres of corn, and the other has 1000 acres of corn. Each farmer's combine can harvest 100 acres per day. Write two equations for the number of acres y of corn not harvested after x days. Are the graphs of the equations *parallel, perpendicular,* or *neither*? How do you know?

Understanding the Problem

1. What is the difference between the two farms? What is the same?

   _____

2. How can you determine if the graphs of two equations are parallel, perpendicular, or neither?

   _____

Planning the Solution

3. What is an algebraic expression that represents the amount of corn each farmer can harvest per day?

   _____

4. Write an equation representing the number of acres y of corn not harvested after x days on the farm with 600 acres.

   _____

5. Write an equation representing the number of acres y of corn not harvested after x days on the farm with 1000 acres.

   _____

Getting an Answer

6. Write the equations in Steps 4 and 5 in slope-intercept form.

   _____

7. What are the slopes of the equations?

   _____

8. Are the graphs of the equations parallel, perpendicular, or neither? Explain.

   _____

5-6

Practice

Form G

Parallel and Perpendicular Lines

Write an equation of the line that passes through the given point and is parallel to the graph of the given equation.

1. $(3, 2); y = 3x - 2$

2. $(-4, -1); y = 2x + 14$

3. $(-8, 6); y = -\frac{1}{4}x + 5$

4. $(6, 2); y = \frac{2}{3}x + 19$

5. $(10, -5); y = \frac{3}{2}x - 7$

6. $(-3, 4); y = 2$

Determine whether the graphs of the given equations are *parallel*, *perpendicular*, or *neither*. Explain.

7. $y = 4x + 5$
$-4x + y = -13$

8. $y = \frac{7}{9}x - 7$
$y = -\frac{7}{9}x + 3$

9. $y = \frac{7}{8}$
$x = -4$

10. $y = -6x - 8$
$-x + 6y = 12$

11. $3x + 6y = 12$
$y - 4 = -\frac{1}{2}(x + 2)$

12. $y = 4x + 12$
$x + 4y = 32$

Determine whether each statement is *always*, *sometimes*, or *never* true. Explain.

13. Two lines with different slopes are perpendicular.

14. The slopes of vertical lines and horizontal lines are opposite reciprocals.

15. A vertical line is perpendicular to the *x*-axis.

5-6

Practice (continued)   Form G

Parallel and Perpendicular Lines

Write an equation of the line that passes through the given point and is perpendicular to the graph of the given equation.

16. $(2, -1); y = -2x + 1$

17. $(5, 7); y = \frac{1}{3}x + 2$

18. $(3, -6); x + y = -4$

19. $(-9, 3); 3x + y = 5$

20. $(-8, 3); y + 4 = -\frac{2}{3}(x - 2)$

21. $(0, -5); x - 6y = -2$

22. Open-Ended Write the equations of three lines whose graphs are parallel to one another.

23. Open-Ended Write the equations of two lines whose graphs are perpendicular to one another.

24. What is the slope of a line that is parallel to the x-axis?

25. What is the slope of a line that is perpendicular to the x-axis?

26. What is the slope of a line that is parallel to the y-axis?

27. What is the slope of a line that is perpendicular to the y-axis?

28. On a map, Sandusky St. passes through coordinates $(2, -1)$ and $(4, 8)$. Pennsylvania Ave. intersects Sandusky St. and passes through coordinates $(1, 3)$ and $(6, 2)$. Are these streets perpendicular? Explain.

29. Writing Explain how you can determine if the graphs of two lines are parallel or perpendicular without graphing the lines.

5-6 Standardized Test Prep

Parallel and Perpendicular Lines

Multiple Choice

For Exercises 1–5, choose the correct letter.

1. Which equation has a graph parallel to the graph of $9x + 3y = -22$?

   A. $y = 3x - 22$ **B.** $y = -3x + 8$ **C.** $y = \frac{1}{3}x + 12$ **D.** $y = -\frac{1}{3}x - 2$

2. Which equation has a graph perpendicular to the graph of $7x = 14y - 8$?

   F. $y = -2x - 7$ **G.** $y = -\frac{1}{2}x + 4$ **H.** $y = \frac{1}{2}x - 1$ **I.** $y = 2x + 9$

3. Which equation is the equation of a line that passes through $(-10, 3)$ and is perpendicular to $y = 5x - 7$?

   A. $y = 5x + 53$ **B.** $y = -\frac{1}{5}x - 7$ **C.** $y = -\frac{1}{5}x + 1$ **D.** $y = \frac{1}{5}x + 5$

4. Which of the following coordinates for P will make $\overleftrightarrow{MN}$ perpendicular to $\overrightarrow{OP}$ in the diagram at the right?

   F. $(-2, -5)$ **H.** $(3, 2)$
   G. $(-3, 6)$ **I.** $(3, 5)$

5. Segment XY represents the path of an airplane that passes through the coordinates $(2, 1)$ and $(4, 5)$. What is the slope of a line that represents the path of another airplane that is traveling parallel to the first airplane?

   A. -2 **C.** $\frac{1}{2}$
   B. $-\frac{1}{2}$ **D.** 2

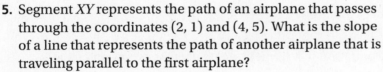

Short Response

6. A city designer is drawing the road map for a new housing development. Palm St. runs through the coordinates $(11, 5)$ and $(-1, 1)$ on the map. Pepperdine St. is going to run perpendicular to Palm St. The coordinates of Pepperdine St. are $(4, 7)$ and $(7, y)$. What is the value of y? What is the equation for the line representing Pepperdine St. in slope-intercept form?

5-7 Think About a Plan

Scatter Plots and Trend Lines

U.S. Population Use the data below.

Estimated Population of the United States (thousands)

Year	2000	2001	2002	2003	2004	2005	2006
Male	138,482	140,079	141,592	142,937	144,467	145,973	147,512
Female	143,734	145,147	146,533	147,858	149,170	150,533	151,886

Source: U.S. Census Bureau

a. Make a scatter plot of the data pairs (male population, female population).

b. Draw a trend line and write its equation.

c. Use your equation to predict the U.S. female population if the U.S. male population increases to 150,000,000.

d. **Reasoning** Consider a scatter plot of the data pairs (year, male population). Would it be reasonable to use this scatter plot to predict the U.S. male population in 2035? Explain your reasoning.

1. Make a scatter plot of the data pairs using the male population for the *x*-coordinates and the female population for the *y*-coordinates for each year.

2. Draw the trend line onto the scatter plot.

3. How do you determine the equation of a trend line? What is the equation of this trend line? Show your work.

_____

4. Substitute 150 for *x* to predict the female population. _____

5. Make a scatter plot of the data pairs (year, male population).

6. Would it be reasonable to use this scatter plot to predict the U.S. male population in 2035? Explain your reasoning.

_____

_____

5-7 Practice
Scatter Plots and Trend Lines

Form G

For each table, make a scatter plot of the data. Describe the type of correlation the scatter plot shows.

1.

Test Scores					
Test Score	76	85	83	97	92
Study Time (min)	33	52	49	101	65

2.

Tickets Sold					
Adult Tickets	10	20	30	40	50
Children Tickets	30	55	80	112	137

Use the table below and a graphing calculator for Exercises 3 through 6.

Florida Resident Population									
Year	1980	1990	1995	2000	2002	2003	2004	2005	2006
Population (in thousands)	9746	12,938	14,538	15,983	16,682	16,982	17,367	17,768	18,090

SOURCE: U.S. Census Bureau

3. Make a scatter plot of the data pairs (years since 1980, population).

4. Draw the line of best fit for the data.

5. Write an equation for the trend line.

6. According to the data, what will the estimated resident population in Florida be in 2020?

5-7 Practice (continued)   Form G

Scatter Plots and Trend Lines

Use the table below and a graphing calculator for Exercises 7 through 10.

Total Box Office Gross									
Year	1999	2000	2001	2002	2003	2004	2005	2006	2007
Gross Revenue (in million $)	7500	7750	8370	9320	9300	9450	8960	9300	9680

Source: www.mediabynumbers.com

7. Make a scatter plot of the data pairs (years since 1999, revenue).

8. Draw the line of best fit for the data.

9. Write an equation for the line of best fit.

10. According to the data, what will the estimated gross revenue be in 2015?

In each situation, tell whether a correlation is likely. If it is, tell whether the correlation reflects a causal relationship. Explain your reasoning.

11. the number of practice free throws you take and the number of free throws you make in a game

12. the height of a mountain and the average elevation of the state it is in

13. the number of hours worked and an employee's wages

14. a drop in the price of a barrel of oil and the amount of gasoline sold

15. Open-Ended Describe a real world situation that would show a strong negative correlation. Explain your reasoning.

16. Writing Describe the difference between interpolation and extrapolation. Explain how both could be useful.

17. Writing Describe how the slope of a line relates to a trend line. What does the *y*-intercept represent?

5-7 Standardized Test Prep

Scatter Plots and Trend Lines

Multiple Choice

For Exercises 1–5, choose the correct letter.

1. For the following situation, determine if there is a correlation. If there is a correlation, is it a causal relationship?
   the number of hours practicing at the batting cages and your batting average
   A. negative correlation and a causal relationship
   B. positive correlation but not a causal relationship
   C. positive correlation and a causal relationship
   D. no correlation

2. When evaluating data on a scatter plot, what can be used to make predictions about the future?
   F. interpolation   H. correlation coefficient
   G. extrapolation   I. causation

3. Mr. Bolton has worked for the same company for 17 years. What relationship would you expect between the number of years he has been with the company and his annual salary?
   A. positive correlation   C. no correlation
   B. negative correlation   D. none of the above

4. A city had a population of 150,000 people in 1990. The population growth of the city is represented by the equation $p = 5t + 150$ where p is the population in thousands and t is the time in years since 1990. In what year will the population have doubled?
   F. 1993   G. 2000   H. 2020   I. 2030

5. What type of correlation is represented by the data in the scatter plot?
   A. positive correlation   C. no correlation
   B. negative correlation   D. none of the above

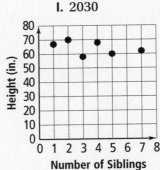

Number of Siblings

Short Response

6. Use the scatter plot to answer the following questions.
   a. What is an equation of the trend line for the data?

   b. What would the earnings be for 40 hours worked?

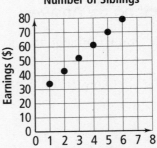

Hours Worked

5-8 | Think About a Plan

Graphing Absolute Value Functions

What point(s) do the graphs of $y = -|x| + 7$ and $y = |x - 3|$ have in common?

Understanding the Problem

1. What is the parent function of both equations?

_____

2. What shape is the graph of the parent function of both equations?

_____

3. What transformations occur in $y = -|x| + 7$?

_____

4. What translations occur in $y = |x - 3||$?

_____

Planning the Solution

5. Could a table help you answer the question? Explain.

_____

_____

6. Could a graph help you answer the question? Explain.

_____

_____

7. Which method is better? Why?

_____

_____

Getting an Answer

8. Graph both equations on the same coordinate grid.

9. What point(s) do the graphs have in common?

_____

5-8 Practice

Form G

Graphing Absolute Value Functions

Describe how each graph is related to $y = |x|$.

1.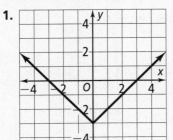

2.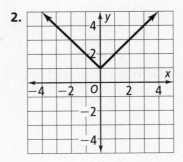

3.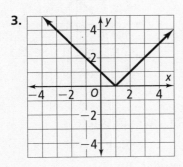

4.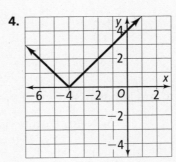

Graph each function by translating $y = |x|$.

5. $y = |x| + 3$

6. $y = |x| - 2$

7. $y = |x| - 1.5$

Write an equation for each translation of $y = |x|$.

8. 2 units down

9. 1 unit up

10. 1.18 units up

Graph each function by translating $y = |x|$.

11. $y = |x + 6|$

12. $y = |x - 5|$

13. $y = |x + 3.2|$

5-8 Practice (continued) Form G

Graphing Absolute Value Functions

Write an equation for each translation of $y = |x|$.

14. left 7 units

15. left $\frac{1}{2}$ unit

16. right $\frac{2}{3}$ unit

At the right is the graph of $y = -|x|$. Graph each function by translating $y = -|x|$.

17. $y = -|x + 2|$

18. $y = -|x| - 2$

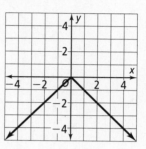

Write an equation for each translation of $y = -|x|$.

19. 5 units down

20. 8 units right

21. 3.25 units left

22. Reasoning Examine the expressions $|m - n|$ and $|n - m|$. Substitute $m = 2$ and $n = 3$ in each expression and simplify. Now, substitute $m = 3$ and $n = 2$ in each expression and simplify. Repeat this process with 3 other sets of numbers for m and n. What is your conclusion?

23. Writing Can the absolute value of a number equal a negative number? Explain your reasoning.

Graph each translation of $y = |x|$. Describe how the graph is related to the graph of $y = |x|$.

24. $y = |x + 3| - 2$

25. $y = |x - 2| + 4$

5-8 Standardized Test Prep

Graphing Absolute Value Functions

Multiple Choice

For Exercises 1–6, choose the correct letter.

1. Which equation represents a translation of 6 units right of $y = |x|$?

   A. $y = |x| - 6$ **B.** $y = |x - 6|$ **C.** $y = |x| + 6$ **D.** $y = |x| + 6$

2. How is the graph shown at the right is related to $y = |x|$?

   F. translated 5 units left
   G. translated 5 units right
   H. translated 5 units up
   I. translated 5 units down

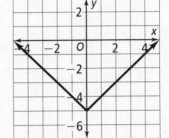

3. What is the y-intercept of $y = |x| - 3$?

   A. -3 **C.** $\frac{1}{3}$

   B. $-\frac{1}{3}$ **D.** 3

4. Which equation represents $y = |x|$ translated 4 units up?

   F. $y = |x| - 4$ **G.** $y = |x - 4|$ **H.** $y = |x| + 4$ **I.** $y = |x + 4|$

5. Which equation represents the graph shown at the right?

   A. $y = |x + 2|$ **C.** $y = -|x + 2|$
   B. $y = |x| + 2$ **D.** $y = -|x| + 2$

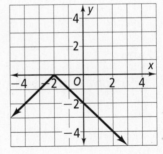

6. What is the y-intercept of $y = |x + 8|$?

   F. -8 **H.** $\frac{1}{8}$

   G. $-\frac{1}{8}$ **I.** 8

Short Response

7. Let $f(x) = |x - 3| + 1$.

   a. What is the graph of the function?
   b. How is the graph related to the graph of $y = |x|$?

6-1 Think About a Plan

Solving Systems by Graphing

Cell Phone Plans A cell phone provider offers plan 1 that costs $40 per month plus $.20 per text message sent or received. A comparable plan 2 costs $60 per month but offers unlimited text messaging.

    a. How many text messages would you have to send or receive in order for the plans to cost the same each month?

    b. If you send and receive an average of 50 text messages each month, which plan would you choose? Why?

Know

1. What equations can you write to model the situation?

	times		plus	=	y (total)

    Cell phone plan #2 cost per month _____

    Cell phone plan #1 cost per month _____

2. How will graphing the equations help you find the answers?

_____

Need

3. How will you find the best plan?

_____

Plan

4. What are the equations that represent the two plans? _____ and _____

5. Graph your equations.

6. Where will the solution be on the graph?

_____

_____

7. What is the solution?

_____

6-1 Practice   Form G

Solving Systems by Graphing

Solve each system by graphing. Check your solution.

1. $x + y = 3$
$2x + 5y = 12$

2. $4x + 3y = 2$
$3x - 2y = 10$

3. $5x - 8y = -4$
$2x - 7y = 6$

4. $x + 6y = 11$
$2x - 3y = 7$

5. $3x = y$
$2x + 3y = 10$

6. $3x - 5y + 1 = 0$
$2x - y + 3 = 0$

7. $x + 3y = 0$
$2x + 3y = 12$

8. $2x + 4y = 6$
$x + 2y = 3$

9. $x - 2y = 1$
$x + y = 4$

10. Reasoning Can there be more than one point of intersection between the graphs of two linear equations? Why or why not?

11. Reasoning If the graphs of the equations in a system of linear equations coincide with each other, what does that tell you about the solution of the system? Explain.

12. Writing Explain the method used to graph a line using the slope and y-intercept.

13. Reasoning If the ordered pair $(3, -2)$ satisfies one of the two linear equations in a system, how can you tell whether the point satisfies the other equation of the system? Explain.

14. Writing If the graphs of two lines in a system do not intersect at any point, what can you conclude about the solution of the system? Why? Explain.

15. Reasoning Without graphing, decide whether the following system of linear equations has one solution, infinitely many solutions or no solution. Explain.

$y = 3x - 5$
$6x = 2y + 10$

16. Five years from now, a father's age will be three times his son's age, and 5 years ago, he was seven times as old as his son was. What are their present ages?

6-1

Practice (continued)
Solving Systems by Graphing

17. The denominator of a fraction is greater than its numerator by 9. If 7 is subtracted from both its numerator and denominator, the new fraction equals $\frac{2}{3}$. What is the original fraction?

18. The sum of the distances two hikers walked is 53 mi, and the difference is 25 mi. What are the distances?

19. The result of dividing a two-digit number by the number with its digits reversed is $\frac{7}{4}$. If the sum of the digits is 12, what is the number?

Solve each system by graphing. Tell whether the system has *one solution*, *infinitely many solutions*, or *no solution*.

20. $x + y + 3 = 0$
  $3x - 2y + 4 = 0$

21. $x + 2y = 7$
  $2x - y = -1$

22. $2x + y = 8$
  $x + 1 = 2y$

23. $x + y = -2$
  $3x - 4y = 15$

24. $3x - 5y = -18$
  $3x + 5y = 12$

25. $2x - y = 3$
  $x + 3y = 5$

26. $5x - y = 15$
  $5x - 6y = -10$

27. $y = 6x + 4$
  $-2 + y = 6x$

28. $5x - y = 2$
  $2x - \frac{1}{2}y = 3$

29. $18x - 3y = 21$
  $-y = -6x + 7$

30. $7x - y = -1$
  $-x + 2y = 6$

31. $-x + 2y = 5$
  $x + y = 1$

32. The measure of one of the angles of a triangle is 35. The sum of the measures of the other two angles is 145 and the difference between their measures is 15. What are the measures of the unknown angles?

6-1 Standardized Test Prep

Solving Systems by Graphing

Multiple Choice

For Exercises 1–4, choose the correct letter.

1. Which best describes a system of equations that has no solution?
   A. consistent, independent
   B. inconsistent, dependent
   C. consistent, dependent
   D. inconsistent

2. How many solutions does this system have? $\begin{array}{l} 2x + y = 3 \\ 6x = 9 - 3y \end{array}$

   F. 1   **G.** none   **H.** infinite   **I.** 2

3. What is the approximate solution of the linear system represented by the graph at the right?
   A. $(4, -3)$ **B.** $(6, -1)$ **C.** $(-1, 4)$ **D.** $(4, -1)$

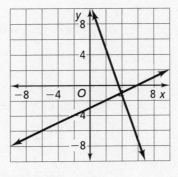

4. Which cannot describe a system of linear equations?
   F. no solution
   G. exactly two solutions
   H. infinite solutions
   I. exactly one solution

Extended Response

5. A farmer feeds his cows 200 pounds of feed each day and has 700 pounds of feed in his barn. Another farmer feeds his cows 350 pounds of feed each day and has 1000 pounds of feed in his barn.

   a. In how many days will the two farmers have the same amount of feed left?

   _____

   b. Does your answer make sense? Explain.

   _____

   _____

   c. How would your answer change if both farmers got an additional 1000 pounds of feed?

   _____

   _____

6-2 · Think About a Plan

Solving Systems Using Substitution

Art An artist is going to sell two sizes of prints at an art fair. The artist will charge $20 for a small print and $45 for a large print. The artist would like to sell twice as many small prints as large prints. The booth the artist is renting for the day costs $510. How many of each size print must the artist sell in order to break even at the fair?

Understanding the Problem

1. How much will the artist spend to rent a booth? _____

2. What do you know about selling prices of the prints? _____

3. What do you know about the number of prints the artist would like to sell? _____

4. What is the problem asking you to determine? _____
_____

Planning the Solution

5. What variables are needed? _____

6. What equation can be used to determine the number of prints that the artist would like to sell based on size? _____

7. What equation can be used to determine how many prints the artist has to sell to break even? _____

Getting an Answer

8. What is the solution to the system of equations?

$\dfrac{6\text{-}2}{}$ **Practice**   *Form G*

Solving Systems Using Substitution

Solve each system by substitution. Check your solution.

1. $x = y$
   $x + 2y = 3$

2. $y = -x + 4$
   $y = 3x$

3. $y = 2x - 10$
   $2y = x - 8$

4. $2y = x + 1$
   $-2x - y = 7$

5. $x + 2y = 14$
   $y = 3x - 14$

6. $x2x - 3y = 13$
   $y = \frac{1}{2}x - \frac{7}{2}$

7. $-3x - 2y = 5.5$
   $x + 3y = 7.5$

8. $6x - 4y = 54$
   $-9x + 2y = -69$

9. $y = \frac{-x}{2} - 4$
   $-2x - y = -5$

10. **Writing** How do you know that substitution gives the answer to a system of equations? Explain.

11. **Reasoning** With the substitution method, which variable should you solve for first? Explain.

12. **Writing** How can you use substitution method to solve a system of equations that does not have a variable with a coefficient of 1 or −1?

13. **Writing** When solving the system of equations $\begin{array}{l} 6y + 2x = 3 \\ 2x + y = 8 \end{array}$ using substitution, which variable will you solve for and which equation will you use to substitute into?

14. **Reasoning** Can you tell that there is no solution for a system by just looking at the equations? Explain and give an example.

15. If the difference in the side lengths of two squares is 10, and the sum of the side lengths is 18, what are the side lengths?

16. A shopper purchased 8 T-Shirts and 5 pairs pants for $220. The next day, he purchased 5 T-shirts and 1 pair of pants for $112. How much does each T-shirt and each pair of pants cost?

Prentice Hall Gold Algebra 1 • Practice and Problem Solving Workbook

6-2 Practice (continued) Form G
Solving Systems Using Substitution

17. A student bought 1 box of crayons and 5 reams of paper for $54. She bought 5 boxes of crayons and 3 reams of paper for $50. What is the cost of each box of crayons and each ream of paper?

18. Suppose you got 8 mangoes and 3 apples for $18 and 3 mangoes and 5 apples for $14.50. How much does each mango and each apple cost?

19. A shopper purchased 4 tables and 2 chairs for $200 and 2 tables and 7 chairs for $400. What is the cost of each table and each chair?

20. If the length of the rectangle is twice the width, and the perimeter of the rectangle is 30 cm, what is length and width of the rectangle?

21. The population of a city is 2,500. If the number of males is 240 more than the number of females, how many males and females are there in the city?

Solve each system by substitution. Tell whether the system has *one solution*, *infinitely many solutions*, or *no solution*.

22. $7x + 2y = -13$
$-3x - 8y = -23$

23. $x - 9y = -10$
$6x + y = -5$

24. $x = \dfrac{y}{4} + 1$
$y = 4x - 5$

25. $x - 2y - 1 = 0$
$y - 5x + 14 = 0$

26. $y = -8x - 37$
$x + 3y = 4$

27. $3x + 6y = 18$
$3y = -\dfrac{3}{2}x + 9$

28. $5x - 9y = 29$
$12x + y = 47$

29. $2x = 3y - 9$
$-3x + y = 10$

30. $5y = 7x + 22$
$x = -6y + 17$

31. $x = 6y + 16$
$9x - 2y = -12$

32. $4x - y - 4 = 0$
$3x + 2y - 14 = 0$

33. $x + 3y = -5$
$-2x - y = 5$

6-2 Standardized Test Prep

Solving Systems Using Substitution

Gridded Response

Solve each exercise and enter your answer on the grid provided.

1. For the following system of equations, what is the x-value of the solution?
$$-x + 2y = 6$$
$$6y = x + 18$$

2. The sum of the measures of angle X and angle Y is 90. If the measure of angle X is 30 less than twice the measure of angle Y, what is the measure of angle X?

3. One number is 4 less than 3 times a second number. If 3 more than two times the first number is decreased by 2 times the second number, the result is 11. Use the substitution method. What is the first number?

4. An investor bought 3 shares of stock A and 2 shares of stock B for a total of $41. Stock A costs $2.00 more per share than stock B. What is the cost of a share of stock A in dollars?

5. Solve the following system of equations using substitution. What is the value of y?
$$2x + 3y = 105$$
$$x + 2y = 65$$

1. 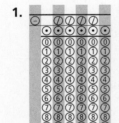 2. 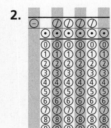 3. 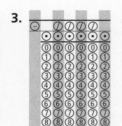 4. 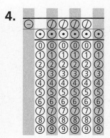 5.

6-3 Think About a Plan

Solving Systems Using Elimination

Nutrition Half a pepperoni pizza plus three fourths of a ham-and-pineapple pizza contains 765 Calories. One fourth of a pepperoni pizza plus a whole ham-and-pineapple pizza contains 745 Calories. How many Calories are in a whole pepperoni pizza? How many Calories are in a whole ham-and-pineapple pizza?

Know

1. What equation will represent the 765 Calories combination of pizza? _____

2. What equation will represent the 745 Calories combination of pizza? _____

Need

3. What possible methods can you use to solve the system of equations?

_____

Plan

4. How can you solve the system of equations by elimination?

_____

_____

5. How can you eliminate one of the variables to solve the system of equations?

_____

6. Solve the system of equations.

7. What is the solution of the system?

_____

8. How many Calories are in each kind of pizza?

_____

_____

6-3

Practice

Form G

Solving Systems Using Elimination

Solve each system using elimination.

1. $x + y = 2$
$x - y = 4$

2. $x + 2y = 3$
$x - y = 6$

3. $2x - y = 4$
$3x - y = 2$

4. $x - 2y = -2$
$-x + y = 3$

5. $-x - 3y = -3$
$2x + 3y = 5$

6. $x + 2y = -4$
$x + y = 2$

7. $3x - 2y = 8$
$2x - 2y = 5$

8. $x - 2y = 3$
$3x - y = 2$

9. $2x - 4y = -6$
$x - y = -1$

10. Writing For the system $\begin{matrix} 3x - 5y = 9 \\ 2x + y = 3 \end{matrix}$, which variable should you eliminate first and why? How will you eliminate that variable?

11. Open-Ended If you do not have equal coefficients for both variables, can you still use the elimination method? Explain.

12. In a class, 45 students take the SAT exam. The number of boys is 8 more than the number of girls.

a. Write a system that models the above situation.

b. Do you need to multiply any of the equations by a constant? If so, which equation and what is the constant?

13. Open-Ended Write a system for which using the elimination method to solve the system is easier than the substitution method. Explain.

14. Error Analysis A student solved a system of linear equations using the elimination method as follows. Describe and correct the error made by the student.

$3x - 5y = 4$	$6x - 10y = 8$	Multiply equation 1 by 2.
$-2x + 3y = 2$	$\underline{-6x + 3y = 6}$	Multiply equation 2 by 3.
	$-7y = 14$	Add the equations.
	$y = -2$	Divide by -7.

6-3 Practice (continued) Form G

Solving Systems Using Elimination

15. A farm raises a total of 220 chickens and pigs. The number of legs of the stock in the farm totals 520. How many chickens and pigs are at the farm?

16. You drive a car that runs on ethanol and gas. You have a 20-gallon tank to fill and you can buy fuel that is either 25 percent ethanol or 85 percent ethanol. How much of each type of fuel should you buy to fill your tank so that it is 50 percent ethanol?

17. Your math test has 38 questions and is worth 200 points. The test consists of multiple-choice questions worth 4 points each and open-ended questions worth 20 points each. How many of each type of question are there?

18. A student bought 3 boxes of pencils and 2 boxes of pens for $6. He then bought 2 boxes of pencils and 4 boxes of pens for $8. Find the cost of each box of pencils and each box of pens.

Solve each system using elimination. Tell whether the system has *one solution*, *infinitely many solutions,* or *no solution.*

19. $x - 3y = -7$
$2x = 6y - 14$

20. $3x - 5y = -2$
$x + 3y = 4$

21. $x + 2y = 6$
$2x - 4y = -12$

22. $5x + y = 15$
$3y = -15x + 6$

23. $3x = 4y - 5$
$12y = 9x + 15$

24. $3x - y = -2$
$-2x + 2y = 8$

25. $x + 2y = -4$
$-3x + 2y = 4$

26. $x + y = -2$
$-x - y = 4$

27. $3x - 2y = -3$
$6y = 9x + 9$

28. $-4x - 3y = 5$
$3x - 2y = -8$

29. $x - 3y = 1$
$2x + 2y = 10$

30. $-4x - 2y = 20$
$2x + y = 19$

31. How is the multiplication or division property of equality used in the elimination method? Are the properties always needed? Explain.

6-3 Standardized Test Prep

Solving Systems Using Elimination

Multiple Choice

For Exercises 1–5, choose the correct letter.

1. What is the solution for the following system of equations?
$$5x + 7y = 3$$
$$2x + 3y = 1$$

   A. $(-2, 1)$ **B.** $(1, -2)$ **C.** $(2, -1)$ **D.** $(-1, 2)$

2. The perimeter of a rectangle is 24 in. and its length l is 3 times the width w. What is the length and width (l, w) of the rectangle?

   F. $(3, 9)$ **G.** $(14.4, 4.8)$ **H.** $(12, 4)$ **I.** $(9, 3)$

3. What do both dependent and inconsistent systems have in common?
   A. no solution   **C.** same slope
   B. same y-intercept   **D.** same slope and y-intercept

4. Two linear equations have the same y-intercept and different slopes. How would you classify the system?
   F. consistent, independent   **H.** dependent, inconsistent
   G. consistent, dependent   **I.** independent, inconsistent

5. What is the solution of the following system of equations?

   $$5x + 7y = 3$$
   $$2x = -3y + 1$$

   A. $(11, 17)$ **B.** $(2, -1)$ **C.** $(11.5, 8)$ **D.** $(-2, 1)$

Short Response

6. A hotel is offering the two weekend specials described below.

   Plan 1: 3 nights and 4 meals for $233

   Plan 2: 3 nights and 3 meals for $226.50.

   For accounting purposes, the hotel will record income for the stay and the meals separately. So the cost per night for each special must be the same, and the cost per meal for each special must be the same.

   a. What is a system of equations for the situation?
   b. Solve the system. What is the cost per night and the cost per meal?

6-4 Think About a Plan

Applications of Linear Systems

Chemistry In a chemistry lab, you have two vinegars. One is 5% acetic acid, and one is 6.5% acetic acid. You want to make 200 mL of a vinegar with 6% acetic acid. How many milliliters of each vinegar do you need to mix together?

Know

1. What types of vinegar do you have available?

2. What amount of mixed vinegar do you need?

3. What percentage of acetic acid do you want in the mixed vinegar?

Need

4. What do you need to find to solve the problem?

Plan

5. How will you define the two variables for this problem?

6. What is an equation for the total amount of vinegar you want to make?

7. What is an equation for the acetic acid content?

8. What method will you use to solve?

9. What is the solution of the system of equations?

10. How much of each type of vinegar should you mix together?

Name _____ Class _____ Date _____

6-4

Practice

Form G

Applications of Linear Systems

Solve each word problem

1. You have $6000 to invest in two stock funds. The first fund pays 5% annual interest and the second account pays 9% annual interest. If after a year you have made $380 in interest, how much money did you invest in each account?

2. During a sale at the local department store, you buy three sweatshirts and two pairs of sweatpants for $85.50. Later you return to the same store and buy three more sweatshirts and four more pairs of sweatpants for $123. What is the sale price of each sweatshirt and each pair of sweatpants?

3. The sum of two numbers is 27. The larger number is 3 more than the smaller number. What are the two numbers?

4. One plane at 520 feet is ascending at a rate of 40 feet per minute, while another plane at 3800 feet is descending at a rate of 120 feet per minute. How long will it take the two planes to be at the same altitude?

5. The perimeter of a rectangle is 24 in. and its length is 3 times its width. What are the length and the width of the rectangle?

6. You are getting ready to move and have asked some friends to help. For lunch, you buy the following sandwiches at the local deli for $30: six tuna sandwiches and six turkey sandwiches. Later at night, everyone is hungry again and you buy four tuna sandwiches and eight turkey sandwiches for $30.60. What is the price of each sandwich?

7. You have a cable plan that costs $39 a month for a basic plan plus one movie channel. Your friend has the same basic plan plan plus two movie channels for $45.50. What is the basic plan charge that you both pay?

8. At an all-you-can-eat barbeque fundraiser that you are sponsoring, adults pay $6 for a dinner and children pay $4 for a dinner. 212 people attend and you raise $1128. What is the total number of adults and the total number of children attending?

   a. What is a system of equations that you can use to solve this problem?

   b. What method would you use to solve the system? Why?

6-4 Practice (continued)   Form G

Applications of Linear Systems

Solve each system. Explain why you chose the method you used.

9. $2y = x + 1$
$-2x - y = 7$

10. $6x - 4y = 54$
$-9x + 2y = -69$

11. $3x - 2y = 8$
$2x - 2y = 5$

12. $2x - y = 4$
$3x - y = 2$

13. $2x - 3y = 13$
$y = \frac{1}{2}x - \frac{7}{2}$

14. $-x - 3y = -3$
$2x + 3y = 5$

15. Open-Ended What are three differences between an inconsistent system and a consistent and independent system? Explain.

16. Reasoning One number is 4 less than 3 times a second number. If 3 more than two times the first number is decreased by two times the second, the result is 11. What are both numbers?

17. Error Analysis In Exercise 16, what kind of errors are likely to occur when solving the problem?

18. A plane leaves Chicago and flies 750 miles to New York. If it takes 2.5 hours to get to New York flying against the wind, but only 2 hours to fly back to Chicago, what is the plane's rate of speed and what is the wind speed?

19. A coin bank has 250 coins, dimes and quarters, worth $39.25. How many of each type of coin are there?

20. In 4 years, a mother will be 5 times as old as her daughter. At present, the mother is 9 times as old as the daughter. How old are the mother and the daughter today?

6-4 Standardized Test Prep

Applications of Linear Systems

Multiple Choice

For Exercises 1–5, choose the correct letter.

1. You solved a linear system with two equations and two variables and got the equation $-6 = -6$. How many solutions does the system of equations have?
   A. no solution
   B. infinitely many solutions
   C. exactly 1 solution
   D. 2 solutions

2. The sum of two numbers is 12. The difference of the same two numbers is 4. What is the larger of the two numbers?
   F. 4
   H. 7
   G. 5
   I. 8

3. You solved a linear system and got the equation $-6 = 0$. How many solutions does the system of equations have?
   A. no solution
   B. infinitely many solutions
   C. exactly 1 solution
   D. 2 solutions

4. What is the solution of the system of equations?
   $$-y + 3x = 6$$
   $$y = -6x + 12$$
   F. $(-2, 0)$
   H. $(2, 0)$
   G. $(0, -2)$
   I. $(0, 2)$

5. A kayaker paddles upstream for 1.5 hours, then turns his kayak around and returns to his tent in 1 hour. He travels 3 miles each way. What is the rate of the river's current?
   A. 0.5 mi/h
   B. 2 mi/h
   C. 1 mi/h
   D. 1.5 mi/h

Short Response

6. Rectangle *EFGH* has a perimeter of 24 inches, and triangle *BCD* has a perimeter of 18 inches.

   a. What is a system of equations for the perimeters of the figures?

   b. Without solving, what method you would use to solve the system? Explain.

6-5

Think About a Plan

Linear Inequalities

Employment A student with two summer jobs earns $10 per hour at a café and $8 per hour at a market. The student would like to earn at least $800 per month.
  a. Write and graph an inequality to represent the situation.
  b. The student works at the market for 60 h per month and can work at most 90 h per month. Can the student earn at least $800 each month? Explain how you can use your graph to determine this.

Understanding the Problem

1. What do you know about the student's hourly rates?

_____

2. What do you know about how much the student would like to earn each month?

_____

3. What do you know about the number of hours the student can work each month?

_____

_____

Planning the Solution

4. What inequality represents the number of hours that the student can work each month? _____

5. What inequality represents the amount that the student can earn each month?

_____

Getting an Answer

6. How can you use these two inequalities to find out if the student working 60 hours a month at the market can make $800 per month?

_____

_____

7. How can you determine the number of hours that the student should work each month? What are the number of hours the student should work at the market and at the cafe to make at least $800 per month?

_____

_____

6-5 Practice

Form G

Linear Inequalities

Graph each linear inequality.

1. $x \geq -4$

2. $y < 2$

3. $3x - y \geq 6$

4. $-4x + 5y < -3$

5. $3x + 2y > 6$

6. $y < x$

7. $3x - 5y > 6$

8. $x \leq \dfrac{y}{9}$

9. $\dfrac{x}{4} < 4y - 3$

10. Error Analysis A student graphed $y \leq -4x + 3$ as shown. Describe and correct the student's error.

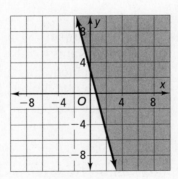

11. Writing How do you decide which half-plane to shade when graphing an inequality? Explain.

6-5

Practice (continued)   Form G

Linear Inequalities

Determine whether the ordered pair is a solution of the linear inequality.

12. $7x + 2y > -5, (-1, 1)$

13. $x - y \leq 3, (2, -1)$

14. $y + 2x > 5, (4, 1)$

15. $x + 4y \leq -2, (-8, -2)$

16. $y < x + 4, (-9, -5)$

17. $y < 3x + 2, (3, 10)$

18. $x - \frac{1}{2}y > 3, (9, 12)$

19. $0.3x - 2.4y > 0.9, (8, 0.5)$

Write an inequality that represents each graph.

20.

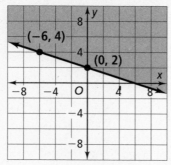

21.

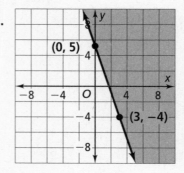

22. You and some friends have $30. You want to order large pizzas (*p*) that are $9 eachand drinks (*d*) that cost $1 each. Write and graph an inequality that shows how many pizzas and drinks can you order.?

23. Tickets to a play cost $5 at the door and $4 in advance. The theater club wants to raise at least $400 from the play. Write and graph an inequality for the number of tickets the theater club needs to sell. If the club sells 40 tickets in advance, how many do they need to sell at the door to reach their goal?

24. Reasoning Two students did a problem as above, but one used *x* for the first variable and *y* for the second variable and the other student used *x* for the second variable and *y* for the first variable. How did their answers differ and which one, if either, was incorrect?

6-5 Standardized Test Prep

Linear Inequalities

Multiple Choice

For Exercises 1–5, choose the correct letter.

1. What point on the axes satisfies the inequality $y < x$?
   A. $(0, 1)$ **B.** $(-1, 0)$ **C.** $(1, 0)$ **D.** $(0, 0)$

2. For the graph of the inequality $x - 2y \geq 4$, what is a value of x for a point that is on the boundary line and the axes?
   F. 4   **G.** -2 **H.** 2   **I.** -4

3. If $x \geq 0$ and $y \geq 0$, then which quadrant holds the solutions?
   A. IV   **B.** III   **C.** I   **D.** II

4. Which is the y-value of a boundary point that is an intersecting point not on the axes for this region: $x \geq 0, y \geq 0, x \leq 4$ and $y \leq 3$?
   F. 4   **G.** 0   **H.** 1   **I.** 3

5. How do you decide where to shade an inequality whose boundary does not go through the origin?
   A. For $<$, shade above the boundary.
   B. If $(0, 0)$ is a solution, shade where $(0, 0)$ is.
   C. For $>$, shade below the boundary.
   D. If $(0, 0)$ is a solution, shade the boundary.

Short Response

6. A school fundraiser sells holiday cards and wrapping paper. They are trying to raise at least $400. They make a profit of $1.50 on each box of holiday cards and $1.00 on each pack of wrapping paper.

   a. What is an inequality for the profit the school wants to make for the fundraiser?
   b. If the fundraiser sells 100 boxes of cards and 160 packs of wrapping paper, will they reach their goal? Show your work.

6-6 Think About a Plan

Systems of Linear Inequalities

Gift Certificates You received a $100 gift certificate to a clothing store. The store sells T-shirts for $15 and dress shirts for $22. You want to spend no more than the amount of the gift certificate. You want to leave at most $10 of the gift certificate unspent. You need at least one dress shirt. What are all of the possible combinations of T-shirts and dress shirts you could buy?

Understanding the Problem

1. What do you know about the cost of each type of shirt that you want to buy?

   _____

2. What do you know about how much you can spend? What do you know about how much you want to leave unspent?

   _____

3. What do you know about the number of dress shirts that you want to buy?

   _____

Planning the Solution

4. What inequality represents the amount of shirts you can buy? _____

5. What inequality represents the amount of the gift certificate which could be unspent? _____

6. What inequality represents the number of dress shirts you want to buy? _____

Getting an Answer

7. How can you use these inequalities to find out the number of T-shirts and dress shirts you can buy? _____

   _____

8. Graph the system of linear inequalities. Point out the region that shows the answer.

9. What combinations of T-shirts and dress shirts are possible? _____

10. Are there any other possible combinations? Explain.

   _____

   _____

6-6 Practice

Form G

Systems of Linear Inequalities

Solve each system of inequalities by graphing.

1. $3x + y \le 1$
$\quad x - y \le 3$

2. $5x - y \le 1$
$\quad x + 3y \le -2$

3. $4x + 3y \le 1$
$\quad 2x - y \le 2$

4. Writing What is the difference between the solution of a system of linear inequalities and the solution of a system of linear equations? Explain.

5. Open-Ended When can you say that there is no solution for a system of linear inequalities? Explain your answer and show with a system and graph.

6. Error Analysis A student graphs the system below. Describe and correct the student's error.

$x - y \ge 3$

$y < -2$

$x \ge 1$

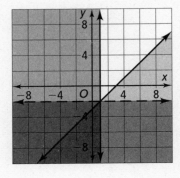

Determine whether the ordered pair is a solution of the given system.

7. $(0, 1)$;
$\quad 1 - x \ge 3y$
$\quad 3y - 1 > 2x$

8. $(-2, 3)$;
$\quad 2x + 3y > 2$
$\quad 3x + 5y > 1$

9. $(1, 4)$;
$\quad 2x + y > 3$
$\quad -3x - y \le 5$

6-6 **Practice** (continued) *Form G*

Systems of Linear Inequalities

10. Mark is a student, and he can work for at most 20 hours a week. He needs to earn at least $75 to cover his weekly expenses. His dog-walking job pays $5 per hour and his job as a car wash attendant pays $4 per hour. Write a system of inequalities to model the situation, and graph the inequalities.

11. Britney wants to bake at most 10 loaves of bread for a bake sale. She wants to make banana bread that sells for $1.25 each and nut bread that sells for $1.50 each and make at least $24 in sales. Write a system of inequalities for the given situation and graph the inequalities.

12. Write a system of inequalities for the following graph.

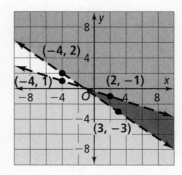

Solve each system of inequalities by graphing.

13. $5x + 7y > -6$
$x + 3y < -1$

14. $x + 4y - 2 \geq 0$
$2x - y + 1 > 2$

15. $\frac{x}{2} - 5 > -6y$
$3x + y > 2$

6-6 Standardized Test Prep

Systems of Linear Inequalities

Multiple Choice

For Exercises 1–4, choose the correct letter.

1. You and a friend both would like a salad and a small drink. Between the two of you, you have $8.00. A salad costs $2.49 and a small drink is $.99. Can either of you have a second salad or drink?

   A. yes, 1 salad   **B.** yes, 1 of each   **C.** yes, 1 drink   **D.** no, you cannot

2. Which of the following systems of inequalities represents the graph?

   F. $\begin{array}{l} y > 2x + 4 \\ y \le -x + 2 \end{array}$ **G.** $\begin{array}{l} 2x - y \ge 4 \\ y < -x + 2 \end{array}$

   H. $\begin{array}{l} y \ge 2x + 4 \\ -x + y < 2 \end{array}$ **I.** $\begin{array}{l} -2x + y \ge 4 \\ x + y < 2 \end{array}$

   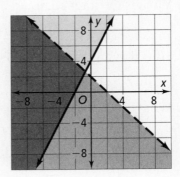

3. For the graph above, what is the approximate y-value of the point of intersection?

   A. -1 **B.** 4   **C.** 3   **D.** 2

4. A student spends no more than 2 hours on his math and English homework. If math takes about twice as long as English, what is the maximum time that the student can spend on English?

   F. $\frac{1}{3}$ hour   **G.** $\frac{1}{2}$ hour   **H.** 1 hour   **I.** $\frac{2}{3}$ hour

Short Response

5. A young woman wants to make at least $200 a week and can work no more than 30 hours a week. She works at the library for $8 an hour and babysits for $6 an hour.

   a. What system of inequalities shows the possible combination of hours and jobs she can work?

   b. Why did you exclude points to the left of the y-axis and below the x-axis?

7-1

Think About a Plan

Zero and Negative Exponents

Manufacturing A company is making metal rods with a target diameter of 1.5 mm. A rod is acceptable when its diameter is within 10^{-3} mm of the target diameter. Write an inequality for the acceptable range of diameters.

Understanding the Problem

1. What is the target diameter for the metal rods? _____

2. How do you know if a rod is acceptable? _____

3. What is the problem asking you to determine? _____

_____

Planning the Solution

4. What does the word "within" tell you about the acceptable range of diameters? _____

_____

5. What does this tell you about the type of inequality that you should use?

_____

Getting an Answer

6. Write 10^{-3} as a fraction and as a decimal.

7. Find the acceptable range for the diameters of the rods.

8. Write your answer as a single inequality. _____

7-1

Practice
Zero and Negative Exponents

Form G

Simplify each expression.

1. 13^0

2. 5^{-3}

3. $\dfrac{3}{3^{-4}}$

4. $\dfrac{2}{4^{-1}}$

5. $-(7)^{-2}$

6. 46^{-1}

7. -6^0

8. $-(12x)^{-2}$

9. $\dfrac{1}{8^0}$

10. $6bc^0$

11. $-(11x)^0$

12. $\left(\dfrac{2}{9}\right)^{-2}$

13. $3m^{-8}p^0$

14. $\dfrac{5a^{-4}}{2c}$

15. $\dfrac{-3k^{-3}(mn)^3}{p^{-8}}$

16. $\left(\dfrac{2m}{3n}\right)^{-3}$

17. $8^{-2}q^3r^{-5}$

18. $-(10a)^{-4}b^0$

19. $\dfrac{11xy^{-1}z^0}{v^{-3}}$

20. $\dfrac{5m^{-1}}{9(ab)^{-4}c^7}$

7-1 Practice (continued)   Form G
Zero and Negative Exponents

Evaluate each expression for $a = -4$, $b = 3$, and $c = 2$.

21. $3a^{-1}$ **22.** b^{-3}

23. $4a^2 b^{-2} c^3$ **24.** $9a^0 c^4$

25. $-a^{-2}$ **26.** $(-c)^{-2}$

Write each number as a power of 10 using negative exponents.

27. $\dfrac{1}{1000}$ **28.** $\dfrac{1}{10}$

Write each expression as a decimal.

29. 10^{-3} **30.** $8 \cdot 10^{-4}$

31. The number of people who vote early doubles every week leading up to an election. This week 1200 people voted early. The expression $1200 \cdot 2^w$ models the number of people who will vote early w weeks after this week. Evaluate the expression for $w = -3$. Describe what the value of the expression represents in the situation.

32. A pizza shop makes large pizzas with a target diameter of 16 inches. A pizza is acceptable if its diameter is within $3 \cdot 2^{-2}$ in. of the target diameter. Let d represent the diameter of a pizza. Write an inequality for the range of acceptable large pizza diameters in inches.

33. Open-Ended Choose a fraction to use as a value for the variable c. Find the values of c^{-1}, c^{-3}, and c^3.

7-1 Standardized Test Prep

Zero and Negative Exponents

Multiple Choice

For Exercises 1–6, choose the correct letter.

1. What is the simplified form of $3a^4b^{-2}c^3$?

   A. $\dfrac{81a^4c^3}{b^2}$ 　　**B.** $\dfrac{81a^4}{b^2c^3}$ 　　**C.** $\dfrac{3a^4}{b^2c^3}$ 　　**D.** $\dfrac{3a^4c^3}{b^2}$

2. What is $-a^{-2}$ if $a = -5$?

   F. -25 　　**G.** 25 　　**H.** $-\dfrac{1}{25}$ 　　**I.** $\dfrac{1}{25}$

3. Which of the following simplifies to a negative number?

   A. -4^{-4} 　　**B.** $(-4)^{-4}$ 　　**C.** 4^{-4} 　　**D.** $\dfrac{1}{4^{-4}}$

4. What is the simplified form of $-(14x)^0 y^{-7} z$?

   F. $-\dfrac{14z}{y^7}$ 　　**G.** $\dfrac{14z}{y^7}$ 　　**H.** $\dfrac{z}{y^7}$ 　　**I.** $-\dfrac{z}{y^7}$

5. What is $(-m)^{-3}n$ if $m = 2$ and $n = -24$?

   A. 3 　　**B.** -3 　　**C.** 4 　　**D.** -4

6. What is the simplified form of $\left(-\dfrac{5a}{3}\right)^{-3}$?

   F. $\dfrac{27}{125a^3}$ 　　**G.** $-\dfrac{27}{125a^3}$ 　　**H.** $\dfrac{125a^3}{27}$ 　　**I.** $-\dfrac{125a^3}{27}$

Short Response

7. The number of bacteria in a culture quadruples every hour. There were 65,536 bacteria in the culture at 8:00 A.M. The expression $65{,}536 \cdot 4^h$ models the number of bacteria in the culture h hours after 8:00 A.M.

   a. What is the value of the expression for $h = -4$?

   b. What does the value of the expression in part a represent?

7-2   Think About a Plan

Scientific Notation

Physics The radius of a water molecule is about 1.4 angstroms. One angstrom is 0.00000001 cm. What is the diameter of a water molecule in centimeters? Use scientific notation.

1. What geometric facts and arithmetic operation(s) are you going to need to use to solve the problem? What is the relationship between diameter and radius? How do you convert between the given units?

_____

_____

_____

_____

2. How many angstroms are there in the diameter of a water molecule? _____

How will you turn angstroms into centimeters? _____

_____

3. Rewrite 0.00000001 in scientific notation. Recall that a number written in scientific notation is in the form $a \times 10^n$.

$a =$ _____ $n =$ _____   0.00000001 = _____

4. Multiply the number of angstroms in the diameter of a water molecule by the length of an angstrom in centimeters to find the number of centimeters in the diameter of a water molecule.

_____

7-2

Practice

Scientific Notation

Form G

Is the number written in scientific notation? If not, explain.

1. 32.1×10^5

2. 5.6×10^{12}

3. 4.6×10^{-5}

4. 0.7×10^{34}

Write each number in scientific notation.

5. 3,200,000,000,000

6. 0.00000802

7. 70,030,000

8. 8.7 billion

Write each number in standard notation.

9. 3.37×10^{12}

10. 3.060×10^7

11. 4.2×10^{-6}

12. 4.56×10^0

Simplify. Write each answer using scientific notation.

13. $5(3.2 \times 10^{-4})$

14. $0.7(8.54 \times 10^4)$

15. $87(6.4 \times 10^5)$

16. $0.03(6 \times 10^{-7})$

17. **Writing** Scientific notation is often used for working with very small or very large numbers. Describe two situations where using scientific notation might be appropriate.

18. **Reasoning** How does a number in scientific notation change when you multiply it by 100?

19. Country A has a population of 8.7×10^9. You hear that country B has twice as many people as country A and country C has twice as many people as country B. How many people live in country C?

7-2

Practice (continued)

Form G

Scientific Notation

Write a number in scientific notation that is between the two given numbers.

20. $6.2 \times 10^5, 9.6 \times 10^4$

21. $3.7 \times 10^{-3}, 9.4 \times 10^{-2}$

22. $7.94 \times 10^6, 7.93 \times 10^7$

23. $9 \times 10^{-6}, 6 \times 10^{-7}$

Write a number in standard notation that is between the two given numbers.

24. $3.42 \times 10^8, 3.421 \times 10^8$

25. $1.3 \times 10^{-4}, 1 \times 10^{-3}$

26. $5.708 \times 10^{-6}, 5.7008 \times 10^{-6}$

27. $1.2 \times 10^0, 1.3 \times 10^0$

Write a number in words that is between the two given numbers.

28. $6.52 \times 10^7, 1.2 \times 10^8$

29. $3.9 \times 10^{-5}, 2.8 \times 10^{-4}$

30. Open-Ended Write two factors that, when multiplied together, produce a product of 3.6×10^8. One of the factors should be written in scientific notation.

31. Light travels at 1.86×10^5 miles per second. If a particle is traveling at half the speed of light, how fast is it moving?

32. An atom of carbon has a mass of 1.99×10^{-23} grams.
   a. What is the mass of two atoms of carbon?
   b. What is the mass of five atoms of carbon?

7-2 Standardized Test Prep

Scientific Notation

Multiple Choice

For Exercises 1–6, choose the correct letter.

1. Which of the following expressions is written in scientific notation?

   A. 73.4×10^5 **B.** 0.09×10^7 **C.** 80×10^3 **D.** 4.22×10^{-5}

2. Which of the following is 0.0000000708 written in scientific notation?

   F. 7.08×10^{-8} **G.** 7.8×10^{-8} **H.** 708×10^{-10} **I.** 70.8×10^{-9}

3. Which expression represents the largest number?

   A. 40.1×10^{-6} **B.** 4.1×10^{-7} **C.** 0.411×10^{-6} **D.** 0.04001×10^{-5}

4. Which expression is equal to $\dfrac{1}{8000}$ written in scientific notation?

   F. 8.0×10^3 **G.** 1.25×10^{-4} **H.** 125×10^{-5} **I.** 1.25×10^4

5. Which of the following statements is *not* true regarding an expression written in scientific notation in the form $a \times 10^n$?

   A. The value of a must be greater than or equal to 1 and smaller than 10.
   B. The value of n must be an integer.
   C. Doubling n results in a doubling of the value of the expression.
   D. Doubling a results in a doubling of the value of the expression.

6. Which number is equal to $7(3.5 \times 10^4)$ written in scientific notation?

   F. 24.5×70^4 **G.** 2.45×10^5 **H.** 24.5×10^4 **I.** 1.05×10^5

Short Response

7. A state government has 5.7×10^7 dollars invested in a pension fund for retired employees. It expects this investment to double in value every 8 years. What is the value of the investment after 8 years, 16 years and 24 years? Write your response in scientific notation.

7-3

Think About a Plan

Multiplying Powers With the Same Base

Chemistry In chemistry, a *mole* is a unit of measure equal to 6.02×10^{23} atoms of a substance. The mass of a single neon atom is about 3.35×10^{-23}g. What is the mass of 2 moles of neon atoms? Write your answer in scientific notation.

Understanding the Problem

1. What is the mass of a single atom of neon?

_____

2. How many atoms are in 1 mole?

_____

Planning the Solution

3. Without solving, explain how you can determine the mass of 1 mole of neon atoms. How about 2 moles of neon atoms?

_____

_____

4. What exponent rules and guidelines will help you with your calculations?

_____

_____

Getting an Answer

5. Demonstrate how the numbers can be arranged to simplify the multiplication.

_____

_____

6. Complete your calculations.

_____

_____

7. Is your answer in scientific notation? Explain.

_____

_____

7-3

Practice

Form G

Multiplying Powers With the Same Base

Rewrite each expression using each base only once.

1. $4^5 \cdot 4^3$

2. $2^4 \cdot 2^6 \cdot 2^2$

3. $5^6 \cdot 5^{-2} \cdot 5^{-1}$

4. $10^{-4} \cdot 10^4 \cdot 10^2$

5. $7^9 \cdot 7^3 \cdot 7^{-10}$

6. $9^2 \cdot 9^{-8} \cdot 9^6$

Simplify each expression.

7. $z^8 z^5$

8. $-4k^{-3} \cdot 6k^4$

9. $(-5b^3)(-3b^6)$

10. $(13x^{-8})(3x^{10})$

11. $(-2h^5)(4h^{-3})$

12. $-8n \cdot 11n^9$

13. $(t^3)(t^6)(t^9)$

14. $(-f^{-8})(4f^{12})$

15. $(-5d^{-5})(6d^2)$

16. $mn^2 \cdot m^2n^{-4} \cdot mn^{-1}$

17. $(6a^3b^{-2})(-4ab^{-8})$

18. $(12mn)(-m^3n^{-2}p^5)(2m)$

19. $q^4 \cdot r^{-5} \cdot q^3 \cdot r^5$

20. $-3c^7d^{-2} \cdot 5c^{-3}d$

21. $fg^{-1} \cdot f^3g^5h^2 \cdot 2h^{-1}$

Simplify each expression. Write each answer in scientific notation.

22. $(5 \times 10^4)(1 \times 10^7)$

23. $(3 \times 10^{-6})(2 \times 10^{12})$

24. $(6 \times 10^7)(4 \times 10^{-5})$

25. $(7 \times 10^4)(7 \times 10^{-5})$

26. $(8 \times 10^3) \cdot 10^{-8}$

27. $(9 \times 10^{-6})(2 \times 10^{-7})$

Write each answer in scientific notation.

28. The population of a country in 1950 was 6.2×10^7. The population in 2030 is projected to be 3×10^2 times the 1950 population. If the projection is correct, what will the population of the country be in 2030?

29. The area of land that Rhode Island covers is approximately 1.5×10^3 square miles. The area of land that Alaska covers is a little more than 4.3×10^2 times the land area of Rhode Island. What is the approximate area of Alaska in square miles?

Complete each equation.

30. $9^{-2} \cdot 9^4 = 9^{\square}$

31. $5^{\square} \cdot 5^3 = 5^{-5}$

32. $2^8 \cdot 2^{\square} = 2^{-2}$

33. $z^{\square} \cdot z^{-5} = z^3$

34. $m^{-3} \cdot m^6 \cdot m^{\square} = m^2$

35. $d^7 \cdot d^{-13} \cdot d^{-9} = d^{\square}$

7-3

Practice (continued)   Form G

Multiplying Powers With the Same Base

Find the area of each figure.

36.
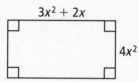
$3x^2 + 2x$
$4x^2$

37.
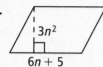
$3n^2$
$6n + 5$

38.

$5b$
$2b^2 - 4$

39.
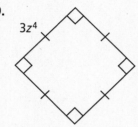
$3z^4$

Simplify each expression. Write each answer in scientific notation.

40. $(7 \times 10^{17})(8 \times 10^{-28})$ 41. $(4 \times 10^{-11})(0.8 \times 10^7)$ 42. $(0.9 \times 10^{15})(0.1 \times 10^{-6})$

43. $(0.8 \times 10^5)(0.6 \times 10^{-17})$ 44. $(0.5 \times 10^3)(0.6 \times 10^0)$ 45. $(0.2 \times 10^{11})(0.4 \times 10^{-14})$

46. The diameter of the moon is approximately 3.5×10^3 kilometers.
   a. The diameter of Earth is approximately 3.7 times the diameter of the moon.
      Determine the diameter of Earth. Write your answer in scientific notation.
   b. The distance from the center of Earth to the center of the moon is
      approximately 30 times the diameter of Earth. Determine the distance
      from the center of Earth to the center of the moon. Write your answer in
      scientific notation.

Simplify each expression.

47. $\dfrac{1}{n^{-8} \cdot n^3}$

48. $\dfrac{1}{x^4 \cdot x^{-9}}$

49. $7k^4(-2k^6 - k)$

50. $-2x^2(-3x^4 + 5)$

51. $4^x \cdot 4^{x+1} \cdot 4$

52. $(n + 2)^5(n + 2)^{-3}$

53. **Writing** Explain what moving the decimal point 4 places to the right or to
    the left does to the value of a number. In scientific notation, what power of 10
    would you multiply by to make up for the movement of the decimal point?

7-3

Standardized Test Prep

Multiplying Powers With the Same Base

Multiple Choice

For Exercises 1–5, choose the correct letter.

1. What is the simplified form of $(-3x^3y^2)(5xy^{-1})$?

   A. $\dfrac{-15x^3}{y^2}$ **B.** $-15x^3y^2$ **C.** $-15x^4y$ **D.** $15x^4y$

2. What is the simplified form of $-9m^{-2}n^5 \cdot 2m^{-3}n^{-6}$?

   F. $-18m^5n$ **G.** $\dfrac{-18}{m^5n}$ **H.** $\dfrac{-18m^6}{n^{30}}$ **I.** $-18m^6n^{30}$

3. A rectangular pasture has a fence around the perimeter. The length of the fence is $16x^7$ and the width is $48x^4$. What is the area of the pasture?

   A. $3x^3$ **B.** $128x^{11}$ **C.** $768x^{11}$ **D.** $768x^{28}$

4. What is the simplified form of $(3.25 \times 10^3)(7.8 \times 10^6)$ written in scientific notation?

   F. 2.535×10^{10} **G.** 2.535×10^{18} **H.** 2.535×10^{19} **I.** 25.35×10^9

5. The size of a certain cell is 2.5×10^{-9} m. Another cell is 1.5×10^3 times larger. How large is the larger cell in scientific notation?

   A. 4×10^{-27} m   **B.** 4×10^{-12} m   **C.** 3.75×10^6 m   **D.** 3.75×10^{-6} m

Extended Response

6. The distance between two astronomical bodies is 6.75×10^6 miles. The distance from the first body to a third body is 3.56×10^4 times the distance between the first two bodies.

   a. Write an expression that represents the distance between the first and third bodies.

   b. Simplify the distance in part a.

   c. Write an expression that represents the distance light would travel from the first body to the third body and back to the first.

   d. Simplify the distance the light travels in part c.

7-4 Think About a Plan

More Multiplication Properties of Exponents

a. **Geography** Earth has a radius of about 6.4×10^6 m. What is the approximate surface area of Earth? Use the formula for the surface area of a sphere, $S = 4\pi r^2$. Write your answer in scientific notation.

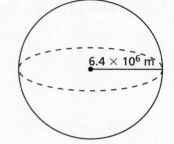

b. Oceans cover about 70% of the surface of the Earth. About how many square meters of Earth's surface are covered by ocean water?

c. The oceans have an average depth of 3790 m. Estimate the volume of water in Earth's oceans.

1. What can you substitute into the formula?

_____

2. What numbers need to be squared?

_____

3. Calculate the surface area using 3.14 for π. Show your work. Write your answer in scientific notation.

_____

_____

4. For part b, set up a percent proportion with the appropriate units.

_____

5. Solve your proportion. Show your work. Leave your answer in scientific notation.

_____

_____

6. Since you calculated the surface area of the ocean, how can you use your calculation to determine the volume of the water?

_____

_____

7. Determine the volume. Show your work. Write your answer in scientific notation.

_____

_____

7-4

Practice

Form G

More Multiplication Properties of Exponents

Simplify each expression.

1. $(z^5)^3$

2. $(m^4)^{10}$

3. $(v^7)^2$

4. $(k^4)^3$

5. $(x^7)^{-2}$

6. $(r^4)^{-6}$

7. $b(b^{-8})^{-3}$

8. $h^2(h^7)^0$

9. $(m^2)^7 n^5$

10. $(x^6)^2(y^3)^0$

11. $(g^5)^{-5}(g^6)^{-2}$

12. $(v^2)^3(w^4)^{-3}$

13. $(6a)^4$

14. $(5f)^{-3}$

15. $(9z)^{-4}$

16. $(10m^3)^{-2}$

17. $(6j^{-2})^{-3}$

18. $(9d^{10})^{-2}$

19. $(gh)^0$

20. $(qr^6)^4$

21. $(4a^3)^2 a^5$

22. $(m^4 n^3)^7(m^4)^3$

23. $(xy^2)(xy^2)^{-1}$

24. $z(y^{-5}z^7)^{-1}y^{-5}$

25. $(7t^{-3})^3(s^5 t^4)^2$

26. $m^{-9}(m^{-1}n)^2 n^8$

27. $(3b^{-4}c^{-2})^6 c^3$

28. $5x^{-5}y^2(2x^{-14})^2$

Simplify. Write each answer in scientific notation.

29. $(5 \times 10^7)^2$

30. $(2 \times 10^4)^6$

31. $(9 \times 10^{-12})^2$

32. $(3 \times 10^{-8})^3$

33. $(3.6 \times 10^5)^2$

34. $(9.3 \times 10^{-6})^{-2}$

35. $(1.7 \times 10^{-8})^3$

36. $(6.24 \times 10^{13})^3$

37. The radius of a cylinder is 5.4×10^6 cm. The height of the cylinder is 2.5×10^3 cm. What is the volume of the cylinder? (Hint: $V = \pi r^2 h$)

38. The side length of a square is 9.6×10^5 in. What is the area of the square?

39. The side length of a cube is 3.78×10^3 ft. What is the volume of the cube?

7-4 Practice (continued)   Form G
More Multiplication Properties of Exponents

Complete each equation.

40. $(p^4)^\square = p^8$

41. $(z^\square)^6 = z^{-24}$

42. $(t^{12})^\square = 1$

43. $(w^3)^\square = w^{-12}$

44. $(n^{-8})^\square = n^8$

45. $10(g^2)^\square = 10g^6$

46. $(3a^\square)^3 = 27a^{-9}$

47. $(6q^4r^\square)^2 = 36q^8$

48. $(x^4y^3)^\square = \dfrac{1}{x^8y^6}$

49. Writing Is $(y^m)^n = (y^n)^m$ a true statement? Explain your reasoning.

50. Reasoning What is the difference between x^4x^3 and $(x^4)^3$? Justify your answer.

Simplify each expression.

51. $2^3(2m)^2$

52. $(68.68)^8(68.68)^{-8}$

53. $(d^2)^{-5}d^3$

54. $(-7p)^3 + 7p^3$

55. $4a(0^8)b^4(-b)^{-7}$

56. $(10^{-5})^3(9.9 \times 10^{-12})^2$

57. The volume of a circular cone can be determined by the formula $V = \dfrac{1}{3}3.14r^2h$, where r is the radius of the base and h is the height of the cone. Find the volume of the cone shown at the right in terms of x.

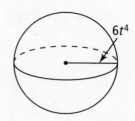

58. The volume of a sphere can be determined by the formula $V = \dfrac{4}{3}3.14r^3$, where r is the radius. Find the volume of the sphere shown at the right in terms of t.

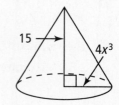

7-4

Standardized Test Prep

More Multiplication Properties of Exponents

Gridded Response

Solve each exercise and enter your answer on the grid provided.

1. What is the simplified form of $(2 \times 10^2)^2$ in standard notation?

2. What is the simplified form of $(0.00038 \times 10^3)^2$ in standard notation?

3. The side of a square measures $2x^2y^3$. What is the area of the square if $x = -2$ and $y = 2$?

4. The side of a square measures $3mn^2$. What is the area of the square if $m = 4$ and $n = -2$?

5. The radius of a circle is 0.00012×10^5 ft. What is the area of the circle? Use the formula $A = \pi r^2$.

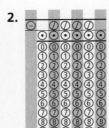

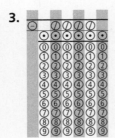

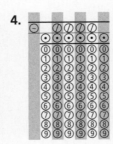

7-5 **Think About a Plan**

Division Properties of Exponents

Physics The wavelength of a radio wave is defined as speed divided by frequency. An FM radio station has a frequency of 9×10^7 waves per second. The speed of the waves is about 3×10^8 meters per second. What is the wavelength of the station?

1. Wavelength is speed divided by frequency. Which of the given values needs to be divided by the other?

   _____ divided by _____

2. What is the quotient of the first part of the numbers?

3. What is the quotient of the powers of 10?

4. What is the quotient, written in scientific notation, of the speed divided by the frequency?

5. How many meters is the wavelength of the station?

7-5

Practice

Form G

Division Properties of Exponents

Simplify each expression.

1. $\dfrac{5^6}{5^2}$

2. $\dfrac{5^5}{5^2}$

3. $\dfrac{x^7}{x^4}$

4. $\dfrac{m^{-3}}{m^{-5}}$

5. $\dfrac{x^6 y^9}{x^2 y^5}$

6. $\dfrac{21m^8}{3m^2}$

7. $\left(\dfrac{3}{5}\right)^4$

8. $\left(\dfrac{3x}{2y}\right)^3$

9. $\left(\dfrac{4}{7}\right)^{-2}$

10. $\left(-\dfrac{3x^4}{2y^5}\right)^{-3}$

11. $\left(\dfrac{12p^3}{15p}\right)^4$

12. $\left(\dfrac{ab^3}{a^5 b}\right)^{-2}$

13. $\left(\dfrac{3x^2 y^5 z^{-2}}{5xz^5}\right)^{-3}$

14. $\dfrac{(4m^2)(3n^5)}{(2m^{-3})(-mn)^3}$

Explain why each expression is *not* in simplest form.

15. $2^4 r^3$

16. $(3x)^2$

17. $m^3 n^0$

18. $\dfrac{y^5}{y}$

Simplify each quotient. Write each answer in scientific notation.

19. $\dfrac{3.6 \times 10^7}{1.5 \times 10^3}$

20. $\dfrac{4.5 \times 10^{-6}}{5 \times 10^{-2}}$

7-5

Practice (continued)   Form G
Division Properties of Exponents

21. Writing Explain how you divide expressions with numerators and denominators written in scientific notation. How do you handle the exponents? What do you do with the coefficients? Connect your response to the rules you have learned regarding the division properties of exponents.

22. A computer can do a computation in 6.8×10^{-9} seconds. How many computations can the computer do in 5 minutes?

23. Error Analysis A student simplifies the expression $\left(\dfrac{6^4}{3^2}\right)^3$ as follows: $\left(\dfrac{6^4}{3^2}\right)^3 = [(6 \div 3)^{4-2}]^3 = (2^2)^3 = 64$. What mistake did the student make in simplifying the expression? What is the correct simplification?

24. Reasoning The division property of exponents says that to simplify powers with the same base you subtract the exponents. Use examples to show why powers need to have the same base in order for this technique to work.

25. The area of a triangle is $80x^5y^3$. The height of the triangle is x^4y. What is the length of the base of the triangle?

26. Open-Ended First simplify the expression $\left(\dfrac{12m^5}{15m}\right)^3$ by raising each factor in the parentheses to the third power and next reducing the result. Then simplify by some other method. Explain your method. Are the results the same? Which method do you prefer?

7-5

Standardized Test Prep

Division Properties of Exponents

Multiple Choice

For Exercises 1–6, choose the correct letter.

1. Which of the following is equivalent to $\dfrac{x^5y^2}{xy^2}$ when $x \neq 0$ and $y \neq 0$?

   A. x^6y^5 **B.** x^5y **C.** x^4y **D.** x^4

2. Which expression is *not* equal to 125?

   F. $5\left(\dfrac{5^3}{\frac{2}{5}}\right)^2$ **G.** $\left(\dfrac{5^3}{5^4}\right)^{-3}$ **H.** $\dfrac{5^{-2}}{5^{-5}}$ **I.** $5\left(\dfrac{5^5}{5^3}\right)$

3. A fraction reduces to 36. If its numerator is $(6x)^5$, what is its denominator?

   A. 6^3x **B.** 6^3x^5 **C.** $6x^5$ **D.** 6^7x^5

4. Which is the correct simplification of $\dfrac{5.4 \times 10^{12}}{1.2 \times 10^3}$ written in scientific notation?

   F. 4.5×10^7 **G.** 4.5×10^9 **H.** 45×10^6 **I.** 6.48×10^7

5. Which of the following statements is *not* true regarding operations with exponents?
   A. To divide powers with the same base, subtract the exponents.
   B. To subtract powers with the same base, divide the exponents.
   C. To multiply powers with the same base, add the exponents.
   D. To raise a power to a power, multiply the exponents.

6. Which of the following expressions is written in simplest form?
   F. 3^5x^2 **G.** $(5y)^3$ **H.** a^0b **I.** x^2y^3z

Short Response

7. A rectangle has an area of $12x^3y^4$ cm^2. It has a width of $3xy$ cm. What ratio would you set up to determine the length? What is the length of the rectangle?

7-6 Think About a Plan

Exponential Functions

Computers A computer valued at $1500 loses 20% of its value each year.
    a. Write a function rule that models the value of the computer.
    b. Find the value of the computer after 3 yr.
    c. In how many years will the value of the computer be less than $500?

1. Make a table for which one column represents the number of years since the computer was purchased and the other represents the value of the computer at the end of each year.

Years Since Purchase	Value of Computer
0	$1500
1	
2	
3	
4	

2. Use the table to determine whether the function is exponential. Is there a common ratio? If so, what is it? What does the common ratio have to do with the situation represented in the problem? Where does it show up in an exponential function?

3. Remember the general form of an exponential function: $f(x) = a \cdot b^x$. Given your table and situation, determine values for a and b. Write the appropriate exponential function.

4. Use the exponential function to answer part b.

5. Set your exponential function equal to $500 and solve or extend your table to determine the answer to part c.

7-6 Practice   *Form G*

Exponential Functions

Determine whether each table or rule represents an exponential function. Explain why or why not.

1.

x	1	2	3	4
y	3	9	27	81

2.

x	1	2	3	4
y	3	9	15	21

3. $y = 5 \cdot 2^x$

4. $y = 6 \cdot x^3$

5. $y = 3x - 8$

6. $y = 4 \cdot 0.3^x$

Evaluate each function for the given value.

7. $f(x) = 5^x$ for $x = 4$

8. $h(t) = 3 \cdot 4^t$ for $t = -3$

9. $y = 8 \cdot 0.7^x$ for $x = 3$

Graph each exponential function.

10. $f(x) = 3^x$

11. $y = 0.25^x$

12. $y = 8 \cdot 1.2^x$

13. An investment of \$8000 in a certain Certificate of Deposit (CD) doubles in value every seven years. The function that models the growth of this investment is $f(x) = 8000 \cdot 2^x$, where x is the number of doubling periods. If the investor does not withdraw any money from this CD, how much money will be available for withdrawal after 28 years?

14. A population of amoebas in a petri dish will triple in size every 20 minutes. At the start of an experiment the population is 800. The function $y = 800 \cdot 3^x$, where x is the number of 20 minute periods, models the population growth. How many amoebas are in the petri dish after 3 hours?

15. A new car costs \$15,000 to build in 2010. The company's financial analysts expect costs to rise by 6% per year for the 10 years they are planning to build the car. The cost to build the car can be modeled by the function $f(t) = 15{,}000\,(1.06)^t$, where t is the number of years after 2010. How much will it cost the company to build the car in 2017?

7-6

Practice (continued)

Form G

Exponential Functions

Evaluate each function over the domain {−2, −1, 0, 1, 2, 3}. As the values of the domain increase, do the values of the range *increase* or *decrease*?

17. $f(x) = 3^x$

18. $y = 4.2^x$

19. $m(x) = 0.3^x$

20. $g(t) = 4 \cdot 3^x$

21. $y = 50 \cdot 0.1^x$

22. $f(x) = 2 \cdot 4^x$

Which function has the greater value for the given value of *x*?

23. $y = 5^x$ or $y = x^5$ for $x = 2$

24. $y = 300 \cdot x^3$ or $y = 100 \cdot 3^x$ for $x = 4$

Solve each equation.

25. $3^x = 81$

26. $5 \cdot 2^x = 40$

27. $4^x + 4 = 68$

28. $3 \cdot 2^x − 16 = 80$

29. Reasoning The function that models the growth of a $1000 investment that earns 7% per year is $f(x) = 1000(1.07)^x$. How do you think you would write a function that models the growth of $1500 that earns 8% per year? Use that function to determine how much money a person would have after 5 years if she invested $1500 in an account earning 8% per year.

30. Writing Discuss the differences between exponential functions with a base of 2 and 3, $y = 2^x$ and $y = 3^x$, and quadratic and cubic functions $y = x^2$ and $y = x^3$. Focus on the shapes of the different graphs and rates of growth.

31. Open-Ended Find the value of each of the functions a) $f(x) = 2x^2$ and b) $f(x) = 2 \cdot 2^x$ for $x = 5$. Write another quadratic function and another exponential function with a base of two whose values at $x = 5$ are between the values you found for functions a and b.

7-6 Standardized Test Prep

Exponential Functions

Multiple Choice

For Exercises 1–6, choose the correct letter.

1. Which of the following equations represents an exponential function?

   A. $y = 3x^2$ **B.** $y = 3(2^x)$ **C.** $y = 2x^3$ **D.** $y = 5x + 4$

2. What is the solution to $4 \cdot 3^x = 36$?

   F. 2 **G.** 3 **H.** 4 **I.** 6

3. Which function has the greatest value for $x = 3$?

   A. $f(x) = 2 \cdot 4^x$ **B.** $f(x) = 4 \cdot 2^x$ **C.** $f(x) = 4 \cdot x^2$ **D.** $f(x) = 2 \cdot x^4$

4. When graphed, which function will not have an x-intercept?

   F. $y = 2x + 3$ **G.** $y = 2x^3$ **H.** $y = 3x^2$ **I.** $y = 3 \cdot 2^x$

5. Which of the following statements is *not* true regarding the function $y = 2^x$?

   A. The function is an exponential function.
   B. The function has a domain of all real numbers.
   C. As the value of x gets very large, the value of y gets close to zero.
   D. As the value of x increases by one, the value of y doubles.

6. Which of the following ordered pairs is on the graph of $y = 3 \cdot 4^x$?

   F. $(0, 0)$ **G.** $(1, 81)$ **H.** $(2, 24)$ **I.** $(2, 48)$

Short Response

7. You invest $1000 at 7% interest compounded annually. What is the exponential equation that models this situation? According to your equation, how much will the investment be worth 3 years later?

7-7   Think About a Plan

Exponential Growth and Decay

Business You open a bank account to save for college and deposit $400 in the account. Each year, the balance in your account will increase 5%.

    a. Write a function that models your annual balance.

    b. What will be the *total* amount in your account after 7 yr?

1. Make a table that has one column representing the number of years the account has been open, a second column representing the balance in the given year, and a third column representing the *total* balance.

Years Account Open	Balance this Year	Total Balance
0		
1		
2		
3		

2. The first row of the table represents year 0. Year 0 is the start up year, the year with a balance of $400. If you want to know how much you have after three years, you will read your balance from the fourth line of the table, which starts with the number 3. In order to answer the question in part b, what line of the table should you use? What number would start that line? Why?

_____

_____

_____

3. Recall that the general form of an exponential function is $f(x) = a \cdot b^x$. Given the situation described, what is a? What is b? Write the function that models your annual balance. Check to make sure the function you created provides the same values you put into your table for years 1, 2 and 3.

    $a = $ _____ $b = $ _____ $f(x) = $ _____

4. Use the exponential function and extend the table to answer part b.

7-7 Practice   Form G

Exponential Growth and Decay

Identify the initial amount a and the growth factor b in each exponential function.

1. $f(x) = 3 \cdot 5^x$

2. $y = 250 \cdot 1.065^x$

3. $g(t) = 3.5^t$

4. $h(x) = 5 \cdot 1.02^x$

Find the balance in each account after the given period.

5. $8000 principal earning 5% compounded annually, after 6 yr

6. $2000 principal earning 5.4% compounded annually, after 4 yr

7. $500 principal earning 4% compounded quarterly, after 10 yr

8. $6500 principal earning 2.8% compounded monthly, after 2 yr

Identify the initial amount a and the decay factor b in each exponential function.

9. $y = 8 \cdot 0.8^x$

10. $f(x) = 12 \cdot 0.1^x$

State whether the equation represents *exponential growth, exponential decay,* or *neither.*

11. $y = 0.82 \cdot 3^x$

12. $f(x) = 5 \cdot 0.3^x$

13. $f(x) = 18 \cdot x^2$

14. $y = 0.9^x$

15. The town manager reports that revenue for a given year is $2.5 million. The budget director predicts that revenue will increase by 4% per yr. If the director's prediction holds true, how much revenue will the town have available 10 years from the date of the town manager's report?

16. A wildlife manager determines that there are approximately 200 deer in a certain state park.
   a. The population is growing at a rate of 7% per year. How many deer will live in the park after 4 years?
   b. If the carrying capacity of this park is 350 deer, how long will it take for the deer population to reach carrying capacity?

7-7 **Practice** (continued)   Form G

Exponential Growth and Decay

17. Open-Ended Write an exponential function that begins its rapid increase
when $2 \leq x \leq 3$. Write another that begins its rapid increase when $3 \leq x \leq 4$.
Write a third that begins its rapid increase when $6 \leq x \leq 8$.

18. A business purchases a computer system for $3000. If the value of the system
decreases at a rate of 15% per year, how much is the computer worth after
4 years?

19. Writing Explain the difference in how you would model the following
situations. Person A puts $1000 in a safe in his home, and puts in an additional
$50 per year. Person B puts $1000 in an investment that earns 5% per year.
Why is one exponential and the other linear? How would their graphs
compare? How would their values compare over time?

**State whether each graph shows an *exponential growth function,* an *exponential
decay function,* or *neither.***

20.
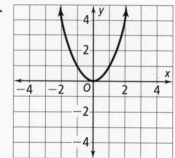

21.
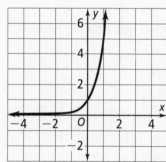

22.
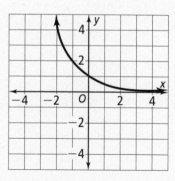

23.
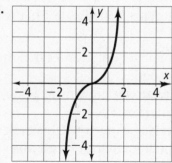

24. Reasoning Can the graph of an exponential function ever have a *y*-intercept
of 0? Why or why not?

7-7 Standardized Test Prep

Exponential Growth and Decay

Multiple Choice

For Exercises 1–5, choose the correct letter.

1. Which of the following functions models exponential decay?
   A. $f(x) = 12 \cdot 3^x$ **B.** $y = 2 \cdot 0.8^x$ **C.** $y = -3x^2$ **D.** $f(x) = 1.8^x$

2. Suppose you deposit $500 into an account earning 7.8% interest compounded annually. How long will it take for the account to be worth $1000?
   F. between 6 and 7 years **H.** between 8 and 9 years
   G. between 7 and 8 years **I.** between 9 and 10 years

3. What is always true regarding functions that model exponential growth?
   A. Their graphs are always symmetric about the y-axis.
   B. The range depends on the growth factor.
   C. The value of y is always greater than the value of x.
   D. The value of y decreases as x gets more negative.

4. What is $3 \cdot 2^x$ if $x = 3$?
   F. 18 **G.** 24 **H.** 125 **I.** 216

5. Where will the graphs of $y = 4^x$, $y = 1.2^x$ and $y = 0.6^x$ intersect?
   A. $(0, 0)$ **B.** $(1, 0)$ **C.** $(0, 1)$ **D.** $(1, 1)$

Short Response

6. Suppose you deposit $2000 into an account earning 5% interest compounded quarterly. To the nearest dollar, what is the balance after 4 years?

8-1 Think About a Plan

Adding and Subtracting Polynomials

Geometry The perimeter of a trapezoid is $39a - 7$. Three sides have the following lengths: $9a$, $5a + 1$, and $17a - 6$. What is the length of the fourth side?

Understanding the Problem

1. What is the perimeter of the trapezoid? _____

2. What are the lengths of the sides you are given? _____, _____, _____

3. How many sides does a trapezoid have? _____

4. How do you find the perimeter of a trapezoid? _____

5. What is the problem asking you to determine? _____

_____

Planning the Solution

6. Draw a diagram of the trapezoid and label the information you know.

7. Write an equation that can be used to determine the length of the fourth side.

_____

Getting an Answer

8. Solve your equation to find the length of the fourth side of the trapezoid.

8-1

Practice

Form G

Adding and Subtracting Polynomials

Find the degree of each monomial.

1. $2b^2c^2$ **2.** $5x$ **3.** $7y^5$ **4.** $19ab$

5. 12 **6.** $\frac{1}{2}z^2$ **7.** t **8.** $4d^4e$

Simplify.

9. $2a^3b + 4a^3b$ **10.** $5x^3 - 4x^3$ **11.** $3m^6n^3 - 5m^6n^3$

12. $-6ab + 3ab$ **13.** $4c^2d^6 - 7c^2d^6$ **14.** $315x^2 - 30x^2$

Write each polynomial in standard form. Then name each polynomial based on its degree and number of terms.

15. $15x - x^3 + 3$ **16.** $5x + 2x^2 - x + 3x^4$ **17.** $9x^3$

18. $7b^2 + 4b$ **19.** $-3x^2 + 11 + 10x$ **20.** $12t^2 + 1 - 3x + 8 - 2x$

Simplify.

21. $\begin{array}{r} 8z - 12 \\ + \ 6z + 90 \\ \hline \end{array}$ **22.** $\begin{array}{r} 9x^3 + 3 \\ + \ 4x^3 + 7 \\ \hline \end{array}$ **23.** $\begin{array}{r} 6j^2 - 2j + 5 \\ + \ 3j^2 + 4j - 6 \\ \hline \end{array}$

24. $(3k^2 + 5) + (16x^2 + 7)$ **25.** $(g^4 - 4g^2 + 11) + (-g^3 + 8g)$

26. A local deli kept track of the sandwiches it sold for three months. The polynomials below model the number of sandwiches sold, where s represents days.

Ham and Cheese: $4s^3 - 28s^2 + 33s + 250$
Pastrami: $-7.4s^2 + 32s + 180$

Write a polynomial that models the total number of these sandwiches that were sold.

8-1

Practice (continued)   Form G

Adding and Subtracting Polynomials

Simplify.

27.
$$\begin{array}{r} 11n - 4 \\ - (5n + 2) \\ \hline \end{array}$$

28.
$$\begin{array}{r} 7x^4 + 9 \\ - (8x^4 + 2) \\ \hline \end{array}$$

29.
$$\begin{array}{r} 3d^2 + 8d - 2 \\ - (2d^2 - 7d + 6) \\ \hline \end{array}$$

30. $(28e^3 + 3e^2) + (19e^3 + e^2)$ 31. $(-12h^4 + h) - (-6h^4 + 3h^2 - 4h)$

32. A small town wants to compare the number of students enrolled in public and private schools. The polynomials below show the enrollment for each:

        Public School: $-19c^2 + 980c + 48{,}989$
        Private School: $40c + 4046$

Write a polynomial for how many more students are enrolled in public school than private school.

Simplify. Write each answer in standard form.

33. $(3a^2 + a + 5) - (2a - 5)$ 34. $(6d - 10d^3 + 3d^2) - (5d^3 + 3d - 4)$

35. $(-4s^3 + 2s - 3) + (-2s^2 + s + 7)$ 36. $(8p^3 - 6p + 2p^2) + (9p^2 - 5p - 11)$

37. The fence around a quadrilateral-shaped pasture is $3a^2 + 15a + 9$ long. Three sides of the fence have the following lengths: $5a$, $10a - 2$, $a^2 - 7$. What is the length of the fourth side of the fence?

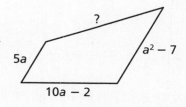

38. **Error Analysis** Describe and correct the error in simplifying the sum shown at the right.

39. **Open-Ended** Write three different examples of the sum of a quadratic trinomial and a cubic monomial.

8-1 Standardized Test Prep

Adding and Subtracting Polynomials

Multiple Choice

For Exercises 1–6, choose the correct letter.

1. What is the degree of the monomial $3x^2y^3$?

   A. 2   **B.** 3   **C.** 5   **D.** 6

2. What is the simplified form of $8b^3c^2 + 4b^3c^2$?

   F. $12bc$ **G.** $12b^3c^2$ **H.** $12b^6c^4$ **I.** $12b^9c^4$

3. How is $6d - 8 + 4d^2$ written in standard form?

   A. $4d^2 + 6d - 8$ **B.** $4d^2 + 6d + 8$ **C.** $4d^2 - 6d - 8$ **D.** $4d^2 - 6d + 8$

4. What is the simplified form of $(4j^2 + 6) + (2j^2 - 3)$?

   F. $6j^2 - 3$ **G.** $6j^2 + 3$ **H.** $6j^2 + 9$ **I.** $4j^4 + 3$

5. What is the difference of the following polynomials?

$$\begin{aligned} 6x^3 - 2x^2 + 4 \\ - \ (2x^3 + 4x^2 - 5) \end{aligned}$$

   A. $4x^3 - 2x^2 - 1$ **B.** $8x^3 + 6x^2 - 1$ **C.** $4x^3 - 2x^2 + 1$ **D.** $4x^3 - 6x^2 + 9$

6. What is the simplified form of $(3x^2 - 4x + 6x) + (5x^3 + 2x^2 - 3x)$ in standard form?

   F. $5x^3 + 10x^2 - x$ **G.** $8x^3 - 2x^2 + 3x$ **H.** $5x^3 + 10x^2 - 5x$ **I.** $5x^3 + 5x^2 - x$

Short Response

7. Suppose you have been given this polynomial.
$$5b + 4b^2 - 3b^4 + 3$$

   a. How can you write this polynomial in standard form?

   _____

   b. What is the degree of this polynomial? Explain. _____

   _____

Prentice Hall Algebra 1 • Practice and Problem Solving Workbook
225

8-2 Think About a Plan

Multiplying and Factoring

a. Factor $n^2 + n$.

b. Writing Suppose n is an integer. Is $n^2 + n$ *always*, *sometimes*, or *never* an even integer? Justify your answer.

1. Factor out n from the expression.

$$n\left(\boxed{} + \boxed{}\right)$$

2. What are the two factors? _____ , _____

3. What is an integer? _____

_____

4. Are n and $n + 1$ consecutive integers? Explain. _____

_____

5. What do you know about the product of odd and even integers?

EVEN $\times$ EVEN = _____

ODD $\times$ ODD = _____

EVEN $\times$ ODD = _____

ODD $\times$ EVEN = _____

6. Out of two consecutive integers, how many are odd? _____

7. Is the product of consecutive integers *odd* or *even*? Explain. _____

_____

8. $n^2 + n$ is $\boxed{}$ an even integer because _____

_____ .

8-2

Practice

Multiplying and Factoring

Form G

Simplify each product.

1. $2x(x + 8)$

2. $(n + 7)5n$

3. $6h^2(7 + h)$

4. $-b^2(b - 10)$

5. $-3c(8 + 2c - c^3)$

6. $y(2y^2 - 3y + 6)$

7. $4t(t^2 - 6t + 2)$

8. $-m(4m^3 - 8m^2 + m)$

9. $7j(-2j^2 - 8j - 3)$

10. $-t^2(2t^4 + 4t - 8)$

11. $2k(-3k^3 + k^2 - 10)$

12. $8a^2(-a^7 + 7a - 7)$

13. $4v^3(2v^2 - 3v + 5)$

14. $5d(-d^3 + 2d^2 - 3d)$

15. $11w(w^2 + 2w + 6)$

Find the GCF of the terms of each polynomial.

16. $15x + 27$

17. $6w^3 - 14w$

18. $63s + 45$

19. $72y^5 + 18y^2$

20. $-18q^3 - 6q^2$

21. $108f^3 - 54$

22. $b^3 + 5b^2 - 20b$

23. $9m^3 + 30m - 24$

24. $4p^3 + 12p^2 - 18p$

25. $2e^2 + 12e - 22$

26. $14b^3 + 21b^2 - 42b$

27. $-12x^3 + 24x^2 - 16x$

28. $8a^4 + 24a^3 - 40a^2$

29. $36j^3 - 3j^2 - 15j$

30. $12j^8 + 30j^4 - 6j^3$

Factor each polynomial.

31. $12x - 9$

32. $18s^2 + 54$

33. $108t^2 - 60t$

34. $-20w^2 + 16w$

35. $32y^3 + 8y^2$

36. $300d^2 - 175d$

37. $12n^3 - 36n^2 + 18$

38. $40t^3 + 25t^2 + 80t$

39. $42x^4 - 56x^3 + 28x^2$

40. $15c^4 + 24c^3 - 6c^2 + 12c$

41. $8m^3 + 14m^2 + 6m$

42. $10x^2 + 50x - 25$

43. $36p^4 + 14p^3 + 35p^2$

44. $9a^5 + 27a^4 + 63a^2$

45. $4b^4 + 20b^3 + 12b$

46. $x^6 - x^4 + x^2$

47. $34g^3 + 51g^2 + 17g$

48. $18h^4 - 27h^2 + 18h$

8-2

Practice (continued)   Form G

Multiplying and Factoring

49. A circular hedge surrounds a sculpture on a square base. The radius of the hedge is $6x$. The side length of the square sculpture base is $4x$. What is the area of the hedge? Write your answer in factored form.

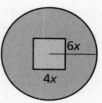

50. Suppose you are making a giant chocolate chip cookie for a raffle. You roll out a square slab of cookie dough. Then you use a circular plate that touches the edges of the square slab of cookie dough and cut the cookie out of the dough. What is the area of the extra dough? Write your answer in factored form.

Simplify. Write in standard form.

51. $-3x(4x^2 - 6x + 12)$ 52. $-7y^2(-4y^3 + 6y)$ 53. $9a(-3a^2 + a - 5)$

54. $p(p + 4) - 2p(p - 8)$ 55. $t(t + 4) - t(4t^2 - 2)$ 56. $6c(2c^2 - 4) - c(8c)$

57. $-5m(2m^3 - 7m^2 + m)$ 58. $2q(q + 1) - q(q - 1)$ 59. $-n^2(-6n^2 + 2n)$

Factor each polynomial.

60. $15xy^4 + 60x^2y^3$ 61. $8m^3n^4 + 32mn^2$ 62. $26a^5b^2 + 51a^4$

63. $36j^2k^4 + 24j^4k^2$ 64. $12w^4x^3 - 42wx^2$ 65. $54c^2d^3 - 36c^3d^2$

66. $12st^4 + 46s^3t^4$ 67. $9v^6w^3 + 33v^4w^5$ 68. $11e^3f^3 + 132e^2f^4$

69. **Error Analysis** A student factored the polynomial at the right. Describe and correct the error made in factoring.

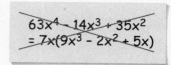

70. **Reasoning** The GCF of two numbers j and k is 8. What is the GCF of $2j$ and $2k$? Justify your answer.

71. A cylinder has a radius of $3m^2n$ and a height of $7mn$. The formula for the volume of a cylinder is $V = \pi r^2 h$, where r is the radius and h is the height. What is the volume of the cylinder? Simplify your answer.

8-2 Standardized Test Prep

Multiplying and Factoring

Multiple Choice

For Exercises 1–5, choose the correct letter.

1. How can this product be simplified?
$$5x^2(2x - 3)$$
   A. $5x^2 + 2x - 3$ **B.** $10x^3 - 15x^2$ **C.** $-5x^2$ **D.** $7x^3 - 15x^2$

2. What is the GCF of the terms of $8c^3 + 12c^2 + 10c$?
   F. 2   **G.** 4   **H.** $2c$ **I.** $4c$

3. How can the polynomial $6d^4 + 9d^3 - 12d^2$ be factored?
   A. $3d^2(2d^2 + 3d - 4)$
   B. $3d^2(3d^2 + 6d - 9)$
   C. $3d(d^3 + 3d^2 - 4)$
   D. $6d^2(d^2 + 3d^3 - 6)$

4. There is a circular garden in the middle of a square yard. The radius of the circle is $4x$. The side length of the yard is $20x$. What is the area of the part of the yard that is not covered by the circle?
   F. $4x(5)$ **G.** $8x^2(5 - \pi)$ **H.** $16x(25 + \pi)$ **I.** $16x^2(25 - \pi)$

5. What is the simplified form of $-3z^2(z + 2) - 4(z^2 + 1)$?
   A. $-7z^2 + 1$
   B. $-3z^3 - 4z^2 - 6z - 4$
   C. $-3z^3 - 2z^2 - 4$
   D. $-3z^3 - 10z^2 - 4$

Short Response

6. A rectangular blacktop with a length of $5x$ and a width of $3x$ has been erected inside a rectangular field that has a length of $12x$ and a width of $7x$.
   a. What is the area of the part of the field that is not blacktop?

   b. There is a circular fountain in the rectangular field that has a radius of $3x$. What is the area of the part of the field that does not include the blacktop or the fountain? Factor your answer.

8-3 Think About a Plan

Multiplying Binomials

Geometry The dimensions of a rectangular prism are n, $n + 7$, and $n + 8$. Use the formula $V = lwh$ to write a polynomial in standard form for the volume of the prism.

Know

1. What are the dimensions of the rectangular prism? _____, _____, _____

2. What is the formula for the volume of a rectangular prism? _____

3. In the volume formula, what do l, w, and h represent? _____, _____, _____

4. Explain how to write a polynomial in standard form. _____

_____

Need

5. To solve the problem you need to find _____

_____.

Plan

6. Draw a diagram of the rectangular prism and label the information you know.

7. Write an expression for the volume of the rectangular prism.

_____

8. Write the volume of the rectangular prism as a polynomial in standard form.

8-3

Practice

Form G

Multiplying Binomials

Simplify each product using the Distributive Property.

1. $(x + 3)(x + 8)$

2. $(y - 4)(y + 7)$

3. $(m + 9)(m - 3)$

4. $(c - 6)(c - 4)$

5. $(2r - 5)(r + 3)$

6. $(3x + 1)(5x - 3)$

7. $(d + 2)(4d - 3)$

8. $(5t - 1)(3t - 2)$

9. $(a + 11)(11a + 1)$

Simplify each product using a table.

10. $(x + 3)(x - 5)$

11. $(a - 2)(a - 13)$

12. $(w - 4)(w + 8)$

13. $(5h - 3)(h + 7)$

14. $(x - 3)(2x + 3)$

15. $(2p + 1)(6p + 4)$

Simplify each product using the FOIL method.

16. $(2x - 6)(x + 3)$

17. $(n - 5)(3n - 4)$

18. $(4p^2 + 2)(3p - 1)$

19. $(a + 7)(a - 3)$

20. $(x + 3)(3x - 2)$

21. $(k - 9)(k + 5)$

22. $(b - 5)(b - 11)$

23. $(4m - 1)(m + 4)$

24. $(7z + 3)(4z - 6)$

25. $(2h + 6)(5h - 3)$

26. $(3w + 12)(w + 3)$

27. $(6c - 2)(9c - 8)$

8-3 Practice (continued) Form G
Multiplying Binomials

28. What is the surface area of the cylinder at the right? Write your answer in simplified form.

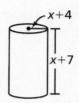

29. The radius of a cylindrical popcorn tin is $(3x + 1)$ in. The height of the tin is three times the radius. What is the surface area of the cylinder? Write your answer in simplified form.

30. The radius of a cylindrical tennis ball can is $(2x + 1)$ cm. The height of the tennis ball can is six times the radius. What is the surface area of the cylinder? Write your answer in simplified form.

Simplify each product.

31. $(x + 3)(x^2 - 2x + 4)$

32. $(k^2 - 5k + 2)(k - 5)$

33. $(3a^2 + a + 4)(2a - 6)$

34. $(2x^2 + 2x - 6)(3x - 4)$

35. $(4g + 5)(2g^2 - 7g + 3)$

36. $(m^2 - 2m + 7)(3m + 6)$

37. $(2c + 8)(2c^2 - 4c - 1)$

38. $(t + 8)(3t^2 + 4t + 5)$

39. A medical center's rectangular parking lot currently has a length of 30 meters and a width of 20 meters. The center plans to expand both the length and the width of the parking lot by $2x$ meters. What polynomial in standard form represents the area of the expanded parking lot?

40. Error Analysis Describe and correct the error made in finding the product.

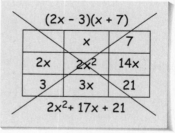

41. Multi Step The height of a painting is twice its width x. You want a 3 inch wide wooden frame for the painting. The area of the frame alone is 216 square inches.
  a. Draw a diagram that represents this situation.
  b. Write a variable expression for the area of the frame alone.

  c. What are the dimensions of the frame?

8-3

Standardized Test Prep

Multiplying Binomials

Multiple Choice

For Exercises 1–5, choose the correct letter.

1. What is the simplified form of $(x - 2)(2x + 3)$? Use the Distributive Property.

   A. $2x^2 - x - 6$ **B.** $2x^2 - 6$ **C.** $2x^2 - 7x - 6$ **D.** $2x^2 + x - 6$

2. What is the simplified form of $(3x + 2)(4x - 3)$? Use a table.

   F. $12x^2 + 18x + 6$ **G.** $12x^2 + x - 6$ **H.** $12x^2 + 18x - 6$ **I.** $12x^2 - x - 6$

3. What is the simplified form of $(4p - 2)(p - 4)$?

   A. $4p^2 + 6p - 16$ **B.** $4p^2 - 18p + 8$ **C.** $4p^2 - 14p - 6$ **D.** $4p^2 - 6p + 16$

4. The radius of a cylinder is $3x - 2$ cm. The height of the cylinder is $x + 3$ cm. What is the surface area of the cylinder?

   F. $2\pi(3x^2 + 10x - 8)$

   G. $2\pi(12x^2 + 7x - 2)$

   H. $2\pi(12x^2 - 2x + 13)$

   I. $2\pi(12x^2 - 5x - 2)$

5. What is the simplified form of $(2x^2 + 4x - 3)(3x + 1)$?

   A. $6x^3 + 10x^2 - 5x + 3$

   B. $6x^3 + 14x^2 + 5x - 3$

   C. $6x^3 + 14x^2 - 5x - 3$

   D. $6x^3 - 10x^2 - 5x - 3$

Short Response

6. A soup can that is a cylinder has a radius of $2x - 1$ and a height of $3x$. What is the surface area of the soup can? Show your work.

8-4 | Think About a Plan

Multiplying Special Cases

Construction A square deck has a side length of $x + 5$. You are expanding the deck so that each side is four times as long as the side length of the original deck. What is the area of the new deck? Write your answer in standard form.

Understanding the Problem

1. What is the shape of the deck? _____

2. How long is each side of the deck? _____

3. The new deck has sides that are _____ times longer than the original sides.

4. What is the problem asking you to find? _____

_____

Planning the Solution

5. Write an expression for the new side length of the deck.

6. Write an expression for the area of the new deck.

Getting an Answer

7. What is the standard form of the expression for the area of the new deck?

8-4

Practice

Form G

Multiplying Special Cases

Simplify each expression.

1. $(x + 7)^2$

2. $(w + 9)^2$

3. $(h + 3)^2$

4. $(2s + 4)^2$

5. $(3s + 1)^2$

6. $(5s + 2)^2$

7. $(a - 5)^2$

8. $(k - 10)^2$

9. $(n - 4)^2$

10. $(3m - 4)^2$

11. $(6m - 2)^2$

12. $(4m - 2)^2$

The figures below are squares. Find an expression for the area of each shaded region. Write your answers in standard form.

13.
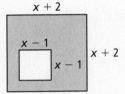

14.
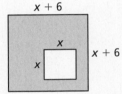

15.
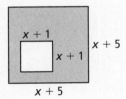

16.
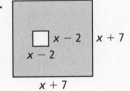

17. A square brown tarp has a square green patch green in the corner. The side length of the tarp is $(x + 8)$ and the side length of the patch is x. What is the area of the brown part of the tarp?

18. A square red placemat has a gold square in the center. The side length of the gold square is $(x - 2)$ inches and the width of the red region is 4 inches. What is the area of the red part of the placemat?

8-4

Practice (continued)   Form G

Multiplying Special Cases

Mental Math Simplify each product.

19. 48^2

20. 31^2

21. 29^2

22. 52^2

23. 63^2

24. 41^2

25. 89^2

26. 199^2

27. 302^2

Simplify each product.

28. $(v + 7)(v - 7)$

29. $(b + 2)(b - 2)$

30. $(z - 9)(z + 9)$

31. $(x + 12)(x - 12)$

32. $(8 + y)(8 - y)$

33. $(t - 15)(t + 15)$

34. $(m + 1)(m - 1)$

35. $(a + 4)(a - 4)$

36. $(5 + g)(5 - g)$

37. $(p + 20)(p - 20)$

38. $(f - 18)(f + 18)$

39. $(2c + 3)(2c - 3)$

Mental Math Simplify each product.

40. $61 \cdot 59$

41. $27 \cdot 33$

42. $202 \cdot 198$

43. $74 \cdot 66$

44. $597 \cdot 603$

45. $85 \cdot 75$

Simplify each product.

46. $(m + 4n)^2$

47. $(3a + b)^2$

48. $(6s - t)^2$

49. $(s + 7t^2)^2$

50. $(p^5 - 8q^3)^2$

51. $(e^4 + f^2)^2$

52. $(r^2 + 5s)(r^2 - 5s)$

53. $(6p^2 + 2q)(6p^2 - 2q)$

54. $(3w^4 - z^3)(3w^4 + z^3)$

55. Error Analysis Describe and correct the error made in simplifying the product.

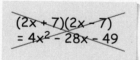

56. The formula $V = \frac{4}{3}\pi r^3$ gives the volume of a sphere with radius r. Find the volume of a sphere with radius $x + 9$. Write your answer in standard form.

8-4

Standardized Test Prep

Multiplying Special Cases

Gridded Response

Solve each exercise and enter your answer on the grid provided.

1. What is coefficient of the x-term in the simplified form of $(2x + 4)^2$?

2. What is 27^2? Use mental math.

3. What is constant in the simplified form of $(x - 6)^2$?

4. What is the product of 38 and 42? Use mental math.

`5. How much greater is the product of 73 and 67 than the product of 74 and 66?

1. 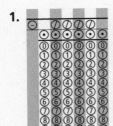 2. 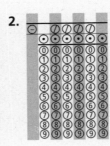 3. 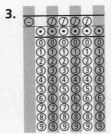 4. 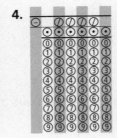 5.

8-5 | Think About a Plan

Factoring $x^2 + bx + c$

Recreation A rectangular skateboard park has an area of $x^2 + 15x + 54$. What are possible dimensions of the park? Use factoring.

Know

1. The area of the skateboard park is _____ .

2. The dimensions of a rectangle are its _____ and _____ .

3. The _____ of the area polynomial are possible dimensions of the skateboard park.

Need

4 To solve the problem I need to find _____

_____

Plan

5. Complete the table. List the pairs of factors of ☐ .

   Identify the pair that has a sum of ☐ .

Factors of 54	Sum of Factors

6. Write the factored polynomial.

7. What are possible dimensions of the skateboard park?

8. Justify your answer.

_____

_____

_____

8-5 Practice

Form G

Factoring $x^2 + bx + c$

Complete.

1. $k^2 + 11k + 30 = (k + 5)(k + \boxed{})$

2. $x^2 + 6x + 9 = (x + 3)(x + \boxed{})$

3. $t^2 + 7t + 10 = (t + 2)(t + \boxed{})$

4. $n^2 + 9n + 14 = (n + 7)(n + \boxed{})$

5. $w^2 + 13w + 36 = (w + 4)(w + \boxed{})$

6. $y^2 + 18y + 65 = (y + 13)(y + \boxed{})$

7. $s^2 - 12s + 32 = (s - 8)(s - \boxed{})$

8. $g^2 - 14g + 45 = (g - 9)(g - \boxed{})$

9. $v^2 - 17v + 60 = (v - 12)(v - \boxed{})$

10. $q^2 - 13q + 42 = (q - 6)(q - \boxed{})$

11. $d^2 - 9d + 8 = (d - 8)(d - \boxed{})$

12. $r^2 - 9r + 20 = (r - 5)(r - \boxed{})$

Factor each expression. Check your answer.

13. $y^2 + 5y + 6$

14. $t^2 + 9t + 18$

15. $x^2 + 16x + 63$

16. $n^2 - 12n + 35$

17. $r^2 - 12r + 27$

18. $q^2 - 12q + 20$

19. $w^2 + 19w + 60$

20. $b^2 - 11b + 24$

21. $z^2 - 13z + 12$

Complete.

22. $q^2 + q - 56 = (q - 7)(q + \boxed{})$

23. $z^2 - 3z - 18 = (z - 6)(z + \boxed{})$

24. $n^2 - 6n - 40 = (n + 4)(n - \boxed{})$

25. $y^2 + 3y - 4 = (y + 4)(y - \boxed{})$

26. $v^2 - 5v - 36 = (v - 9)(v + \boxed{})$

27. $d^2 + 2d - 15 = (d - 3)(d + \boxed{})$

28. $m^2 - 5m - 14 = (m + 2)(m - \boxed{})$

29. $p^2 - 6p - 16 = (p - 8)(p + \boxed{})$

8-5 Practice (continued) Form G

Factoring $x^2 + bx + c$

Factor each expression. Check your answer.

30. $r^2 + 3r - 10$ **31.** $w^2 + 2w - 8$ **32.** $z^2 + 3z - 40$

33. $d^2 - 4d - 12$ **34.** $p^2 - 7p - 8$ **35.** $s^2 - 5s - 24$

36. $x^2 + 5x - 6$ **37.** $v^2 + 3v - 28$ **38.** $n^2 + 2n - 63$

39. $t^2 - 2t - 24$ **40** $a^2 - 7a - 18$ **41.** $c^2 - c - 30$

42. The area of a rectangular door is given by the trinomial $x^2 - 14x + 45$. The door's width is $(x - 9)$. What is the door's length?

43. The area of a rectangular painting is given by the trinomial $a^2 - 6a - 16$. The painting's length is $(a + 2)$. What is the painting's width?

Write the correct factored form for each expression.

44. $k^2 + 4kn - 96n^2$ **45.** $g^2 - 13gh + 42h^2$ **46.** $m^2 - 4mn - 32n^2$

47. $x^2 + 5xy - 14y^2$ **48.** $s^2 + 17st + 72t^2$ **49.** $h^2 + 3hj - 88j^2$

50. Error Analysis Describe and correct the error made in factoring the trinomial.

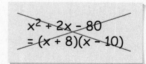

$$x^2 + 2x - 80$$
$$= (x + 8)(x - 10)$$

51. A rectangular pool cover has an area of $p^2 + 9p - 36$. What are possible dimensions of the pool cover? Use factoring.

8-5

Standardized Test Prep

Factoring $x^2 + bx + c$

Multiple Choice

For Exercises 1–7, choose the correct letter.

1. Which number makes this equation true?
$$v^2 + 10v + 16 = (v + 8)(v + \square)$$

   A. 2   **B.** 4   **C.** 6   **D.** 8

2. What is the factored form of $x^2 + 6x + 8$?

   F. $(x + 5)(x + 3)$ **G.** $(x + 4)(x + 2)$ **H.** $(x + 7)(x + 1)$ **I.** $(x + 3)(x + 3)$

3. What is the factored form of $x^2 - 7x + 12$?

   A. $(x - 5)(x - 3)$ **B.** $(x - 6)(x - 1)$ **C.** $(x - 2)(x - 5)$ **D.** $(x - 4)(x - 3)$

4. Which number makes this equation true?
$$q^2 + 3q - 18 = (q + 6)(q - \square)$$

   F. 1   **G.** 2   **H.** 3   **I.** 12

5. What is the factored form of $x^2 + 3x - 10$?

   A. $(x + 5)(x - 2)$ **C.** $(x - 2)(x - 5)$
   B. $(x - 5)(x + 2)$ **D.** $(x + 5)(x + 2)$

6. The area of a garden is given by the trinomial $g^2 - 2g - 24$. The garden's length is $g + 4$. What is the garden's width?

   F. $g - 2$ **G.** $g - 6$ **H.** $g - 8$ **I.** $g + 2$

7. What is the factored form of $x^2 + 3xy - 28y^2$?

   A. $(x + 14y)(x - 2y)$**B.** $(x + 2y)(x - 14y)$ **C.** $(x + 4y)(x - 7y)$ **D.** $(x - 4y)(x + 7y)$

Short Response

8. The area of a rectangular backyard is given by the trinomial $b^2 + 5b - 24$. What are possible dimensions of the backyard? Show why your answer is correct.

8-6

Think About a Plan

Factoring $ax^2 + bx + c$

Carpentry The top of a rectangular table has an area of $18x^2 + 69x + 60$. The width of the table is $3x + 4$. What is the length of the table?

Know

1. The area of the table top is _____ .

2. The width of the table top is _____ .

3. Some quadratic trinomials can be written as the product of two _____ .

4. One of the factors of the polynomial $18x^2 + 69x + 60$ is _____ .

Need

5. To solve the problem I need to find _____

_____ .

Plan

6. Find the missing factor.

   What can you multiply by $3x$ to get $18x^2$? $3x \cdot \boxed{} = 18x^2$

   What can you multiply by 4 to get 60? $4 \cdot \boxed{} = 60$

7. What is the factored form of $18x^2 + 69x + 60$? _____

8. What is the length of the table? Check your answer.

_____

_____

_____

8-6

Practice

Form G

Factoring $ax^2 + bx + c$

Factor each expression.

1. $2w^2 + 13w + 15$

2. $3d^2 + 20d + 12$

3. $4n^2 + 62n - 32$

4. $3p^2 - 7p - 40$

5. $6r^2 - 10r - 24$

6. $5z^2 - 17z + 14$

7. $14k^2 - 67k + 63$

8. $2m^2 - m - 15$

9. $3x^2 + 9x - 84$

10. $4y^2 + 26y + 30$

11. $5t^2 - 24t - 5$

12. $7c^2 - 2c - 9$

13. $8k^2 - 42k + 27$

14. $6g^2 - 2g - 20$

15. $2c^2 - 23c + 11$

16. The area of a rectangular computer screen is $4x^2 + 20x + 16$. The width of the screen is $2x + 8$. What is the length of the screen?

17. The area of a rectangular granite countertop is $12x^2 + 10x - 12$. The width of the countertop is $2x + 3$. What is the length of the countertop?

18. The area of a rectangular book cover is $4x^2 - 6x - 40$. The width of the book cover is $2x - 8$. What is the length of the book cover?

19. The area of a rectangular parking lot is $21x^2 - 44x + 15$. The width of the parking lot is $3x - 5$. What is the length of the parking lot?

Factor each expression completely.

20. $6x^2 - 10x - 4$

21. $6d^2 + 21d + 15$

22. $8n^2 + 68n + 84$

23. $20p^2 - 115p - 30$

24. $15r^2 + 141r - 90$

25. $12z^2 - 14z + 4$

26. $20k^2 + 110k + 120$

27. $9m^2 - 66m + 21$

28. $40x^2 - 136x - 96$

29. $42y^2 + 28y - 14$

30. $8t^2 - 16t - 90$

31. $24c^2 + 96c + 90$

8-6

Practice (continued)   Form G

Factoring $ax^2 + bx + c$

Open-Ended Find two different values that complete each expression so that the trinomial can be factored into the product of two binomials. Factor your trinomials.

32. $4x^2 + \boxed{}x + 12$

33. $6t^2 - \boxed{}t - 4$

34. $9m^2 - \boxed{}m + 8$

35. $8n^2 + \boxed{}n - 10$

36. $12v^2 - \boxed{}v + 15$

37. $5w^2 - \boxed{}w - 24$

38. Error Analysis Describe and correct the error made in factoring the expression at the right.

$$
\begin{aligned}
(6x^2 + 3x - 9) &= 3(2x^2 + x - 3) \\
&= 3(2x^2 - 3x + 2x - 3) \\
&= 3(2x^2 - 3x + (2x - 3) \\
&= 3[\, x(2x - 3) + 1(2x - 3)\,] \\
&= 3(x + 1)(2x - 3)
\end{aligned}
$$

39. A parallelogram has an area of $4x^2 + 7x - 15$. The base of the parallelogram is $x + 3$. What is the height of the parallelogram?
 a. Write the formula for the area of a parallelogram.

 b. Writing Explain how factoring the trinomial helps you solve the problem.

40. A rectangular window pane has an area of $15x^2 - 19x + 6$. The width of the window pane is $3x - 2$. What is the length of the window pane?

Factor each expression completely.

41. $28y^2 + 43y - 48$

42. $16z^2 - 54z + 35$

43. $27n^2 - 54n + 15$

44. $36p^2 + 63p + 20$

45. $28r^2 - 20r - 33$

46. $30z^2 - 53z + 12$

47. $32x^3 + 28x^2 + 5x$

48. $25p^2 + 20pq - 12q^2$

49. $72g^2h - 43gh + 6h$

8-6 Standardized Test Prep
Factoring $ax^2 + bx + c$

Multiple Choice

For Exercises 1–5, choose the correct letter.

1. What is the factored form of $4x^2 + 12x + 5$?
   A. $(2x + 4)(2x + 3)$ **B.** $(4x + 5)(x + 1)$ **C.** $(2x + 1)(2x + 5)$ **D.** $(4x + 1)(x + 5)$

2. What is the factored form of $2x^2 + x - 3$?
   F. $(2x + 3)(x - 1)$ **G.** $(2x + 1)(x - 3)$ **H.** $(2x - 3)(x + 1)$ **I.** $(2x - 1)(x + 3)$

3. The area of a rectangular swimming pool is $10x^2 - 19x - 15$. The length of the pool is $5x + 3$. What is the width of the pool?
   A. $2x - 18$ **B.** $2x - 5$ **C.** $5x - 5$ **D.** $5x - 22$

4. What is the factored form of $16x^2 - 16x - 12$?
   F. $4(2x - 2)(2x + 2)$
   G. $4(4x - 6)(x + 2)$
   H. $4(2x - 2)(2x + 3)$
   I. $4(2x - 3)(2x + 1)$

5. What is the factored form of $3x^2 + 21x - 24$?
   A. $3(x + 8)(x - 1)$
   B. $3(x + 6)(x + 1)$
   C. $3(x + 5)(x - 3)$
   D. $3(x + 7)(x - 3)$

Short Response

6. The perimeter around a dog's running space is $20x^2 + 28x + 8$. The length of the dog's running space is $10x + 4$. What is the width of the dog's running space? Show why your answer is correct.

8-7 Think About a Plan

Factoring Special Cases

Interior Design A square rug has an area of $49x^2 - 56x + 16$. A second square rug has an area of $16x^2 + 24x + 9$. What is an expression that represents the difference of the areas of the rugs? Show two different ways to find the solution.

1. What are two methods you could use to solve this problem?_____

2. How would you find the difference without factoring?_____

3. What polynomial do you get when you use this method?_____

4. Can you factor that polynomial?_____

5. How could you use factoring to solve the problem?_____

6. What do the shape of the rug and the polynomials tell you about how to factor

   the polynomials for the area of the rugs? _____

   _____

7. Factor each trinomial.

   $49x^2 - 56x + 16 = (\square - \square)(\square - \square) = (\square\square\square)^2$

   $16x^2 + 24x + 9 = (\square + \square)(\square + \square) = (\square\square\square)^2$

8. Use your results from Exercise 7 to write an expression for the difference in the areas.

   _____

9. Factor the expression from Exercise 8 using the difference of two squares. Simplify the expressions within each set of parentheses.

   _____

10. Do the two methods give you the same result?

8-7 Practice

Form G

Factoring Special Cases

Factor each expression.

1. $h^2 + 10h + 25$ 2. $v^2 - 14v + 49$ 3. $d^2 - 22d + 121$

4. $m^2 + 4m + 4$ 5. $q^2 + 6q + 9$ 6. $p^2 - 24p + 144$

7. $36x^2 + 60x + 25$ 8. $64x^2 + 48x + 9$ 9. $49n^2 + 14n + 1$

10. $16s^2 - 72s + 81$ 11. $25r^2 - 80r + 64$ 12. $9g^2 - 24g + 16$

13. $81w^2 + 144w + 64$ 14. $16e^2 - 88e + 121$ 15. $25j^2 + 100j + 100$

16. $144f^2 - 24f + 1$ 17. $4a^2 - 36a + 81$ 18. $49d^2 - 84d + 36$

The given expression represents the area. Find the side length of the square.

19.

$64x^2 + 80x + 25$

20.

$9y^2 - 24y + 16$

21.

$4t^2 + 36t + 81$

22.

$36n^2 + 84n + 49$

23.

$100w^2 + 20w + 1$

24.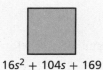

$16s^2 + 104s + 169$

25. **Error Analysis** Describe and correct the error made in factoring the expression at the right.

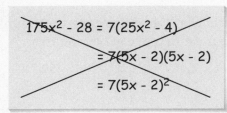

$175x^2 - 28 = 7(25x^2 - 4)$

$= 7(5x - 2)(5x - 2)$

$= 7(5x - 2)^2$

8-7 · Practice (continued) · Form G

Factoring Special Cases

Factor each expression.

26. $m^2 - 49$

27. $c^2 - 100$

28. $p^2 - 16$

29. $4a^2 - 25$

30. $64n^2 - 1$

31. $25x^2 - 144$

32. $50g^2 - 8$

33. $8d^2 - 8$

34. $27x^2 - 48$

35. $24e^2 - 54$

36. $245k^2 - 20$

37. $112h^2 - 63$

38. $48x^2 + 72x + 27$

39. $8b^2 + 80b + 200$

40. $48w^2 + 48w + 12$

41. $45s^2 - 210s + 245$

42. $45t^2 - 72t + 24$

43. $100z^2 - 120z + 36$

44. Writing Explain how to recognize a perfect-square trinomial.

45. a. Open-Ended Write an expression that shows the factored form of a difference of two squares.

    b. Explain how you know that your expression is a difference of two squares.

Factor each expression.

46. $36s^8 - 60s^4 + 25$

47. $c^{10} - 30c^5d^2 + 225d^4$

48. $25n^6 + 40n^3 + 16$

Mental Math For Exercises 49–51, find a pair of factors for each number by using the difference of two squares.

49. 24

50. 28

51. 72

52. Reasoning Explain how reversing the rules for multiplying squares of binomials can help you factor a perfect-square trinomial.

53. Writing The area of a square parking lot is $49p^4 - 84p^2 + 36$. Explain how you would find the length of the parking lot.

8-7 Standardized Test Prep

Factoring Special Cases

Multiple Choice

For Exercises 1–6, choose the correct letter.

1. What is the factored form of $q^2 - 12q + 36$?

   A. $(q + 6)(q - 6)$ **B.** $(q - 6)(q - 6)$ **C.** $(q - 9)(q + 4)$ **D.** $(q + 4)(q + 9)$

2. What is the factored form of $9x^2 + 12x + 4$?

   F. $(3x + 2)^2$ **G.** $(3x + 3)^2$ **H.** $(3x - 2)^2$ **I.** $(3x - 3)^2$

3. What is the factored form of $x^2 - 196$?

   A. $(x - 14)^2$ **B.** $(x + 14)^2$ **C.** $(x - 28)(4x + 7)$ **D.** $(x - 14)(x + 14)$

4. What is the factored form of $9x^2 - 64$?

   F. $(3x - 8)^2$ **G.** $(3x + 8)^2$ **H.** $(3x - 8)(3x + 8)$ **I.** $(9x - 8)(x + 8)$

5. What is the factored form of $12m^2 - 75$?

   A. $3(2m - 5)^2$ **B.** $3(2m + 5)(2m - 5)$ **C.** $3(2m + 5)^2$ **D.** $(6m - 25)(2m + 3)$

6. What is the factored form of $49x^2 - 56x + 16$?

   F. $(7x - 4)^2$ **G.** $(7x + 4)(7x - 4)$ **H.** $(7x + 4)^2$ **I.** $(7x - 8)^2$

Extended Response

7. A four-sided building has an area of $36x^2 + 48x + 16$. Explain how to find a possible length and width of the building. What is a possible shape of the building?

8-8   Think About a Plan

Factoring by Grouping

Art The pedestal of a sculpture is a rectangular prism with a volume of $63x^3 - 28x$. What expressions can represent the dimensions of the pedestal? Use factoring.

KNOW

1. The pedestal of the sculpture is shaped like a _____.

2. The volume of the pedestal is _____.

3. The formula you can use to find the dimensions of the pedestal is _____.

NEED

4. To solve the problem you need to find _____

_____

PLAN

5. Factor out the GCF from the volume of the pedestal. _____

6. What type of expression is of the remaining expression? _____

7. Factor the expression completely. _____

8. What expressions represent possible dimensions of the pedestal?

_____

8-8 Practice

Form G

Factoring by Grouping

Find the GCF of the first two terms and the GCF of the last two terms for each polynomial.

1. $12x^3 + 3x^2 + 20x + 5$

2. $6v^3 + 42v^2 + 5v + 35$

3. $8t^3 + 36t^2 + 2t + 9$

4. $10s^3 + 35s^2 + 6s + 21$

5. $9m^3 - 6m^2 + 12m - 8$

6. $8w^3 + 6w^2 - 28w - 21$

7. $7r^3 + 16r^2 - 9r - 72$

8. $21x^3 - 28x^2 - 6x + 8$

Factor each expression.

9. $8j^3 + 4j^2 + 10j + 5$

10. $2m^3 + 8m^2 + 9m + 36$

11. $10s^3 + 25s^2 + 8s + 20$

12. $6x^3 + 9x^2 + 2x + 3$

13. $21x^3 + 6x^2 - 28x - 8$

14. $8w^3 + 12w^2 + 10w + 15$

15. $18r^3 - 12r^2 + 21r - 14$

16. $36n^3 - 27n^2 - 8n + 6$

17. $110b^3 + 77b^2 - 60b - 42$

18. $64d^3 - 40d^2 - 24d + 15$

19. $10s^3 + 80s^2 - 7s - 56$

20. $25j^3 + 15j^2 - 5j - 3$

21. $24c^3 - 84c^2 + 10c - 35$

22. $27f^3 + 9f^2 - 24f - 8$

8-8   **Practice** (continued)   *Form G*
Factoring by Grouping

Factor completely.

23. $32x^3 + 8x^2 + 48x + 12$ **24.** $45w^4 - 36w^3 + 15w^2 - 12w$

25. $32k^4 - 16k^3 + 12k^2 - 6k$ **26.** $6g^3 + 18g^2 + 60g + 180$

27. $30b^4 - 45b^3 - 10b^2 + 15b$ **28.** $32m^3 + 72m^2 - 80m - 180$

29. $63j^4 + 84j^3 - 18j^2 - 24j$ **30.** $96n^3 - 240n^2 - 168n + 420$

31. $12e^4 + 18e^3 + 36e^2 + 54e$ **32.** $60a^5 - 72a^4 - 210a^3 + 252a^2$

Find linear expressions for the possible dimensions of each rectangular prism.

33.
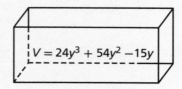
$V = 15x^3 + 52x^2 + 32x$

34.
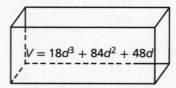
$V = 18d^3 + 84d^2 + 48d$

35.
$V = 24y^3 + 54y^2 - 15y$

36.
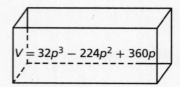
$V = 32p^3 - 224p^2 + 360p$

37. A shipping box in the shape of a rectangular prism has a volume of $12x^3 + 32x^2 + 20x$. What linear expressions can represent possible dimensions of the box?

38. Error Analysis Describe and correct the error made in factoring completely.

$$16x^4 + 24x^3 + 64x^2 + 96x = 4x(4x^3 + 6x^2 + 16x + 24)$$
$$4x[2x^2(2x + 3) + 8(2x + 3)]$$
$$= 4x(2x^2 + 8)(2x + 3)$$

39. Open-Ended Write a 3-term expression for the volume of a rectangular prism that you can factor by grouping. Factor your polynomial.

8-8

Standardized Test Prep

Factoring by Grouping

Multiple Choice

For Exercises 1–5, choose the correct letter.

1. What is the GCF of the first two terms of the polynomial $4y^3 + 8y^2 + 5y + 10$?

   A. $4y$　　　　　　**B.** $4y^2$　　　　　　**C.** $4y^3$　　　　　　**D.** 4

2. What is the factored form of $4x^3 + 3x^2 + 8x + 6$?

   F. $(2x^2 + 3)(2x + 3)$

   G. $(2x^2 + 2)(2x + 3)$

   H. $(x^2 + 2)(2x + 3)$

   I. $(x^2 + 2)(4x + 3)$

3. What is the factored form of $9x^4 - 6x^3 + 18x^2 - 12x$?

   A. $3x(x^2 - 2x)(x - 4)$

   B. $3x(x^2 - 2)(3x + 2)$

   C. $3x(x^2 + 2)(3x - 2)$

   D. $3x(3x^2 - 2x)(6x - 4)$

4. What is the factored form of $20p^3 + 40p^2 + 15p + 30$?

   F. $5(2p^2 + 3)(p + 2)$

   G. $5(2p^2 + 6)(p + 4)$

   H. $5(4p^2 + 3)(p + 2)$

   I. $5(4p^2 + 8p)(3p + 6)$

5. A box in the shape of a rectangular prism has a volume of $9x^3 + 24x^2 + 12x$. Which is not one of the possible dimensions? (Its dimensions are all linear expressions with integer coefficients.)

   A. $2x + 3$　　　　**B.** $3x + 2$　　　　**C.** $3x$　　　　　**D.** $x + 2$

Short Response

6. The polynomial $3\pi x^3 + 24\pi x^2 + 48\pi x$ represents the volume of a cylinder. The formula for the volume of a cylinder with radius r and height h is $V = \pi r^2 h$.

   a. Factor $3\pi x^3 + 24\pi x^2 + 48\pi x$.

   b. Write a linear expression for a possible radius of the cylinder. Explain.

9-1

Think About a Plan

Quadratic Graphs and Their Properties

Physics In a physics class demonstration, a ball is dropped from the roof of a building, 72 feet above the ground. The height h (in feet) of the ball above the ground is given by the function $h = -16t^2 + 72$, where t is the time in seconds.

    a. Graph the function.

    b. How far has the ball fallen from time $t = 0$ to $t = 1$?

    c. Reasoning Does the ball fall the same distance from time $t = 1$ to time $t = 2$ as it does from $t = 0$ to $t = 1$? Explain?

1. Complete the following table of values.

t	$h = -16t^2 + 72$	(t, h)
0		
1		
2		
3		

2. Use the completed table to graph the function $h = -16t^2 + 72$.

3. What was the height of the ball at $t = 0$? _____

    What was the height of the ball at $t = 1$? _____

    How far has the ball fallen from time $t = 0$ to $t = 1$? _____

4. What is the height of the ball at $t = 2$? _____

    How far has the ball fallen from time $t = 1$ to $t = 2$? _____

5. Does the ball fall the same distance from time $t = 1$ to $t = 2$ as it does from $t = 0$ to $t = 1$? Explain.

_____

_____

_____

_____

Prentice Hall Algebra 1 • Practice and Problem Solving Workbook

9-1 Practice

Form G

Quadratic Graphs and Their Properties

Identify the vertex of each graph. Tell whether it is a minimum or a maximum.

1.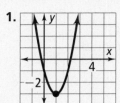

2.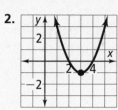

3.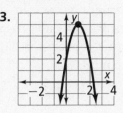

Graph each function.

4. $f(x) = 3x^2$

5. $f(x) = -2.5x^2$

6. $f(x) = -\frac{1}{5}x^2$

Order each group of quadratic functions from widest to narrowest graph.

7. $y = -3x^2, y = -5x^2, y = -1x^2$

8. $y = 4x^2, y = -2x^2, y = -6x^2$

9. $y = x^2, y = \frac{1}{3}x^2, y = 2x^2$

10. $y = \frac{1}{6}x^2, y = \frac{1}{4}x^2, y = \frac{1}{2}x^2$

Graph each function.

11. $f(x) = x^2 + 1$

12. $f(x) = x^2 - 2$

13. $f(x) = 2x^2 + 1$

14. $f(x) = -\frac{1}{2}x^2 + 5$

15. $f(x) = -3x^2 - 4$

16. $f(x) = 5x^2 - 10$

9-1

Practice (continued)   Form G

Quadratic Graphs and Their Properties

17. For a physics experiment, the class drops a golf ball off a bridge toward the pavement below. The bridge is 75 feet high. The function $h = -16t^2 + 75$ gives the golf ball's height h above the pavement (in feet) after t seconds. Graph the function. How many seconds does it take for the golf ball to hit the pavement?

18. A relief organization flew over a village and dropped a package of food and medicine. The plane is flying at 1000 feet. The function $h = -16t^2 + 1000$ gives the package's height h above the ground (in feet) after t seconds. Graph the function. How many seconds does it take for the package to hit the ground?

Identify the domain and range of each function.

19. $y = 5x^2 - 5$

20. $y = -\frac{1}{2}x^2 + 3$

21. $y = \frac{3}{5}x^2 - 2$

22. $f(x) = -9x^2 + 1$

Use a graphing calculator to graph each function. Identify the vertex and axis of symmetry.

23. $y = 2.75x^2 + 3$

24. $y = -\frac{1}{3}x^2 - 8$

25. $y = -2x^2 + 7$

26. Writing Discuss how the function $y = x^2 + 4$ differs from the graph $y = x^2$.

27. Writing Explain how you can determine if the parabola opens up or down by simply examining the equation.

9-1 Standardized Test Prep

Quadratic Graphs and Their Properties

Multiple Choice

For Exercises 1–4, choose the correct letter.

1. What is the vertex of the parabola shown at the right?

   A. $(-1, 0)$ **C.** $(1, -4)$

   B. $(0, -3)$ **D.** $(3, 0)$

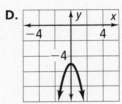

2. Which of the following has a graph that is wider than the graph of $y = 3x^2 + 2$?

   F. $y = 3x^2 + 3$ **H.** $y = -4x^2 - 1$

   G. $y = 0.5x^2 + 1$ **I.** $y = 4x^2 + 1$

3. Which graph represents the function $y = -2x^2 - 5$?

   A. 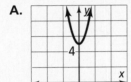 **B.** 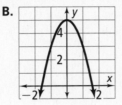 **C.** 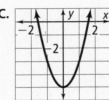 **D.**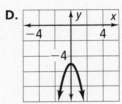

4. What is the order, from narrowest to widest graph, of the quadratic functions $f(x) = -10x^2$, $f(x) = 2x^2$, and $f(x) = 0.5x^2$?

   F. $f(x) = -10x^2$, $f(x) = 2x^2$, and $f(x) = 0.5x^2$

   G. $f(x) = 2x^2$, $f(x) = -10x^2$, and $f(x) = 0.5x^2$

   H. $f(x) = 0.5x^2$, $f(x) = 2x^2$, and $f(x) = -10x^2$

   I. $f(x) = 0.5x^2$, $f(x) = -10x^2$, and $f(x) = 2x^2$

Short Response

5. A ball fell off a cliff into the river from a height of 25 feet. The function $h = -30t^2 + 25$ gives the ball's height h above the water after t seconds. Graph the function. How much time does it take for the ball to hit the water?

9-2 Think About a Plan

Quadratic Functions

Business A cell phone company sells about 500 phones each week when it charges $75 per phone. It sells about 20 more phones per week for each $1 decrease in price. The company's revenue is the product of the number of phones sold and the price of each phone. What price should the company charge to maximize its revenue?

1. Let d = the total amount of dollar decrease to the price. Let r = the company's revenue. Write a quadratic function that reflects the company's revenue.

   Revenue equals 500 phones plus d times 20 phones times $75 less d.

   $$r = \left(\boxed{} + \left(d \times \boxed{} \right) \right) \times \left(\boxed{} - d \right)$$

   $r =$

   _____

   $r =$

   _____

   $r =$

   _____

2. Find the vertex of the quadratic function above. How will finding the vertex help you determine at what price the company should charge to maximize its revenue?

   _____

   _____

3. What price should the company charge?

9-2 Practice   Form G

Quadratic Functions

Find the equation of the axis of symmetry and the coordinates of the vertex of the graph of each function.

1. $y = 4x^2 - 2$

2. $y = -x^2 + 4x - 6$

3. $y = x^2 + 4x + 5$

4. $y = x^2 - 8x + 12$

5. $y = -6x^2 + 3$

6. $y = -3x^2 + 12x - 7$

7. $y = 2x^2 + x - 14$

8. $y = -6x^2 - 8x + 10$

9. $y = -2x^2 + 3x + 6$

Graph each function. Label the axis of symmetry and the vertex.

10. $f(x) = x^2 - 2x - 1$

11. $f(x) = -2x^2 + 8x - 10$

12. $f(x) = 2x^2 - 12x + 19$

13. $f(x) = -3x^2 - 6x - 8$

14. $f(x) = 2x^2 + 2x + 1$

15. $f(x) = -2x^2 + 12x - 2$

16. A punter kicked the football into the air with an upward velocity of 62 ft/s. Its height h in feet after t seconds is given by the function $h = -16t^2 + 62t + 2$. What is the maximum height the ball reaches? How long will it take the football to reach the maximum height? How long does it take for the ball to hit the ground?

17. A disc is thrown into the air with an upward velocity of 20 ft/s. Its height h in feet after t seconds is given by the function $h = -16t^2 + 20t + 6$. What is the maximum height the disc reaches? How long will it take the disc to reach the maximum height? How long does it take for the disc to be caught 3 feet off the ground?

9-2   **Practice** (continued)   *Form G*

Quadratic Functions

Graph each function. Label the axis of symmetry and the vertex.

18. $f(x) = \frac{3}{2}x^2 + 6x + 2$ **19.** $f(x) = \frac{2}{3}x^2 + 8x + 5$ **20.** $f(x) = \frac{1}{4}x^2 + 4x - 10$

21. $f(x) = \frac{1}{2}x^2 - 12x + 11$ **22.** $f(x) = -\frac{3}{4}x^2 + 2x + 3$ **23.** $f(x) = \frac{5}{4}x^2 - 4x + 1$

Open-Ended For Exercises 24–26, give an example of a quadratic function with the given characteristic(s).

24. Its graph opens up and has its vertex at $(0, -3)$.

25. Its graph lies entirely below the x-axis.

26. Its vertex lies on the x-axis and the graph opens down.

27. A fountain that is 5 feet tall sprays water into the air with an upward velocity of 22 ft/s. What function gives the height h of the water in feet t seconds after it is sprayed upward? What is the maximum height of the water?

28. The parabola shown at the right is of the form
$y = ax^2 + bx + c$.

   a. What is the y-intercept?

   b. What is the axis of symmetry?

   c. Use the formula $x = \frac{-b}{2a}$ to find b.

   d. What is the equation of the parabola?

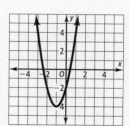

9-2

Standardized Test Prep

Quadratic Functions

Multiple Choice

For Exercises 1–5, choose the correct letter.

1. Which equation represents the axis of symmetry of the function
   $y = -2x^2 + 4x - 6$?

   A. $y = 1$ **B.** $x = 1$ **C.** $x = 3$ **D.** $x = -3$

2. What are the coordinates of the vertex of the graph of the function
   $y = -x^2 + 6x - 11$?

   F. $(3, -2)$ **G.** $(3, 16)$ **H.** $(-3, -29)$ **I.** $(-3, -20)$

3. What are the coordinates of the vertex of the graph of the function
   $y = 3x^2 - 12x + 3$?

   A. $(-2, 29)$ **B.** $(2, -15)$ **C.** $(2, -9)$ **D.** $(3, -6)$

4. Which graph represents the function $y = 3x^2 + 12x - 6$?

   F. 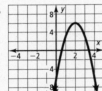   **G.** 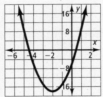   **H.** 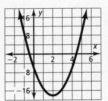   **I.**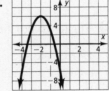

5. Which equation matches the graph shown at the right?
   A. $y = 8x^2 + 2x - 5$
   B. $y = 8x^2 + 2x + 5$
   C. $y = 2x^2 + 8x + 5$
   D. $y = 2x^2 + 8x - 5$

   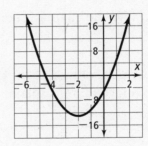

Short Response

6. A golf ball is driven in the air toward the hole from an elevated tee with an
   upward velocity of 160 ft/s. Its height h in feet after t seconds is given by the
   function $h = -16t^2 + 160t + 18$. How long will it take for the golf ball to
   reach its maximum height? What is the ball's maximum height?

9-3 Think About a Plan

Solving Quadratic Equations

Quilting You are making a square quilt with the design shown at the right. Find the side length of the inner square that would make the area of the inner square equal to 50% of the total area of the quilt. Round to the nearest tenth of a foot.

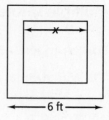

1. What is an expression for the area of the inner

   square?_____

2. What is the area of the entire quilt?_____

3. What is 50% of the area of the entire quilt?_____

4. Write an equation for the area of the inner square using the expressions from

   Steps 1 and 3._____

5. Solve the quadratic equation.

6. Which solution to the quadratic equation best describes the side length of the
   inner square? Explain.

   _____

   _____

   _____

9-3

Practice

Form G

Solving Quadratic Equations

Solve each equation by graphing the related function. If the equation has no real-number solution, write _no solution_.

1. $x^2 - 16 = 0$

2. $x^2 + 12 = 0$

3. $2x^2 - 18 = 0$

4. $7x^2 = 0$

5. $\frac{1}{2}x^2 - 2 = 0$

6. $x^2 + 49 = 0$

7. $x^2 - 15 = -15$

8. $4x^2 - 36 = 0$

9. $x^2 + 36 = 0$

Solve each equation by finding square roots. If the equation has no real-number solution, write _no solution_.

10. $t^2 = 25$

11. $k^2 = 484$

12. $z^2 - 256 = 0$

13. $d^2 - 14 = -50$

14. $9y^2 - 16 = 0$

15. $2g^2 - 32 = -32$

16. $4a^2 = 36$

17. $7x^2 + 28 = 0$

18. $6n^2 - 54 = 0$

19. $81 - c^2 = 0$

20. $16x^2 - 49 = 0$

21. $64 + j^2 = 0$

Model each problem with a quadratic equation. Then solve. If necessary, round to the nearest tenth.

22. Find the side length of a square with an area of 196 ft^2.

23. Find the radius of a circle with an area of 100 in^2.

24. Find the side length of a square with an area of 50 cm^2.

9-3 **Practice** (continued)   *Form G*

Solving Quadratic Equations

25. The square tarp you are raking leaves onto has an area of 150 ft². What is the side length of the tarp? Round your answer to the nearest tenth of a foot if necessary.

26. There is enough mulch to spread over a flower bed with an area of 85 m². What is the radius of the largest circular bed that can be covered by the mulch? Round your answer to the nearest tenth of a meter if necessary.

Mental Math Tell how many solutions each equation has.

27. $q^2 - 22 = -22$ **28.** $m^2 + 15 = 0$ **29.** $b^2 - 12 = 12$

Solve each equation by finding square roots. If the equation has no real-number solution, write *no solution*. If a solution is irrational, round to the nearest tenth.

30. $3.35z^2 + 2.75 = -14$ **31.** $100t^2 + 36 = 100$ **32.** $5a^2 - \frac{1}{125} = 0$

33. $\frac{1}{3}h^2 - 12 = 0$ **34.** $-\frac{1}{2}m^2 + 5 = -10$ **35.** $11x^2 - 0.75 = 3.21$

36. Find the value of n such that the equation $x^2 - n = 0$ has 24 and -24 as solutions.

Find the value of x for the square and triangle. If necessary, round to the nearest tenth.

37.

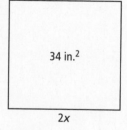

34 in.²

2x

38.

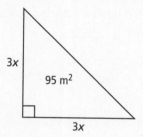

3x

95 m²

3x

39. Writing Explain how the number of solutions for a quadratic equation relates to the graph of the function.

9-3 Standardized Test Prep

Solving Quadratic Equations

Multiple Choice

For Exercises 1–7, choose the correct letter.

1. What is the solution of $n^2 - 49 = 0$?
   A. -7 **B.** 7   **C.** ± 7 **D.** no solution

2. What is the solution of $x^2 + 64 = 0$?
   F. -5 **G.** 8   **H.** ± 8 **I.** no solution

3. What is the solution of $a^2 + 17 = 42$?
   A. -5 **B.** 5   **C.** ± 5 **D.** no solution

4. What is the side length of a square with an area of $144x^2$?
   F. 12   **G.** $12x$ **H.** $\pm 12x$ **I.** no solution

5. What is the value of b in the triangle shown at the right?
   A. -4 in.
   B. 4 in.
   C. ± 4 in.
   D. no solution

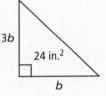

6. What is the radius of a sphere whose surface area is 100 square centimeters? Use the formula for determining the surface area of a sphere, $S = 4\pi r^2$, and 3.14 for π. Round your answer to the nearest hundredth.
   F. 2.82 cm   **G.** 5 cm   **H.** 5.64 cm   **I.** 125,600 cm

7. What is the value of z so that -9 and 9 are both solutions of $x^2 + z = 103$?
   A. -22 **B.** 3   **C.** 22   **D.** 184

Extended Response

8. A ball is dropped from the top of a building that is 250 feet tall. The height h of the ball in feet after t seconds is modeled by the function $h = -16t^2 + 250$. Round to the nearest tenth if necessary.
   a. How long will it take for the ball to reach the ground? Show your work.
   b. How long will it take for the ball to reach a height of 75 feet? Show your work.

9-4 · Think About a Plan

Factoring to Solve Quadratic Equations

Sports You throw a softball into the air with an initial upward velocity of 38 ft/s and an initial height of 5 ft.

a. Use the vertical motion model to write an equation that gives the ball's height h (in feet) at time t (in seconds).

b. The ball's height is 0 ft when it is on the ground. Solve the equation you wrote in part (a) for $h = 0$ to find when the ball lands.

What do you know?

1. Write a vertical motion model that best describes the equation for the ball's height h at time t. What are the values of v and c?

$$h = -16t^2 + v \cdot t + c$$

$$h = -16t^2 + \boxed{} \cdot t + \boxed{}$$

2. How would graphing the quadratic equation help you understand the problem?

_____

_____

_____

How do you solve the problem?

3. The ball's height is 0 ft when it is on the ground. Solve the equation you wrote in part (a) for $h = 0$ to find when the ball lands.

9-4

Practice

Form G

Factoring to Solve Quadratic Equations

Use the Zero-Product Property to solve each equation.

1. $(y + 6)(y - 4) = 0$

2. $(3f + 2)(f - 5) = 0$

3. $(2x - 7)(4x + 10) = 0$

4. $(8t - 7)(3t + 5) = 0$

5. $d(d - 8) = 0$

6. $3m(2m + 9) = 0$

Solve by factoring.

7. $n^2 + 2n - 15 = 0$

8. $a^2 - 15a + 56 = 0$

9. $z^2 - 10z + 24 = 0$

10. $8x^2 + 10x + 3 = 0$

11. $3b^2 + 7b - 6 = 0$

12. $5p^2 - 9p - 2 = 0$

13. $w^2 + w = 12$

14. $s^2 + 12s = -32$

15. $d^2 = 5d$

16. $3j^2 - 20j = -12$

17. $12y^2 + 40y = 7$

18. $27r^2 + 69r = 8$

Use the Zero-Product Property to solve each equation. Write your solutions as a set in roster form.

19. $k^2 - 11k + 30 = 0$

20. $x^2 - 6x - 7 = 0$

21. $n^2 + 17n + 72 = 0$

22. The volume of a sandbox shaped like a rectangular prism is 48 ft^3. The height of the sandbox is 2 feet. The width is w feet and the length is $w + 2$ feet. Use the formula $V = lwh$ to find the value of w.

23. The area of the rubber coating for a flat roof was 96 ft^2. The rectangular frame the carpenter built for the flat roof has dimensions such that the length is 4 feet longer than the width. What are the dimensions of the frame?

24. Ling is cutting carpet for a rectangular room. The area of the room is 324 ft^2. The length of the room is 3 feet longer than twice the width. What should the dimensions of the carpet be?

9-4

Practice (continued)   Form G

Factoring to Solve Quadratic Equations

Write each equation in standard form. Then solve.

25. $21x^2 + 5x - 35 = 3x^2 - 4x$ **26.** $3n^2 - 2n + 1 = -3n^2 + 9n + 11$

Find the value of x as it relates to each rectangle or triangle.

27. Area $= 60 \text{ cm}^2$ **28.** Area $= 234 \text{ yd}^2$

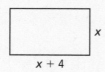

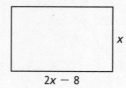

29. Area $= 20 \text{ in.}^2$ **30.** Area $= 150 \text{ m}^2$

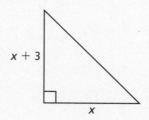

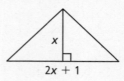

Reasoning For each equation, find k and the value of any missing solutions.

31. $x^2 - kx - 16 = 0$ where -2 is one solution of the equation.

32. $x^2 - 6x = k$ where 10 is one solution of the equation.

33. $kx^2 - 13x = 5$ where $-\frac{1}{3}$ is one solution of the equation.

34. Writing Explain how you solve a quadratic equation by factoring.

9-4 Standardized Test Prep

Factoring to Solve Quadratic Equations

Gridded Response

Solve each exercise and enter your answer on the grid provided.

1. What is the positive solution of $3x^2 - 10x - 8 = 0$?

2. A triangular-shaped wall has a base of $2x + 4$ and a height of $x + 3$. The area of the triangle is 56 in.^{2}. What is the value of x?

3. The product of two consecutive integers, n and $n + 1$, is 42. What is the positive integer that satisfies the situation?

4. One more rectangular-shaped piece of metal siding needs to be cut to cover the exterior of a pole barn. The area of the piece is 30 ft^2. The length is 1 less than 3 times the width. How wide should the metal piece be? Round to the nearest hundredth of a foot.

5. What solution do $2x^2 - 13x + 21 = 0$ and $2x^2 + 9x - 56 = 0$ have in common? Round your answer to the nearest tenth if necessary.

1. 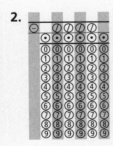 2. 3. 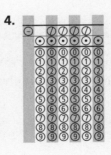 4. 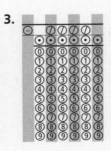 5.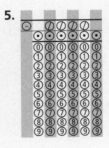

9-5   Think About a Plan

Completing the Square

Landscaping A school is fencing in a rectangular area for a playground. It plans to enclose the playground using fencing on three sides, as shown at the right. The school has budgeted enough money for 75 ft of fencing material and would like to make a playground with an area of 600 ft^2.

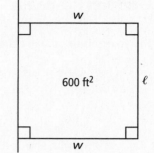

a. Let w represent the width of the playground. Write an expression in terms of w for the length of the playground.

b. Write and solve an equation to find the width w. Round to the nearest tenth of a foot.

c. What should the length of the playground be?

What do you know?

1. Let w represent the width of the playground. Write an expression in terms of w for the length of the playground.

$$w + w + l = \boxed{} \text{ feet}$$

$$l =$$

2. Write an equation for the area of the playground.

$$w \cdot l = \boxed{} \text{ ft}^2$$

What do you need to solve the problem?

3. Substitute the expression for l from Step 1 in the equation from Step 2.

How do you solve the problem?

4. Solve the equation in Step 3 to find the width w. Round to the nearest tenth of a foot. What should the length l of the playground be?

9-5

Practice   Form G

Completing the Square

Find the value of c such that each expression is a perfect-square trinomial.

1. $x^2 + 4x + c$

2. $b^2 + 12b + c$

3. $g^2 - 20g + c$

4. $a^2 - 7a + c$

5. $w^2 + 18w + c$

6. $n^2 - 9n + c$

Solve each equation by completing the square. If necessary, round to the nearest hundredth.

7. $z^2 - 19z = 66$

8. $p^2 - 5p = -4$

9. $b^2 + 6b = 16$

10. $c^2 - 4c = 21$

11. $a^2 - 2a = 15$

12. $v^2 + 8v = 15$

13. $y^2 + 16y = 17$

14. $x^2 + 4x + 3 = 0$

15. $h^2 + 4h = 1$

16. $r^2 + 8r + 13 = 0$

17. $d^2 - 2d - 4 = 0$

18. $m^2 - 24m + 44 = 0$

Solve each equation by completing the square. If necessary, round to the nearest hundredth.

19. $3y^2 + 5y = 12$

20. $2h^2 - 5h = -1$

21. $4k^2 + 4k = 5$

22. $2c^2 + 7c + 3 = 0$

23. $3f^2 - 2f = 1$

24. $9x^2 - 42x + 49 = 0$

25. The rectangle shown at the right has an area of 56 m^2.
What is the value of x?

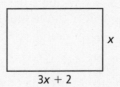

x

$3x + 2$

9-5 Practice (continued) Form G
Completing the Square

26. What are all of the values of c that will make $x^2 + cx + 49$ a perfect square?

27. What are all of the values of c that will make $x^2 + cx + 121$ a perfect square?

Solve each equation. If necessary, round to the nearest hundredth. If there is no solution, write *no solution*.

28. $k^2 - 24k + 4 = -2$

29. $4x^2 - 20x + 25 = 0$

30. $2b^2 + 10b + 15 = 3$

31. $p^2 + 3p + 2 = -1$

32. $5m^2 + 10m - 80 = 75$

33. $2a^2 - 3a + 4 = 0$

34. $5a^2 - 12a + 28 = 0$

35. $5t^2 - 6t = 35$

36. Writing Discuss the strategies of graphing, factoring, and completing the square for solving the quadratic equation $x^2 + 4x - 6 = 0$.

37. The height of a triangle is $4x$ inches and the base is $(5x + 1)$ inches. The area of the triangle is 500 square inches. What are the dimensions of the base and height of the triangle?

38. The formula for finding the volume of a rectangular prism is $V = lwh$. The height h of a rectangular prism is 12 centimeters. The prism has a volume of 10,800 cubic centimeters. The prism's length l is modeled by $3x$ centimeters and its width w by $(2x + 1)$ centimeters. What is the value of x? What are the dimensions of the length and the width?

39. Writing In order to solve a quadratic equation by completing the square, what does the coefficient of the squared term need to be? If the coefficient is not equal to this, what does your first step need to be to complete the square?

9-5

Standardized Test Prep

Completing the Square

Multiple Choice

For Exercises 1–6, choose the correct letter.

1. What is the value of n such that the expression $x^2 + 11x + n$ is a perfect square trinomial?

    A. 11   **B.** 25   **C.** 30.25   **D.** 36

2. What is a solution of $x^2 + 6x = -5$?

    F. $x = -6$ **G.** $x = -1$ **H.** $x = 1$ **I.** $x = 6$

3. Which of the following is a solution of $x^2 + 4x - 1 = 0$? If necessary, round to the nearest hundredth.

    A. $x = -0.94$ **B.** $x = 14.94$ **C.** $x = -14.94$ **D.** no solution

4. Which of the following is a solution of $x^2 + 14x + 112 = 0$? If necessary, round to the nearest hundredth.

    F. $x = -0.24$ **G.** $x = -4.24$ **H.** $x = 4.24$ **I.** no solution

5. The rectangular poster shown at the right has an area of 5400 cm^2. What is the value of w?

    A. -45 cm   **C.** 60 cm

    B. 45 cm   **D.** 90 cm

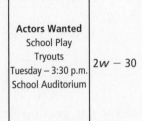

Actors Wanted
School Play
Tryouts
Tuesday – 3:30 p.m.
School Auditorium

$2w - 30$

w

6. A box shaped like a rectangular prism has a height of 17 in. and a volume of 2720 in.^{3}. The length is 4 inches greater than twice the width. What is the width of the box?

    F. -10 in.   **H.** 20 in.

    G. 8 in.   **I.** 40 in.

Short Response

7. The area of a rectangular television screen is 3456 in.^{2}. The width of the screen is 24 inches longer than the length. What is a quadratic equation that represents the area of the screen? What are the dimensions of the screen?

9-6   Think About a Plan

The Quadratic Formula and the Discriminant

Sports Your school wants to take out an ad in the paper congratulating the basketball team on a successful season, as shown at the right. The area of the photo will be half the area of the entire ad. How wide will the border be?

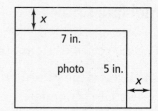

What do you know?

1. What are the dimensions of the photo and the ad? Let $w =$ the width of the photo and $l =$ the length of the photo.

_____

_____

What do you need to solve the problem?

2. What quadratic equation can you write that best describes the relationship between the area of the photo and the area of the ad?

_____

_____

_____

How do you solve the problem?

3. Using the quadratic formula, how will you be able to solve for x, the width of the border? What is the width of the border?

_____

_____

_____

9-6

Practice

Form G

The Quadratic Formula and the Discriminant

Use the quadratic formula to solve each equation.

1. $7c^2 + 8c + 1 = 0$

2. $2w^2 - 28w = -98$

3. $2j^2 - 3j = -1$

4. $2x^2 - 6x + 4 = 0$

5. $2n^2 - 6n = 8$

6. $-7d^2 + 2d + 9 = 0$

7. $2a^2 + 4a - 6 = 0$

8. $-3p^2 + 17p = 20$

9. $4d^2 - 8d + 3 = 0$

Use the quadratic formula to solve each equation. Round answers to the nearest hundredth.

10. $h^2 - 2h - 2 = 0$

11. $5x^2 + 3x = 1$

12. $-z^2 - 4z = -2$

13. $t^2 + 10t = -22$

14. $3n^2 + 10n = 5$

15. $s^2 - 10s + 14 = 0$

16. A basketball is passed through the air. The height h of the ball in feet after the distance d in feet the ball travels horizontally is given by $h = -d^2 + 10d + 5$. How far horizontally from the player passing the ball will the ball land on the ground?

Which method(s) would you choose to solve each equation? Justify your reasoning.

17. $h^2 + 4h + 7 = 0$

18. $a^2 - 4a - 12 = 0$

19. $24y^2 - 11y - 14 = 0$

20. $2p^2 - 7p - 4 = 0$

21. $4x^2 - 144 = 0$

22. $f^2 - 2f - 35 = 0$

23. Writing Explain how the discriminant can be used to determine the number of solutions a quadratic equation has.

9-6

Practice (continued)   Form G

The Quadratic Formula and the Discriminant

Find the number of real-number solutions of each equation.

24. $x^2 - 8x + 7 = 0$ **25.** $x^2 - 6x = 0$ **26.** $2x^2 - 5x + 16 = 0$

27. $-3x^2 - 4x - 8 = 0$ **28.** $7x^2 + 12x - 21 = 0$ **29.** $2x^2 + 4x + 2 = 0$

Use any method to solve each equation. If necessary, round answers to the nearest hundredth.

30. $5m^2 - 3m - 15 = 0$ **31.** $9y^2 + 6y = -12$ **32.** $4a^2 = 36$

33. $6t^2 - 96 = 0$ **34.** $z^2 + 7z = -10$ **35.** $-g^2 + 4g + 3 = 0$

Find the value of the discriminant and the number of real-number solutions of each equation.

36. $x^2 + 11x - 10 = 0$ **37.** $x^2 + 7x + 8 = 0$ **38.** $3x^2 + 5x - 9 = 0$

39. $-2x^2 + 10x - 1 = 0$ **40.** $3x^2 + 6x + 3 = 0$ **41.** $6x^2 + x + 12 = 0$

42. The weekly profit of a company is modeled by the function $w = -g^2 + 120g - 28$. The weekly profit, w, is dependent on the number of gizmos, g, sold. If the break-even point is when $w = 0$, how many gizmos must the company sell each week in order to break even?

43. Reasoning The equation $4x^2 + bx + 9 = 0$ has no real-number solutions. What must be true about b?

44. Open-Ended Describe three different methods to solve $x^2 - x - 56 = 0$. Tell which method you prefer. Explain your reasoning.

9-6

Standardized Test Prep

The Quadratic Formula and the Discriminant

Multiple Choice

For Exercises 1–6, choose the correct letter.

1. Which expression gives the solutions of $-5 + 2x^2 = -6x$?

   A. $\dfrac{2 \pm \sqrt{4 - (4)(6)(-5)}}{12}$

   C. $\dfrac{-6 \pm \sqrt{36 - (4)(2)(-5)}}{4}$

   B. $\dfrac{-5 \pm \sqrt{25 - (4)(2)(6)}}{-10}$

   D. $\dfrac{6 \pm \sqrt{36 - (4)(2)(5)}}{4}$

2. What are the approximate solutions of $2x^2 - x + 10 = 0$?

   F. $-2, 2.5$ **G.** $-1.97, 2.47$ **H.** $-2.5, 2$ **I.** no solution

3. What are the approximate solutions of $7x^2 + 4x - 9 = 0$?

   A. $-1.42, 0.85$ **C.** $-0.88, 1.5$

   B. $-1.5, 0.88$ **D.** no solution

4. Which method is the best method for solving the equation $8x^2 - 13x + 3 = 0$?

   F. square roots   **H.** graphing

   G. factoring   **I.** quadratic formula

5. How many solutions are there for $5x^2 + 7x - 4 = 0$?

   A. 0   **B.** 1   **C.** 2   **D.** 3

6. The perimeter of a rectangle is 54 cm. The area of the same rectangle is $176\ cm^2$. What are the dimensions of the rectangle?

   F. 11 cm by 16 cm   **H.** 5.5 cm by 32 cm

   G. 8 cm by 22 cm   **I.** 4 cm by 44 cm

Short Response

7. The flight of a baseball that has been hit when it was 4 feet off the ground is modeled by the function $h = -16t^2 + 75t + 4$ where h is the height of the baseball in feet after t seconds. Rounding to the nearest hundredth, how long will it take before the ball lands on the ground? Show your work.

9-7 Think About a Plan

Linear, Quadratic, and Exponential Models

Zoology A conservation organization collected the data on the number of frogs in a local wetlands. Which kind of function best models the data? Write an equation to model the data.

Year	Number of Frogs
0	120
1	101
2	86
3	72
4	60

What do you know?

1. Let x = year and y = number of frogs.
   Graph the points in the table.

2. How will graphing the points in the table help you determine which function best models the data?

   _____

What do you need to solve the problem?

3. How will finding the differences or ratios between the data points help you determine which function best models the data?

   _____

   _____

How do you solve the problem?

4. Write an equation that best models the data.

9-7 Practice

Form G

Linear, Quadratic, and Exponential Models

Graph each set of points. Which model is most appropriate for each set?

1. $(-3, -8), (-1, -2), (0, 1), (1, 4), (3, 10)$ **2.** $(-2, 0.75), (-1, 1.5), (0, 3), (1, 6)$

3. $(-2, 1), (-1, 0), (0, 1), (1, 4), (2, 9)$ **4.** $(-2, -11), (-1, -5), (0, -3), (1, -5), (2, -11)$

5. $(-4, 0), (-2, -1), (0, -2), (2, -3), (4, -4)$ **6.** $(-1, -0.67), (0, -2), (1, -6), (2, -18)$

7. $(-3, 10), (-1, 2), (0, 1), (1, 2), (3, 10)$ **8.** $(-2, 4), (-1, 2), (0, 0), (1, -2), (2, -4)$

Which type of function best models the data in each table? Use differences or ratios.

9.

x	y
0	-12
1	-11
2	-8
3	-3
4	4

10.

x	y
0	3
1	-2
2	-7
3	-12
4	17

11.

x	y
0	3
1	12
2	48
3	192
4	768

12. Which type of function best models the ordered pairs $(-1, 6), (0, 1), (1, 2),$ and $(2, 9)$? Use differences or ratios.

13. Which type of function best models the ordered pairs $(-1, -0.25),$ $(0, -0.5), (1, -1),$ and $(2, -2)$? Use differences or ratios.

9-7 Practice (continued) Form G
Linear, Quadratic, and Exponential Models

Which type of function best models the data in each table? Write an equation to model the data.

14.

x	y
0	−7
1	−1
2	5
3	11
4	17

15.

x	y
−4	32
−3	16
−2	8
−1	4
0	2

16.

x	y
0	4
1	0
2	−12
3	−32
4	−60

17.

x	y
−1	22
0	15
1	10
2	7
3	6

18.

x	y
−2	−1
−1	−2
0	−4
1	−8
2	−16

19.

x	y
0	−1
1	−2
2	−3
3	−4
4	−5

Which type of function best models the data in each ordered pair? Write an equation to model the data.

20. $(−3, 33), (−1, 21), (0, 15), (1, 9), (3, −3)$

21. $(−2, −16), (−1, −8), (0, −4), (1, −2), (2, −1)$

22. $(−2, \frac{1}{27}), (−1, \frac{1}{9}), (0, \frac{1}{3}), (1, 1), (2, 3)$

23. $(−2, −2), (−1, −3.5), (0, −4), (1, −3.5), (2, −2)$

24. $(−6, 5), (−3, 4.5), (0, 4), (3, 3.5), (6, 3)$

25. $(−1, 10), (0, 3), (1, 0), (2, 1)$

26. The population of a city for years since 2000 is shown below. Which kind of function best models the data? Write an equation to model the data.

Years since 2000	0	2	4	6	8
Population	1500	6000	24,000	96,000	384,000

9-7 Standardized Test Prep

Linear, Quadratic, and Exponential Models

Multiple Choice

For Exercises 1–4, choose the correct letter.

1. Which kind of function best models the set of data points $(-1, 22)$, $(0, 6)$, $(1, -10)$, $(2, -26)$, $(3, -42)$?

    A. linear   **B.** quadratic   **C.** exponential   **D.** none of the above

2. Which kind of function best models the set of data points $(-3, 18)$, $(-2, 6)$, $(-1, 2)$, $(0, 11)$, $(1, 27)$?

    F. linear   **G.** quadratic   **H.** exponential   **I.** none of the above

3. What function can be used to model data pairs that have a common ratio?

    A. linear   **B.** quadratic   **C.** exponential   **D.** none of the above

4. The attendances at the high school basketball games seemed to be affected by the success of the team. The graph at the right models the attendance over the first half of the season. Which function would also represent the data shown in the graph where a represents the attendance and g represents the number of games the team has won?

    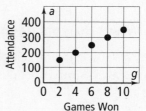

    F. $a = 25(3)^g$ **H.** $a = 25g^2 + 100$

    G. $a = 25g + 100$ **I.** $a = -25g^2 + 100$

Short Response

5. The data in the table show the population growth of a city since the year 2000. What kind of function models the data? How do you know?

Year	Population
0	5275
1	10,550
2	21,100
3	42,200
4	84,400

9-8 Think About a Plan

Systems of Linear and Quadratic Equations

Business The number of customers at a coffee shop can be modeled by the function $y = 0.25x^2 - 5x + 80$, where x is the number of days since the beginning of the month. The number of customers at another coffee shop can be modeled by a linear function. Both shops have the same number of customers on days 10 and 20. What function models the number of customers at the second shop?

What do you know?

1. Using the function $y = 0.25x^2 - 5x + 80$, find the values of y when $x = 10$ and $x = 20$.

When $x = 10$, $y = $ _____.

When $x = 20$, $y = $ _____.

What do you need to solve the problem?

2. How can you use these two data points to write a linear function that models the number of customers at the second coffee shop?

_____

_____

How do you solve the problem?

3. Write the linear function that models the data for the second coffee shop.

4. Check your function in Step 3. Explain the method you used.

_____

_____

9-8

Practice

Form G

Systems of Linear and Quadratic Equations

Solve each system by graphing.

1. $y = x^2 + 2$
   $y = x + 2$

2. $y = x^2$
   $y = 2x$

3. $y = x^2 - 5$
   $y = x - 3$

4. $y = x^2 + 1$
   $y = x + 1$

5. $y = x^2 - 4x - 2$
   $y = -x - 2$

6. $y = x^2 - 6x - 7$
   $y = x + 1$

Solve each system using elimination.

7. $y = x^2$
   $y = x + 2$

8. $y = x^2 - 4$
   $y = -x - 2$

9. $y = x^2 - 2x + 2$
   $y = 2x - 2$

10. $y = -x^2 + 4x - 3$
   $y = -x + 1$

11. $y = -x^2 + 2x + 4$
   $y = -x + 4$

12. $y = x^2 - x - 6$
   $y = 2x - 2$

13. The weekly profits of two different companies selling similar items that opened for business at the same time are modeled by the equations shown below. The profit is represented by y and the number of weeks the companies have been in business is represented by x. According to the projections, what week(s) did the companies have the same profit? What was the profit of both companies during the week(s) of equal profit?
Company A: $y = x^2 - 70x + 3341$
Company X: $y = 50x + 65$

14. The populations of two different cities are modeled by the equations shown below. The population (in thousands) is represented by y and the number of years since 1970 is represented by x. What year(s) did the cities have the same population? What was the population of both cities during the year(s) of equal population?
Baskinville: $y = x^2 - 22x + 350$
Cryersport: $y = 55x - 950$

9-8

Practice (continued)   Form G

Systems of Linear and Quadratic Equations

Solve each system using substitution.

15. $y = x^2 + x - 60$
$y = 2x - 4$

16. $y = x^2 - 3x + 7$
$y = 4x - 3$

17. $y = x^2 - 2x - 5$
$y = x - 5$

18. $y = -x^2 - 2x - 4$
$7x + y = 2$

19. $y = x^2 + 6x$
$x - y = 4$

20. $y = x^2 + 4x - 15$
$y - 25 = x$

Solve each system using a graphing calculator.

21. $y = x^2 + 5x + 13$
$y = -5x + 3$

22. $y = x^2 - x + 82$
$y = -2x + 50$

23. $y = x^2 - 12x + 150$
$y = 15x - 20$

24. $y = x^2 - 2x + 2.5$
$y = 2x - 1.25$

25. $y = x^2 - 0.9x - 1$
$y = 0.5x + 0.76$

26. $y = x^2 - 68$
$y = -5x + 25.75$

27. Reasoning What are the solutions of the system $y = 2x^2 - 11$ and
$y = x^2 + 2x - 8$? Explain how you solved the system.

28. Writing Explain why a system of linear and quadratic equations can only
have 0, 1, or two possible solutions.

29. Reasoning The graph at the right shows a quadratic function
and the linear function $x = b$.
a. How many solutions does this system have?
b. If the linear function were changed to $y = b$, how many
solutions would the system have?
c. If the linear function were changed to $y = b + 3$, how many solutions
would the system have?

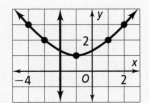

9-8 Standardized Test Prep

Systems of Linear and Quadratic Equations

Multiple Choice

For Exercises 1–4, choose the correct letter.

1. Which system of equations represents the graph shown?

   A. $y = x + 3$
   $y = x^2 - 9$

   C. $y = x + 3$
   $y = 2x^2 - 18$

   B. $y = x - 3$
   $y = x^2 - 9$

   D. $y = x - 3$
   $y = 2x^2 - 18$

   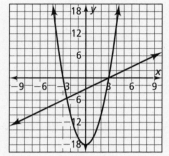

2. What is the solution of the system of equations shown below?
   $y = x - 2$
   $y = x^2 - 8x + 6$

   F. $(-1, -3)$ and $(-8, -10)$ **H.** $(0, -2)$ and $(5, 3)$

   G. $(2, 0)$ and $(-8, -10)$ **I.** $(1, -1)$ and $(8, 6)$

3. What is the solution of the system of equations shown below?
   $y = x^2 - 5x + 18$
   $y = 4x + 4$

   A. $(-2, -4)$ and $(-7, -24)$ **C.** $(2, 12)$ and $(7, 32)$
   B. $(0, 4)$ and $(2, 12)$ **D.** $(4, 20)$ and $(5, 24)$

4. An architect makes a drawing of a parabolic-shaped arch with a linear support intersecting it in two places. The parabola can be modeled by the function $y = x^2 - 5x + 10$. The line intersects the parabola when $x = 2$ and $x = 4$. What is the equation of the line?

   F. $y = x - 6$ **G.** $y = x - 2$ **H.** $y = x + 2$ **I.** $y = x + 6$

Short Response

5. Graph the following system of equations. How many solutions does this system have? Explain your reasoning.
   $y = 2x^2 + 2$
   $y = 2x - 2$

10-1

Think About a Plan

The Pythagorean Theorem

Construction A construction worker is cutting along the diagonal of a rectangular board 15 ft long and 8 ft wide. What will be the length of the cut?

KNOW

1. The board measures ☐ ft long by ☐ ft wide.

2. The board is in the shape of a _____, which has 4 _____ angles.

3. A diagonal cut divides the board into 2 equal _____ triangles.

4. The Pythagorean Theorem states _____.

NEED

5. To solve the problem I need to find _____

_____.

PLAN

6. What drawing can you make to show what you are given and what you are trying to find?

7. What equation can you use to find the length of the cut?

8. Solve the equation.

9. Is the solution reasonable? Explain.

_____

_____

_____

10-1 Practice

The Pythagorean Theorem

Form G

Use the triangle at the right. Find the length of the missing side. If necessary, round to the nearest tenth.

1. $a = 9$, $b = 12$

2. $a = 7$, $c = 25$

3. $b = 12$, $c = 13$

4. $a = \frac{3}{5}$, $b = \frac{4}{5}$

5. $b = 2$, $c = 2.5$

6. $a = 12$, $c = 37$

7. $a = 20$, $b = 21$

8. $a = 3.2$, $c = 13$

9. $a = 1.8$, $c = 8.2$

10. $b = 20$, $c = 25$

11. $a = \frac{6}{5}$, $b = \frac{8}{5}$

12. $a = 0.8$, $b = 1.5$

13. A quilter is cutting along the diagonal of a rectangular piece of fabric $\frac{3}{4}$ yard wide by 1 yard long. What will be the length of the cut?

14. How long is the diagonal of a 12 mm-by-16 mm face of a rectangular prism?

15. A pilot flies a plane south and then 600 miles west, where she lands the plane. How far south did the pilot fly the plane if she lands 610 miles from her starting point?

16. A builder divides a rectangular plot of land in half along the diagonal. If the plot is $\frac{1}{2}$-mile wide and the diagonal measures $1\frac{3}{10}$-miles long, what is the length of the plot?

10-1

Practice (continued)

Form G

The Pythagorean Theorem

Determine whether the given lengths can be side lengths of a right triangle.

17. 16 cm, 30 cm, 34 cm

18. 0.8 m, 1.5 m, 1.7 m

19. 60 in., 91 in., 110 in.

20. 10 ft, 24 ft, 26 ft

21. 12 cm, 36 cm, 37 cm

22. 18 mi, 81 mi, 82 mi

23. 2.0 km, 2.1 km, 2.9 km

24. $\frac{1}{3}$ yd, $\frac{1}{4}$ yd, $\frac{1}{5}$ yd

Any set of three positive integers that satisfies the equation $a^2 + b^2 = c^2$ is a Pythagorean triple. Determine whether each set of numbers is a Pythagorean triple.

25. 36, 77, 85

26. 40, 96, 104

27. 9, 16, 25

28. 54, 72, 85

29. 70, 240, 250

30. 12, 60, 61

31. A landscaper attaches a guy wire 10 ft up the trunk of a newly planted sapling. He stakes the wire between 20 and 25 feet from the tree. What could be the length of the guy wire if it forms a right triangle with the tree?

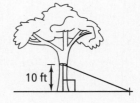

10 ft

32. Writing Summarize the method for finding the measure of the hypotenuse of a right triangle if you are given the measure of both legs.

33. The area of a square is 625 cm^2. What is the measure of the diagonal to the nearest tenth?

34. Open-Ended Draw a right triangle with side lengths that are whole numbers. What equation can you use to prove that you have drawn a right triangle? What theorem will you use to help make your proof?

10-1 **Standardized Test Prep**

The Pythagorean Theorem

Multiple Choice

For Exercises 1–6, choose the correct letter.

1. What is the length of the missing side?
   - **A.** 21.8
   - **B.** 26
   - **C.** 28
   - **D.** 34

2. What is the length of the missing side?
   - **F.** 16 mm
   - **G.** 28 mm
   - **H.** 42 mm
   - **I.** 69.5 mm

3. Which set of lengths could be the side lengths of a right triangle?
   - **A.** 20 cm, 22 cm, 29 cm
   - **B.** 10 ft, 12 ft, 15 ft
   - **C.** 7 km, 24 km, 28 km
   - **D.** 13 in., 84 in., 85 in.

4. A right triangle has a side length that measures 4 m and a hypotenuse that measures 8.5 m. What is the measure of the other side of the triangle?
   - **F.** 7.5 m
   - **G.** 8.1 m
   - **H.** 9.4 m
   - **I.** 9.8 m

5. How long is the diagonal of a 12 ft-by-16 ft rectangular garden?
   - **A.** 6 ft
   - **B.** 14 ft
   - **C.** 18 ft
   - **D.** 20 ft

6. You want to divide a square piece of paper into two equivalent triangles. If the square measures 20 cm on each side, what will the third side of each triangle measure?
   - **F.** 8.9 cm
   - **G.** 20 cm
   - **H.** 28.3 cm
   - **I.** 40 cm

Short Response

7. Joe is cutting three risers for a set of stairs. Each riser is a right triangle with legs $7\frac{1}{2}$ in. and 10 in.

   a. What equation could you use to find the length of the third side of a riser?

   _____

   b. How long will the staircase measure when the 3 risers are installed?

   Explain. _____

   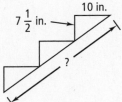

   _____

10-2 Think About a Plan

Simplifying Radicals

Sports The bases in a softball diamond are located at the corners of a 3600 ft^2 square. How far is a throw from second base to home plate?

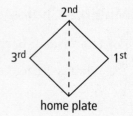

Understanding the Problem

1. What is the area of the softball diamond? _____

2. Where are second base and home plate located? _____

3. What is the problem asking you to determine? _____

_____

Planning the Solution

4. What equation can be used to determine the side length of the softball diamond? _____

5. What equation can be used to determine the length of the throw from second base to home plate? _____

6. How many steps will it take to solve this problem?

Getting an Answer

7. What is the first step in finding the solution? What is the solution of the first step? What is the second step in finding the solution? What is the solution?

10-2 Practice   Form G

Simplifying Radicals

Simplify each radical expression.

1. $\sqrt{169}$

2. $\sqrt{200}$

3. $\sqrt{125}$

4. $-5\sqrt{112}$

5. $\sqrt{68}$

6. $3\sqrt{121}$

7. $\sqrt{63t^4}$

8. $\sqrt{48n^3}$

9. $-\sqrt{60m^7}$

10. $x\sqrt{150x^5}$

11. $-3\sqrt{45y^3}$

12. $-2b\sqrt{136b^2}$

Simplify each product.

13. $\sqrt{6} \cdot \sqrt{30}$

14. $\sqrt{5} \cdot \sqrt{70}$

15. $2\sqrt{3} \cdot \sqrt{96}$

16. $-4\sqrt{7} \cdot \sqrt{42}$

17. $\sqrt{4a} \cdot \sqrt{12a^5}$

18. $\sqrt{2n^2} \cdot \sqrt{30n}$

19. $-3\sqrt{40x} \cdot 2\sqrt{56x^5}$

20. $\frac{3}{4}\sqrt{12t^3} \cdot \sqrt{20t^3}$

21. $4\sqrt{14d^2} \cdot \frac{1}{2}\sqrt{28d^3}$

22. A pool is shaped like a rectangle with a length 4 times its width w. What is an expression for the distance between opposite corners of the pool?

23. Evelyn rode her horse along a triangular path. The distance she traveled south was five times the distance she traveled east. Then she rode directly back to her starting point. What is an expression for the total distance she rode?

10-2 Practice (continued)   Form G
Simplifying Radicals

Simplify each radical expression.

24. $\sqrt{\dfrac{36}{49}}$

25. $\sqrt{\dfrac{81}{16}}$

26. $\sqrt{\dfrac{100}{225}}$

27. $\sqrt{\dfrac{18y}{36y^3}}$

28. $\sqrt{\dfrac{49x^5}{25x}}$

29. $\sqrt{\dfrac{16a^2}{4b^4}}$

30. $\dfrac{\sqrt{5}}{\sqrt{2}}$

31. $\dfrac{\sqrt{12}}{\sqrt{15}}$

32. $\dfrac{\sqrt{72}}{\sqrt{40}}$

33. $\dfrac{\sqrt{25b}}{\sqrt{5b^3}}$

34. $\dfrac{\sqrt{24}}{\sqrt{3n}}$

35. $\dfrac{\sqrt{8}}{\sqrt{30m^2}}$

36. You are making a mosaic design on a square table top. You have already covered half of the table top with 150 1-inch square tile pieces.
  a. What are the dimensions of the table top?
  b. What is the measure of the diagonal from one corner to the opposite corner of the table top?

37. The equation $r = \sqrt{\dfrac{SA}{4\pi}}$ gives the radius r of a sphere with surface area SA. What is the radius of a sphere with the given surface area? Use 3.14 for π.

  a. 1256 in^2 **b.** 200.96 cm^2 **c.** 379.94 ft^2

38. Open-Ended What are three radical expressions that simplify to $2x\sqrt{3}$?

10-2 Standardized Test Prep

Simplifying Radicals

Multiple Choice

For Exercises 1–5, choose the correct letter.

1. What is the simplified form of $\sqrt{140}$?

   A. $4\sqrt{35}$ **B.** $10\sqrt{14}$ **C.** $2\sqrt{70}$ **D.** $2\sqrt{35}$

2. What is the simplified form of $\sqrt{48n^9}$?

   F. $4n^3\sqrt{3}$ **G.** $4n^4\sqrt{3n}$ **H.** $3n\sqrt{4n^8}$ **I.** $4\sqrt{3n^9}$

3. What is the simplified form of $3\sqrt{5c} \cdot \sqrt{15c^3}$?

   A. $15c^2\sqrt{3}$ **B.** $6c^2\sqrt{5}$ **C.** $5c^2\sqrt{3}$ **D.** $12c^4\sqrt{5}$

4. Which radical expression is in simplified form?

   F. $\dfrac{11y}{\sqrt{3}}$ **G.** $\dfrac{\sqrt{6}}{5y}$ **H.** $\dfrac{\sqrt{17}}{\sqrt{4}}$ **I.** $\sqrt{\dfrac{25}{81}}$

5. A gardener is mowing a 20 yd-by-40 yd rectangular pasture using a diagonal pattern. He mows from one corner of the pasture to the corner diagonally opposite. What is the length of this pass with the mower? Give your answer in simplified form.

   A. $10\sqrt{20}$ **B.** $20\sqrt{2}$ **C.** $400\sqrt{5}$ **D.** $20\sqrt{5}$

Short Response

6. Suppose the height of the freight elevator in your building is half its width w when the doors are all the way open.

   a. What is an expression for the maximum side length of a sheet of metal that will fit through the elevator doors?

   _____

   b. If the height of the elevator is 3 meters, what is the maximum length that will fit through the doors?

   _____

10-3

Think About a Plan

Operations with Radical Expressions

Chemistry The ratio of the diffusion rates of two gases is given by the formula $\dfrac{r_1}{r_2} = \dfrac{\sqrt{m_2}}{\sqrt{m_1}}$, where m_1 and m_2 are the masses of the molecules of the gases. Find $\dfrac{r_1}{r_2}$ if $m_1 = 12$ units and $m_2 = 30$ units. Write your answer in simplified radical form.

Understanding the Problem

1. How many gases are involved in the problem? _____

2. What variables represent the masses of the molecules of the two gases? _____

3. What are the masses (in units) of the molecules of the two gases? _____

Planning the Solution

4. What ratio can you simplify to find the ratio $\dfrac{r_1}{r_2}$? _____

5. What values can you substitute for m_1 and m_2? _____

6. How can you simplify the radical expression that results when you substitute values for m_1 and m_2? _____

Getting an Answer

7. Simplify the radical expression. What is the ratio of diffusion rates between the two gases?

_____

8. Is diffusion faster or slower for the molecule with less mass? _____

9. Is the solution reasonable? Explain. _____

_____

10-3 Practice

Form G

Operations with Radical Expressions

Simplify each sum or difference.

1. $3\sqrt{7} + 5\sqrt{7}$

2. $8\sqrt{3} + \sqrt{3}$

3. $11\sqrt{5} - 4\sqrt{5}$

4. $2\sqrt{11} - 6\sqrt{11}$

5. $4\sqrt{13} + 4\sqrt{13}$

6. $\sqrt{7} - 4\sqrt{7}$

7. $4\sqrt{7} - \sqrt{63}$

8. $8\sqrt{3} + 2\sqrt{48}$

9. $6\sqrt{8} - 2\sqrt{50}$

10. $3\sqrt{20} - 2\sqrt{45}$

11. $5\sqrt{18} + 4\sqrt{32}$

12. $\sqrt{12} - 7\sqrt{75}$

Simplify each product.

13. $\sqrt{3}(\sqrt{12} + 4)$

14. $\sqrt{8}(\sqrt{3} + 3)$

15. $\sqrt{7}(\sqrt{7} - 2)$

16. $(\sqrt{3} - 4)^2$

17. $(2\sqrt{3} + \sqrt{5})(6\sqrt{5} - 4\sqrt{3})$

18. $(7 + 3\sqrt{5})(7 - 3\sqrt{5})$

Simplify each quotient.

19. $\dfrac{12}{\sqrt{11} - \sqrt{7}}$

20. $\dfrac{8}{\sqrt{3} + 1}$

21. $\dfrac{32}{\sqrt{7} - \sqrt{3}}$

22. $\dfrac{-2}{\sqrt{15} - \sqrt{7}}$

23. $\dfrac{30}{\sqrt{5} + \sqrt{2}}$

24. $\dfrac{128}{\sqrt{37} + \sqrt{5}}$

10-3

Practice (continued)   Form G

Operations with Radical Expressions

25. A painting is shaped like a golden rectangle. It's length is 24 cm. What is the painting's width to the nearest tenth of a cm?

26. A tomato fits into a 10-in.-long golden rectangle. What is the tomato's width to the nearest tenth of an inch?

27 The length of a golden rectangle is $4 + 4\sqrt{5}$. Use the ratio of length to width $(1 + \sqrt{5}) : 2$ to find the width of the golden rectangle.

28. Error Analysis A student multiplied the radical expressions shown at the right. What mistake did the student make? What is the simplified form of the radical?

$$\sqrt{3} \; (\sqrt{3} + \sqrt{6})$$
$$= \sqrt{9} + \sqrt{18}$$
$$= 6\sqrt{2}$$

29. Writing What is the conjugate of $8\sqrt{3} - \sqrt{7}$? What is the product of the conjugates? Show your work to explain your answer.

30. Find the length of the hypotenuse of the right triangle to the right. Write your answer in simplified radical form.

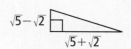

31. Open-Ended Make up three differences that are greater than or equal to 10. Use the square roots of 2, 3, 5, or 7 and whole numbers less than or equal to 10. For example, $10\sqrt{3} - 2\sqrt{7} \geq 10$.

32. A large park is designed as two 10-km squares connected at the corner and with diagonals aligned. If Riley jogs along the diagonal from one end of the park to the other end, how many total kilometers will he jog? Give your answer as a simplified radical and to the nearest tenth of a kilometer.

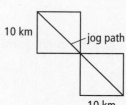

10-3 Standardized Test Prep

Operations with Radical Expressions

Multiple Choice

For Exercises 1–6, choose the correct letter.

1. What is the simplified form of $8\sqrt{5} + 5\sqrt{5}$?

   A. $3\sqrt{5}$ **B.** $13\sqrt{5}$ **C.** $40\sqrt{5}$ **D.** 200

2. What is the simplified form of $\sqrt{2} - 11\sqrt{2}$?

   F. $-10\sqrt{2}$ **G.** $-11\sqrt{2}$ **H.** $-12\sqrt{2}$ **I.** -22

3. What is the simplified form of $4\sqrt{3} - \sqrt{27}$?

   A. $-5\sqrt{3}$ **B.** $-7\sqrt{3}$ **C.** $\sqrt{3}$ **D.** $-\sqrt{9}$

4. What is the simplified form of $\sqrt{8}(\sqrt{5} + 4)$?

   F. $16\sqrt{10}$ **G.** $2\sqrt{10} + 4\sqrt{2}$ **H.** $4\sqrt{10} + 4\sqrt{2}$ **I.** $2\sqrt{10} + 8\sqrt{2}$

5. What is the simplified form of $\dfrac{40}{\sqrt{11} + \sqrt{7}}$?

   A. $10\sqrt{11} - 10\sqrt{7}$ **B.** $\dfrac{20\sqrt{11} - 20\sqrt{7}}{9}$ **C.** $30\sqrt{2}$ **D.** $10\sqrt{11} + 10\sqrt{7}$

6. A golden rectangle is 32 cm long. The ratio of length to width is $(1 + \sqrt{5}) : 2$. What is the width of the rectangle in simplest radical form?

   F. $16\sqrt{5} + 16$ **G.** $8\sqrt{5} - 8$ **H.** $16\sqrt{5} - 16$ **I.** $\dfrac{32\sqrt{5} - 32}{3}$

Short Response

7. The diagram to the right shows the design of the 12-in. quilt block that a quilter is sewing.

   a. What are the dimensions of each triangle in the quilt block? Give your answers as simplified radicals.

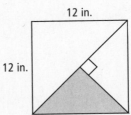

   12 in.

   12 in.

   _____

   b. What are the dimensions of each triangle to the nearest tenth of an inch?

   _____

10-4

Think About a Plan

Solving Radical Equations

Packaging The radius r of a cylindrical can with volume V and height h is given by $r = \sqrt{\dfrac{V}{\pi h}}$. What is the height of a can with a radius of 2 in. and a volume of 75 in.^{3}?

KNOW

1. What equation can you use to find the height of a cylindrical can? _____

2. What known values will you substitute into the equation? _____

3. What is the meaning of the symbol π? _____

NEED

4. Which variable represents the height of the can? _____

PLAN

5. What equation do you get after substituting the known values? _____

6. Can you solve this equation by squaring both sides? _____

7. How can you isolate the remaining variable? _____

   _____

8. Are there any extraneous solutions? If so, what are they? _____

9. What is the height of the can? _____

10. Is the solution reasonable? Explain. _____

    _____

10-4 Practice

Form G

Solving Radical Equations

Solve each radical equation. Check your solution.

1. $\sqrt{x} + 4 = 7$

2. $\sqrt{2t} - 3 = 11$

3. $4 - \sqrt{2s} = -6$

4. $\sqrt{6c + 4} = 8$

5. $\sqrt{3t - 2} = 5$

6. $2 = \sqrt{-3y - 5}$

7. $\sqrt{5n - 4} = 6$

8. $\sqrt{\dfrac{b^4}{16}} = 16$

9. $\sqrt{\dfrac{a}{2}} - 3 = -32$

10. You decide to install a rope swing at the bend in the river. The time t in seconds for the rope swing to make one swing is given by $2\sqrt{\dfrac{l}{3.3}}$, where l is the length of the rope swing in feet. If one swing takes 3.5 seconds, how long is the rope swing? Round your answer to the nearest tenth of a foot.

11. The radius r of a sphere is given by $r = \sqrt{\dfrac{SA}{4\pi}}$, where SA represents the sphere's surface area. If a sphere has a surface area of 531 in.^{2}, what is the length of its radius? Use $\pi = 3.14$. Round to the nearest hundredth of an inch.

12. The speed V in feet per second that an acorn falls from a tree is given by $V = \sqrt{64d}$, where d is the distance in feet that the acorn has fallen. An acorn hits the ground at a speed of 28 feet per second. How far did the acorn fall?

13. Harrison bought a 10-foot ramp to load his dirt bike into the back of his truck. The ramp hooks to the 3-foot-high tailgate. How far away from the tailgate does the ramp sit on the ground? Round your answer to the nearest tenth of a foot.

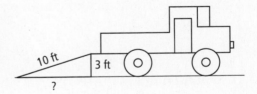

10-4 Practice (continued) Form G
Solving Radical Equations

Solve each radical equation. Check your solution.

14. $\sqrt{4d + 3} = \sqrt{7d - 3}$ **15.** $\sqrt{x + 7} = \sqrt{15 - x}$ **16.** $\sqrt{48 - 3y} = \sqrt{3y - 6}$

17. $\sqrt{a^2 + 20} = \sqrt{9a}$ **18.** $\sqrt{2x^2 + 17} = \sqrt{(x + 3)^2}$ **19.** $\sqrt{d + 7} = 3\sqrt{4d}$

20. $11 = \sqrt{12b - 59}$ **21.** $\dfrac{f}{3} = \sqrt{f - 2}$ **22.** $\dfrac{t}{4} = \sqrt{\dfrac{7t - 10}{16}}$

Solve each radical equation. Check your solution. If there is no solution, write
no solution.

23. $x = \sqrt{2x + 8}$ **24.** $m = \sqrt{-6m + 7}$ **25.** $-n = \sqrt{4n + 12}$

26. $x = \sqrt{3x + 28}$ **27.** $\dfrac{-y}{2} = \sqrt{\dfrac{-5y + 24}{4}}$ **28.** $-f = \sqrt{-f + 56}$

29. Error Analysis A student solved the equation $-t = \sqrt{5t + 14}$ and found the solutions 7 and -2. Describe and correct the error.

30. The distance d in feet that it takes an automobile to stop if it is traveling S miles per hour is given by $S = \sqrt{21d}$. Find the distance it would take an automobile traveling 60 miles per hour to stop. Round your answer to the nearest tenth of a foot.

31. Open-Ended Write two radical equations that have no solutions. Explain why all the solutions are extraneous.

10-4   Standardized Test Prep

Solving Radical Equations

Multiple Choice

For Exercises 1–6, choose the correct letter.

1. What is the solution of the radical equation $\sqrt{t} + 9 = 16$?

   A. 5   **B.** 7   **C.** 25   **D.** 49

2. What is the solution of $\sqrt{6g - 23} = \sqrt{12 - g}$?

   F. 5   **G.** 7   **H.** 11   **I.** 35

3. What are the solutions of $\sqrt{d^2 - 11} = 5$?

   A. 4, −4   **B.** 5, −5   **C.** 5, 6   **D.** 6, −6

4. Which is the extraneous solution of $-x = \sqrt{2x + 15}$?

   F. −5   **G.** −3   **H.** 3   **I.** 5

5. The pendulum of a cuckoo clock completes one full swing every t seconds. The variable t is determined by the function $t = 2\sqrt{\frac{l}{3.3}}$ where l is the length in meters of the pendulum. Each swing takes 0.5 seconds. How many centimeters long is the pendulum?

   A. 20.625 cm   **B.** 41.25 cm   **C.** 82.5 cm   **D.** 330 cm

6. A company invests $15,000 in an account that compounds interest annually. After two years, the account is worth $16,099.44. Use the function $A = P(1 + r)^2$, where r is the annual interest rate, P is the principal, and A is the amount of money after t years. What is the interest rate of the account?

   F. 1.04%   **G.** 3.6%   **H.** 5.4%   **I.** 7.3%

Extended Response

7. The radius of Earth is about 6378 kilometers. The escape velocity V_e is determined by the function $V_e = \sqrt{2gR}$ where g is acceleration due to gravity in m/s^2 and R is the radius of Earth in meters. If g for Earth is 9.8 m/s^2, what is the escape velocity of Earth? Show your work.

10-5 Think About a Plan

Graphing Square Root Functions

Firefighting When firefighters are trying to put out a fire, the rate at which they can spray water on the fire depends on the nozzle pressure. You can find the flow rate f in gallons per minute using the function $f = 120\sqrt{p}$; where p is the nozzle pressure in pounds per square inch.

    a. Graph the function.

    b. What nozzle pressure gives a flow rate of 800 gal/min?

1. What are the independent and dependent variables for this function?

2. What are the domain and range of the function?

    Domain: $p \geq$ [   ]

    Range: $f \geq$ [   ]

3. Use the function to complete the table of values for nozzle pressure and flow rate.

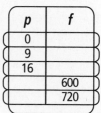

p	f
0	
9	
16	
	600
	720

4. Graph the function.

5. Which nozzle pressure on the graph corresponds to a flow rate of 800 gal/min?

_____

6. Is your answer reasonable? Explain.

_____

_____

10-5

Practice

Form G

Graphing Square Root Functions

Find the domain of each function.

1. $y = 2x\sqrt{x}$

2. $y = \frac{1}{4}\sqrt{x}$

3. $y = \sqrt{x + 3}$

4. $y = 4\sqrt{2x + 10}$

5. $y = \sqrt{x - 9}$

6. $y = 4\sqrt{\frac{x}{2}}$

7. $y = 4.3\sqrt{x + 5}$

8. $y = \sqrt{3x - 18}$

9. $\sqrt{4(x - 7)}$

10. $y = \frac{1}{2}\sqrt{12 - x}$

11. $y = \sqrt{2x + 7} - 3$

12. $y = 3\sqrt{5x - 4}$

Make a table of values and graph each function.

13. $y = \sqrt{x + 2}$

14. $y = 3\sqrt{x}$

15. $y = \sqrt{x - 3} + 1$

16. $y = 5\sqrt{x - 5}$

17. $y = 2\sqrt{x + 3} + 6$

18. $y = 7\sqrt{4x + 12} - 3$

19. The distance d a car skids in feet on dry asphalt is modeled by $S = \sqrt{21d}$, where S is the speed of the car in miles per hour upon sudden braking. What are the domain and range of the function? Graph the function. What braking distance will indicate a speed equal to or greater than 56 miles per hour?

10-5 Practice (continued)   Form G

Graphing Square Root Functions

Graph each function by translating the graph of $y = \sqrt{x}$.

20. $y = \sqrt{x} + 2$

21. $y = \sqrt{x} - 2$

22. $y = \sqrt{x + 5}$

23. $y = \sqrt{x - 4}$

24. $y = \sqrt{x + 1} - 2$

25. $y = 4\sqrt{x} - 6$

26. The distance d in miles that you can see to the horizon when looking out at the ocean is modeled by the function $d = \sqrt{1.5a}$, where a is your altitude in feet. Graph the function. At what altitude can you see 15 miles? 100 miles? Round to the nearest foot.

27. Stacey is designing a soup can. It must hold 32 cubic inches of soup and the radius must be approximately half the height. The function $r = \sqrt{\dfrac{32}{\pi h}}$ shows the radius of the can as a function of its height. What are the domain and range of the function? Graph the function. What height should Stacey design the can?

28. Error Analysis A student graphed the function $y = 6\sqrt{x - 3} + 4$ at the right. What mistake(s) did the student make? Draw the correct graph.

29. Writing Describe the steps for graphing a function of the form $y = a\sqrt{x - h} + k$.

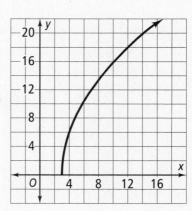

10-5 Standardized Test Prep

Graphing Square Root Functions

Multiple Choice

For Exercises 1–5, choose the correct letter.

1. What is the domain of the function $y = 3\sqrt{6x + 42}$?

   A. $x \geq 0$ **B.** $x \leq 7$ **C.** $x \geq -6$ **D.** $x \geq -7$

2. What are the domain and range of the function $y = 2\sqrt{3x + 4} - 5$?

   F. $x \geq -\frac{4}{3}; y \geq -5$ **G.** $x \geq \frac{4}{3}; y \geq -5$ **H.** $x \leq -\frac{4}{3}; y \leq -5$ **I.** $x \geq -\frac{4}{3}; y \geq 5$

3. When will the dependent variable in the equation $y = \sqrt{x + 4} - 3$ equal or exceed 4?

   A. $x \geq -0.17$ **B.** $x \geq 45$ **C.** $x \geq 48$ **D.** $x \geq 53$

4. Which function is shown on the graph to the right?

   F. $y = \sqrt{2x - 6} - 1$

   G. $y = \sqrt{2x + 6} + 1$

   H. $y = \sqrt{2x - 6} + 1$

   I. $y = \sqrt{2x + 6} - 1$

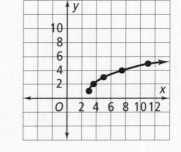

5. The function $t = \sqrt{\dfrac{d}{16}}$ models the time t in seconds that an object has been falling after the object has fallen d feet. When will the time be more than or equal to 1 minute?

   A. $d \geq 16$ ft   **B.** $d \geq 225$ ft   **C.** $d \geq 3600$ ft   **D.** $d \geq 57{,}600$ ft

Short Response

6. An amusement park ride is a spinning cylinder. At a certain speed the riders are pinned against the walls by the force of the spin and the floor drops out safely. The speed s in meters per second that is needed to pin the riders is given by $s = 4.95\sqrt{r}$ where r is the radius of the cylinder in meters.

   a. Graph the function.

   b. What is an estimate for the radius of the ride if $s = 12$ meters per second? Round to the nearest hundredth of a meter.

10-6 Think About a Plan

Trigonometric Ratios

Hobbies Suppose you are flying a kite. The kite string is 60 m long, and the angle of elevation of the string is 65° from your hand. Your hand is 1 m above the ground. How high above the ground is the kite?

KNOW

1. How high above the ground is the base of the triangle made by the kite string?_____

2. What is the length of the hypotenuse of the triangle made by the kite string?_____

3. What is the angle of elevation?_____

NEED

4. What leg of the triangle do you need to find?_____

PLAN

5. What diagram can you draw to help you solve the problem?

6. Which trigonometric ratio can you use to find the length of the missing leg?

_____

7. Write and solve an equation to find the length of the missing leg.

8. Use the distance your hand is above the ground and the length of the missing leg to find how high the kite is above the ground.

9. Is the solution reasonable? Explain.

_____

_____

10-6 Practice

Form G

Trigonometric Ratios

For △JKL and △RST, find the value of each expression.

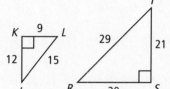

1. sin *J*	**2.** cos *J*	**3.** tan *L*
4. cos *L*	**5.** tan *T*	**6.** sin *T*
7. tan *J*	**8.** cos *R*	**9.** sin *R*
10. tan *R*	**11.** sin *L*	**12.** cos *T*

Find the value of each expression. Round to the nearest ten-thousandth.

13. sin 15°	**14.** tan 45°	**15.** cos 60°
16. tan 72°	**17.** sin 30°	**18.** cos 80°
19. sin 65°	**20.** cos 12°	**21.** tan 87°
22. tan 24°	**23.** sin 35°	**24.** cos 28°

For each triangle, find the missing side length to the nearest tenth.

25. The hypotenuse is 4 m long. How long is the side adjacent to a 40° angle?

26. A 25° angle has an opposite leg 6 cm long. How long is the adjacent leg?

27. A 52° angle has an adjacent leg 10 inches long. How long is the hypotenuse?

28. The hypotenuse is 20 mm long. How long is the side adjacent to a 15° angle?

29. A 60° angle has an adjacent leg 5 cm long. How long is the hypotenuse?

30. The hypotenuse is 13 inches long. How long is the side opposite a 50° angle?

31. A 5° angle has an opposite leg 2 ft long. How long is the adjacent leg?

32. The hypotenuse is 25 mm long. How long is the side adjacent a 70° angle?

10-6 Practice (continued) Form G

Trigonometric Ratios

For each right triangle described, find all three angles to the nearest tenth.

33. The hypotenuse is 8 ft long. The adjacent side is 5 ft long.

34. The opposite side is 12 cm long. The adjacent side is 15 cm long.

35. The hypotenuse is 6 inches long. The opposite side is 3 inches long.

36. The adjacent side is 1 m long. The opposite side is 4 m long.

37. The hypotenuse is 5 inches long. The opposite side is 2 inches long.

38. The adjacent side is 16 mm long. The hypotenuse is 22 mm long.

39. The hypotenuse is 4 m long. The opposite side is 2.5 m long.

40. The opposite side is 7 inches long. The adjacent side is 11 inches long.

41. Gayle stood at the edge of a 120-ft deep canyon. She is approximately 5 ft tall and when she looked across the canyon to the far corner, her line of sight made a 22° angle as shown in the figure. How wide was the canyon?

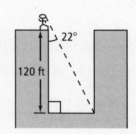

42. A parallelogram has a height of 5 cm and side measures of 8 cm and 12 cm. What are the measures of the angles?

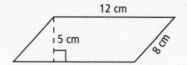

43. Error Analysis A student was finding the measure of an angle. The opposite side measured 6 cm and the hypotenuse measured 13 cm. His work is shown in the box to the right. Describe and correct the student's error.

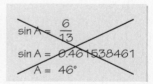

10-6

Standardized Test Prep

Trigonometric Ratios

Gridded Response

Solve each exercise and enter your answer on the grid provided.

1. For △*ABC*, what is the value of cos *C*?

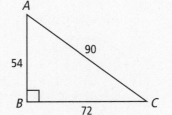

2. A right triangle's hypotenuse is 20 cm long. What is the length of the side opposite a 60° angle? Give your answer to the nearest tenth of a centimeter.

3. A right triangle's legs are 3 and 4 meters long. What is the measure of the angle adjacent to the 4-meter leg to the nearest tenth of a degree?

4. For △*XYZ*, what is the measure of the smallest angle to the nearest tenth of a degree?

5. Suppose that you are watching the tree warden trim branches from a large tree in your yard. He has climbed up 15 meters and his assistant is holding a rope that will be used to guide the branch when it falls. To the nearest meter, how long is the rope?

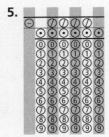

1. 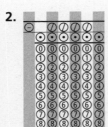   2.   3.   4.   5.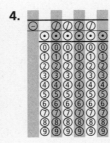

11-1 Think About a Plan

Simplifying Rational Expressions

a. Construction To keep heating costs down for a building, architects want the ratio of surface area to volume to be as small as possible. What is an expression for the ratio of surface area to volume for each shape?

i. square prism

ii. cylinder

b. Find the ratio for each figure when $b = 12$ ft, $h = 18$ ft, and $r = 6$ ft.

Understanding the Problem

1. What is a ratio? _____

2. What are the other two forms of a ratio from 2 to 4? _____

3. What are the formulas for the surface area of a square prism and of a cylinder? What are the formulas for the volume of a square prism and of a cylinder?

_____

_____

Planning the Solution

4. What is the difference between surface area and volume? _____

5. What is the ratio of the surface area to the volume for the square prism?

6. What is the ratio of the surface area to the volume for the cylinder?

Getting an Answer

7. Use the ratio in Exercise 5 to find the ratio for the square prism with the given measurements.

_____

8. Use the ratio in Step 6 to find the ratio for the cylinder with the given measurements. How does your answer compare to your answer for Exercise 7? _____

Prentice Hall Algebra 1 • Practice and Problem Solving Workbook
Copyright © by Pearson Education, Inc., or its affiliates. All Rights Reserved.

11-1 Practice

Form G

Simplifying Rational Expressions

Simplify each expression. State any excluded values.

1. $\dfrac{6p - 36}{18}$

2. $\dfrac{q + 1}{q + 4q + 3}$

3. $\dfrac{8b^5}{64b^4}$

4. $\dfrac{x + 1}{x^2 - 1}$

5. $\dfrac{56c - 14}{24c - 6}$

6. $\dfrac{3b - 6}{b^2 - 4}$

7. $\dfrac{x^2 - 144}{3x^2 - 36x}$

8. $\dfrac{n^2 - n - 12}{n^2 - 4n}$

9. $\dfrac{3x^2 + 19x - 14}{x^2 - 49}$

10. $\dfrac{7d^3 + 14d}{6d^2 - 2d}$

11. $\dfrac{25y^2 - 121}{15y - 33}$

12. $\dfrac{99q^2 - 2q - 1}{9q - 1}$

13. The length of a rectangle is $3h + 2$ and the width is $9h + 6$. What is the ratio of its length to its width? Simplify your answer.

14. The length of a rectangle is $x - 2$. Its area is $2x - 4$. What is a simplified expression for the width?

15. The area of a rectangle is $x^2 - 9$. Its width is $x - 3$. What is a simplified expression for the length?

16. **Writing** Why must the denominator of a rational expression not be equal to 0?

17. The area of a rectangle is $16a^2$. The length is $2a$. What is a simplified expression for the the width?

18. Are the given factors opposites? Explain.
   a. $3d - 7; 7 - 3d$
   b. $-y + 4; y + 4$
   c. $27 + 8x; -27 - 8x$

19. The ratio of the area of a small circle to a larger circle is $\dfrac{\pi(2x)^2}{\pi(6x)^2}$. Simplify the expression.

11-1 **Practice** (continued)   *Form G*

Simplifying Rational Expressions

---

20. A pilot packed two rectangular suitcases for her trip to Hawaii. Both hold the same volume of clothes. Her green suitcase has a length of $2y + 4$, a width of $y + 1$, and a height of $4y$. Her blue suitcase has a length of $8y^2 - 6y$ and a width of $2y$. What is a simplified expression for the height of the blue suitcase? Show your work.

21. The numerical area of a circle with radius c is equal to the numerical volume of a sphere with radius S. What is the radius of the sphere in terms of c? Show your work. (Area circle $= \pi r^2$. Volume sphere $= \frac{4}{3}\pi r^3$).

Simplify each expression. State any excluded values.

22. $\dfrac{x^2 - 9}{2x^2 - 6x}$

23. $\dfrac{n^2 p^2}{n^2 p}$

24. $\dfrac{2x^2 + 17x - 9}{x^2 - 81}$

25. $\dfrac{4d^4 - 6d^3 - 4d^2}{d^2 - 2d}$

26. $\dfrac{11y^2 + 35y - 36}{y^2 - 16}$

27. $\dfrac{6a^5 b + 4ab^3 + 3a^4 c + 2b^2 c}{2ab + c}$

28. Your brother's car is traveling $40\frac{\text{mi}}{\text{h}}$ faster than your car. During the time it takes you to go 150 mi, your brother goes 450 mi. Make a table with the information and find the speeds.

11-1 Standardized Test Prep

Simplifying Rational Expressions

Multiple Choice

For Exercises 1–4, choose the correct letter.

1. What is the simplified form of $\dfrac{x^4 - 81}{x + 3}$?

   A. $x^3 - 3x^2 + 9x - 27$ **C.** $x^3 + 3x^2 + 9x + 27$

   B. $(x^2 + 9)(x^2 - 9)$ **D.** $x^3 + 3x^2 - 9x - 27$

2. What is the simplified form of $\dfrac{(x^2yz)^2\,(xy^2z^2)}{(xyz)^2}$?

   F. $\dfrac{(xyz)^2\,(xyz)}{x}$ **G.** $\dfrac{1}{(xyz)^2}$ **H.** $x^3y^2z^2$ **I.** x^4y^4z

3. What is the excluded value of the rational expression $\dfrac{2x + 6}{4x - 8}$?

   A. -3 **B.** -2 **C.** 0 **D.** 2

4. What is the simplified form of $\dfrac{x^2 - 25}{x^2 - 3x - 10}$?

   F. $\dfrac{x - 3}{x - 5}$ **G.** $\dfrac{(x - 5)(x + 5)}{(x + 5)(x - 3)}$ **H.** $\dfrac{x + 5}{x + 2}$ **I.** $\dfrac{x - 5}{x + 2}$

Short Response

5. When an object is free falling, the equation is $d = 16t^2$ where d is the distance in feet and t is the time in seconds. What happens to the distance d as t increases from 0 to 20? Draw the graph. Plot points for values of t between 0 and 20. ($d = 16t^2$ is a quadratic equation. You can substitute $y = 16x^2$ to graph the equation.)

11-2 | Think About a Plan

Multiplying and Dividing Rational Expressions

Auto Loans You want to purchase a car that costs $18,000. The car dealership offers two different 48-month financing plans. The first plan offers 0% interest for 4 yr. The second plan offers a $2000 discount, but you must finance the rest of the purchase price at an interest rate of 7.9% for 4 yr. For which financing plan will your total cost be less? How much less will it be?

Know

1. The car costs _____.

2. There are 2 different _____-month plans.

3. The purchase price for Plan 1 is _____.

4. The interest rate for Plan 1 is _____.

5. The purchase price for Plan 2 is _____.

6. The interest rate for Plan 2 is _____.

Need

7. To solve the problems for the two plans, you need the _____.

Plan

8. Write the formula to be used by the 2 plans. _____

9. Set up the 2 formulas, 1 for each plan. _____

10. What is the total cost for Plan 1? What is the total cost for Plan 2?

11. For which financing plan will the total cost be less and how much less?

_____

11-2 **Practice** Form G

Multiplying and Dividing Rational Expressions

Multiply.

1. $\dfrac{2-z}{4+5z} \cdot \dfrac{3}{z}$

2. $\dfrac{x-9}{x+7} \cdot \dfrac{x}{x-6}$

3. $\dfrac{5w-25}{5w-10} \cdot \dfrac{w}{w^2-25}$

4. $\dfrac{16u-32}{2u} \cdot \dfrac{3u^3}{56u-24}$

5. $\dfrac{j^2+11j-42}{26j-52} \cdot \dfrac{39j}{j-3}$

6. $\dfrac{15r}{18r^2+9r-27} \cdot \dfrac{3r-3}{r^2}$

7. $\dfrac{45q^2-3q-6}{q^2} \cdot \dfrac{14q^2+10q}{35q^2+11q-10}$

8. $\dfrac{4y+17}{2y-3} \cdot (32y^2-22y-39)$

9. $(12v^2+18v-84) \cdot \dfrac{v}{4v^3-49v}$

10. $(10x^2-7x+2) \cdot \dfrac{6x^2-13x-63}{3x+7}$

11. Which of the following is the reciprocal of x^2-2x-8?

   A. $(x+2)(x-4)$ **B.** $\dfrac{1}{(x+2)(x-4)}$ **C.** $\dfrac{1}{x-8}$

Find the reciprocal of each expression.

12. $x^2-4x+18$

13. $\dfrac{3q^2}{2q^2-13}$

11-2 Practice (continued) Form G

Multiplying and Dividing Rational Expressions

Divide.

14. $\dfrac{5y + 7}{3y + 19} \div \dfrac{5y + 7}{y - 6}$

15. $\dfrac{25i^2 - 36}{56i} \div \dfrac{5i - 6}{8i}$

16. $\dfrac{12j - 36}{2j + 4} \div \dfrac{3j - 9}{4j^2 - 16}$

17. $\dfrac{12x^2 + x - 13}{45x^2 - 20x - 25} \div \dfrac{x - 1}{9x + 5}$

18. $(72k^2 + 29k - 21) \div \dfrac{9k^2 - 92k - 77}{6k - 1}$

Simplify each complex fraction.

19. $\dfrac{1 + 1}{\frac{x}{9}}$

20. $\dfrac{\frac{a}{b} + 1}{\frac{x}{b} + 3}$

21. $\dfrac{\frac{1}{a} + \frac{b}{a}}{\frac{1}{b}}$

22. A rectangular prism has a base area of $3x^2 + 21x - 24$ and a height of $\dfrac{x}{33x - 33}$. What is the volume of the prism?

23. Your friend runs for $(x^2 - 225)$ seconds at a rate of $\dfrac{1}{2x - 30}$ meters per second. How far does your friend run?

24. Writing How do you simplify a complex fraction?

11-2 Standardized Test Prep

Multiplying and Dividing Rational Expressions

Multiple Choice

For Exercises 1–3, choose the correct letter.

1. What is the quotient $\dfrac{x^2 - 16}{2x^2 - 9x + 4} \div \dfrac{2x^2 + 14x + 24}{4x + 4}$?

   A. $\dfrac{1}{x + 3}$ 　　　　**B.** $\dfrac{2x + 2}{x + 3}$ 　　　　**C.** $\dfrac{2x + 2}{2x^2 + 5x - 3}$ 　　　　**D.** $\dfrac{2(x + 1)}{2x^2 - 5x - 3}$

2. What is the simplified form for the product $\dfrac{x + 1}{x^2 - 25} \cdot \dfrac{x + 5}{x^2 + 8x + 7}$?

   F. $\dfrac{x + 1}{(x + 5)(x + 7)}$ 　　　　　　**H.** $\dfrac{1}{(x - 5)(x + 7)}$

   G. $\dfrac{1}{(x + 5)(x + 7)}$ 　　　　　　**I.** $\dfrac{1}{(x - 5)(x - 7)}$

3. What are the coordinates of the x-intercepts of the graph of $y = 2x^2 + 6x - 20$?

   A. $(-5, 0), (2, 0)$ 　　**B.** $(5, 0), (-2, 0)$ 　　**C.** $(-4, 0), (10, 0)$ 　　**D.** $(4, 0)\,(-10, 0)$

Short Response

4. A football is kicked with an upward velocity of $25\,\frac{\text{ft}}{\text{s}}$ from a starting height of 0.5 ft. Use the formula $h = -16t^2 + vt + c$, where h is the ball's height at time t, v is the initial upward velocity, and c is the starting height. What is the height when the time is 1 second? How does the height change as the time increases? What happens at 5 seconds?

11-3 Think About a Plan

Dividing Polynomials

Geometry The volume of the rectangular prism shown at the right is $m^3 + 8m^2 + 19m + 12$. What is the area of the base of the prism?

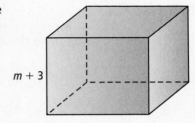

$m + 3$

Understanding the Problem

1. What is a rectangular prism?

   _____

2. What is the literal formula for the volume of a rectangular prism?

   _____

3. What is the formula for the volume of the rectangular prism shown?

   _____

Planning the Solution

4. Using the given information from Step 3, what is the area of the base of the rectangular prism equal to?

   _____

Getting an Answer

5. Divide $(m^3 + 8m^2 + 19m + 12)$ by $(m + 3)$ to find the area of the base of the prism.

   _____

6. What does $m^2 + 5m + 4$ equal?

   _____

11-3 **Practice** *Form G*

Dividing Polynomials

Divide.

1. $(c^2 - c - 1) \div c$

2. $(j^4 - 4j^3 - 8j^2) \div j^2$

3. $(3p^3 - 27p^2) \div 3p^2$

4. $(2m^2 - 5m + 2) \div 2m$

5. $(3b^5 - 9b^4 + 3b^2) \div 6b^2$

6. $(7x^4 - 28x^3) \div 4x^3$

7. $(6t^5 - 3t^4 + 18t^3 - 9t^2) \div 3t$

8. $(-104d^8 + 64d^7 - 86d^6 + 96d^5) \div 2d^4$

9. $(-27q^4 + 51q^3 - 9q^2) \div 3q^2$

10. $(-1040r^{12} - 500r^{11} - 620r^{10} + 1600r^9 + r^8) \div 20r^7$

11. $(-3u^6 - 105u^5 + 147u^4) \div (-3u^3)$

12. $(11y^{26} - 132y^{25} + 121y^{24}) \div (-11y^{24})$

13. $(p^2 + 3p + 2) \div (p + 1)$

14. $(x^2 + 7x + 12) \div (x + 4)$

15. $(p^2 - 5p - 36) \div (p + 4)$

16. $(2q^2 - 4q - 240) \div (q - 12)$

17. $(6x^2 + x - 1) \div (3x - 1)$

18. $(20a^2 + 2a - 4) \div (2a + 1)$

19. $(4t^2 - 64) \div (t + 4)$

20. $(z^2 - 9) \div (z - 3)$

21. $(3x^2 - x^3 + x - 3) \div (-x + 1)$

22. $(c^4 - 16) \div (c - 2)$

23. The area of a rectangle is $x^2 - x - 2$ and the length of the rectangle is $x + 1$.

    a. Find the width of the rectangle.

    b. Find the area of the rectangle if the width is 4 m.

11-3 **Practice** (continued)

Dividing Polynomials

Divide.

24. $(28n^2 - 17n - 3) \div (4n - 3)$

25. $(2t^2 - 8t + 6) \div (t - 3)$

26. $(3c^2 - 5c - 2) \div (6c + 2)$

27. $(3c^2 - 5c - 2) \div (3c + 1)$

28. $(2j^2 - 3j - 9) \div (j - 3)$

29. $(4j^2 - 6j - 18) \div (j - 3)$

30. $(-3x^2 + x^3 - x + 3) \div (x - 1)$

31. $(3x^2 - x^3 + x - 3) \div (-x + 1)$

32. $9d^4 - 729 \div (-3 + d)$

33. $(-3x^2 + 6x^3 + x - 40) \div (-2 + x)$

34. Find the height of a trapezoid if the area of the trapezoid is $2x^2 + 11x + 5$, the length of one base is x, and the length of the other base is $x + 10$. The formula for the area A of a trapezoid with height h and bases b_1 and b_2 is $A = \dfrac{b_1 + b_2}{2} \cdot h$.

35. The area of the rectangle is $x^4 - 9x^3 - 7x^2 - 8x + 2$. The length is given. What is the width?

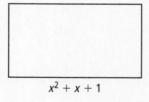

$x^2 + x + 1$

36. Writing If the area of a rectangle is a polynomial and the length of one of the sides is a polynomial, can the measurement of the width of the rectangle be a polynomial quotient with a remainder? Explain.

11-3

Standardized Test Prep

Dividing Polynomials

Multiple Choice

For Exercises 1–4, choose the correct letter.

1. What is the remainder of $(x^3 - 6x^2 - 9x + 3) \div (x - 3)$?

   A. -51 **B.** $\dfrac{-51}{x-3}$ **C.** $\dfrac{-17}{x}$ **D.** $\dfrac{-17}{x-3}$

2. If the area of a rectangle is $x^2 - 9$, can the length be $x - 1$?

   F. Yes; it divides perfectly.

   G. No; the length would be larger.

   H. Yes; but the width will have a remainder.

   I. No; the measurements of the rectangle must multiply and divide evenly.

3. If a line passes through the points $(2, 0)$ and $(-2, -3)$, what is the y-intercept of the line?

   A. $\dfrac{-3}{2}$ **B.** $\dfrac{3}{2}$ **C.** $\dfrac{3}{4}$ **D.** $\dfrac{-3}{4}$

4. What coordinates satisfy the equation of the line $y = -\dfrac{7}{8}x + 2$?

   F. $(-8, 11)$ **G.** $\left(-4, \dfrac{11}{2}\right)$ **H.** both F and G   **I.** $\left(4, \dfrac{11}{2}\right)$

Short Response

5. What are the factors of the expression $x^2 + 12x - 64$? What number would you change to make it a perfect square? Explain.

11-4 Think About a Plan

Adding and Subtracting Rational Expressions

Rowing A rowing team practices rowing 2 mi upstream and 2 mi downstream. The team can row downstream 25% faster than they can row upstream.

a. Let u represent the team's rate rowing upstream. Write and simplify an expression involving u for the total amount of time they spend rowing.

b. Let d represent the team's rate rowing downstream. Write and simplify an expression involving d for the total amount of time they spend rowing.

c. **Reasoning** Do the expressions you wrote in parts (a) and (b) represent the same time? Explain.

Know

1. What is the distance the team rows upstream? _____

2. What is the distance the team rows downstream? _____

3. How much faster does the team row downstream? _____

Need

4. What is the formula for time written in terms of the distance d and the rate r? _____

5. Write expressions for the time rowing upstream and the time rowing downstream by substituting values for the distance and variables for the rate in the formula in Exercise 4.
   a. Time rowing upstream = _____
   b. Time rowing downstream = _____

Plan

6. Write an equation that relates to u and d.

   _____

7. Rewrite the expressions you wrote in Exercise 6 in terms of u.

   a. _____

   b. _____

8. Do the expressions you wrote in Exercise 7 represent the same time? Why or why not?

   _____

   _____

11-4 Practice

Form G

Adding and Subtracting Rational Expressions

Add or subtract.

1. $\frac{1}{a} + \frac{1}{a}$

2. $\frac{11}{2y} + \frac{27}{2y}$

3. $\frac{m}{m+4} + \frac{4}{m+4}$

4. $\frac{t-1}{t} - \frac{t+1}{t}$

5. $\frac{n}{1-n} + \frac{1}{n-1}$

6. $\frac{1-m}{m-4} - \frac{-2m+1}{m+4}$

7. $\frac{2}{y} - \frac{3y}{8}$

8. $\frac{4x}{3} - \frac{3}{4x}$

9. $\frac{2a+1}{a} + \frac{a+2}{2}$

Find the LCM of each pair of expressions.

10. $6x; 3$

11. $40x^2y^2; 8y^2$

12. $3a - 3; 3$

13. $z^2 - 4; z + 2$

14. $4d^2 - 64; 4$

15. $10a^2b^4c^4; 5ab^3c^2$

16. Does it matter whether you use the LCD first or the GCF first when adding or subtracting a rational expression with different denominators and simplifying? Use an example to justify your claim.

17. Is there ever a time when it is all right to add or subtract the denominators when adding or subtracting a rational expression? Explain.

Simplify. Add or subtract.

18. $\frac{x-3}{2(x+5)} + \frac{1}{x}$

19. $\frac{3x}{2x} - 2x$

11-4 Practice (continued) Form G

Adding and Subtracting Rational Expressions

Add, subtract, and/or simplify.

20. $\dfrac{3}{a} + \dfrac{4}{x}$

21. $\dfrac{2}{x-1} + 10$

22. $\dfrac{-x}{2} + 3$

23. $1 + \dfrac{a}{b}$

24. $\dfrac{m}{x} + \dfrac{4}{m(x-1)}$

25. $\dfrac{a}{b} + \dfrac{x}{y}$

26. $\dfrac{21.5}{4x} - \dfrac{5.5}{3x}$

27. $\dfrac{1+2}{x} - \dfrac{12}{5x}$

28. $\dfrac{1}{x-1} + \dfrac{-x+1}{x^2}$

29. Your friend bought $n + 8$ outfits and her sister bought $\dfrac{n+2}{n+3}$ outfits. Write an expression for the number of outfits they bought.

30. What is the perimeter of a rectangular garden that is $\dfrac{5+x}{2}$ ft long and $\dfrac{2x-1}{3}$ ft wide?

31. Your brother ran to school at a rate of 6 mi/h. He walked back home at a rate of 4 mi/h. How far is it to school if the round trip takes 1 hour?

32. Adding two rational expressions leads to a solution of $\dfrac{5x}{6}$. One expression is $\dfrac{x}{3}$. What is the other one? Show your work.

33. Writing Explain how to use opposites to find the sum $\dfrac{8}{1-2x} + \dfrac{x}{2x-1}$.

34. Open-Ended Write a problem that uses addition of rational expressions.

11-4 Standardized Test Prep

Adding and Subtracting Rational Expressions

Multiple Choice

For Exercises 1–5, choose the correct letter.

1. What is the difference $\dfrac{5x-2}{4x} - \dfrac{x-2}{4x}$?

   A. 1 **B.** $\dfrac{x-1}{x}$ **C.** 0 **D.** $\dfrac{3}{2}$

2. What is the sum $\dfrac{1}{2b} + \dfrac{b}{2}$?

   F. $\dfrac{b+1}{2b+2}$ **G.** $2b$ **H.** $\dfrac{1}{4}$ **I.** $\dfrac{b^2+1}{2b}$

3. What is the sum $\dfrac{1}{g+2} + \dfrac{3}{g+1}$?

   A. $\dfrac{3}{g+3}$ **B.** $\dfrac{g+3}{(g+1)(g+2)}$ **C.** $\dfrac{4g+7}{(g+1)(g+2)}$ **D.** $\dfrac{2g+3}{(g+1)(g+2)}$

4. What is the difference $\dfrac{r+2}{r+4} - \dfrac{3}{r+1}$?

   F. $\dfrac{-1}{r+3}$ **G.** $\dfrac{r^2-1}{(r+1)(r+4)}$ **H.** $\dfrac{r^2-10}{(r+1)(r+4)}$ **I.** $\dfrac{r^2+14}{(r+1)(r+4)}$

5. What is the sum $\dfrac{a-1}{abc^3} + \dfrac{3-b}{abc^3}$?

   A. $\dfrac{a-b-3}{abc^3}$ **B.** $\dfrac{a-b+2}{abc^3}$ **C.** $\dfrac{a-4+b}{abc^3}$ **D.** $\dfrac{-3}{c^3}$

Short Response

6. Elena went on a 6-mile walk. She completed the first half of the walk 1 mi/h faster than usual and the second half of the walk 2 mi/h slower than the first half.
   a. If it took her 7.2 h to complete the walk, what is her usual rate?
   b. What is the formula necessary to solve this problem?

11-5

Think About a Plan

Solving Rational Equations

Running You take 94 min to complete a 10-mi race. Your average speed during the first half of the race is 2 mi/h greater than your average speed during the second half of the race. What is your average speed during the first half of the race?

Understanding the Problem

1. What is the distance of the first half of the race? _____

2. What is the distance of the second half of the race? _____

3. What is the total time it takes to complete the race? _____

Planning the Solution

4. Rewrite the distance formula $d = rt$ for time t in terms of distance d and rate r. _____

5. Use your answer to Exercise 4 to write an expression for the time it takes to run each part of the race.

   a. Time for first half of race = _____

   b. Time for second half of race = _____

6. Compare the units of the given time it takes to complete the race with the units of the description of the average speed. Write the time so that it matches the units in the rates.

   _____

Getting an Answer

7. Write an equation for the total time it takes to complete the race. Solve the equation. What is the rate for the first half of the race?

   _____

11-5 Practice

Form G

Solving Rational Equations

Solve each equation. Check your solutions.

1. $\dfrac{1}{2-j} + 2 = \dfrac{4}{2-j}$

2. $\dfrac{8}{c+2} - 6 = \dfrac{4}{c+2}$

3. $\dfrac{3}{2p-2} - 1 = \dfrac{4}{p-1} + 2$

4. $\dfrac{2}{x-2} + \dfrac{3}{4} = \dfrac{2}{x-2}$

5. $\dfrac{5}{d+2} + \dfrac{d}{5} = \dfrac{d+5}{5}$

6. $-\dfrac{3}{a} - \dfrac{3}{a-3} = \dfrac{3}{2}$

7. $\dfrac{4}{n} - 1 = \dfrac{2}{n+2} - 1$

8. $\dfrac{x}{x-3} + \dfrac{2}{x+3} = 1$

9. $\dfrac{p+7}{p+2} - 2 = \dfrac{2-p}{p+4}$

10. $\dfrac{2}{p+3} = \dfrac{7}{28p}$

11. $\dfrac{a}{a+6} = \dfrac{2}{a+6}$

12. $\dfrac{-6}{4-d} = \dfrac{2d}{d-2}$

13. It takes you about an hour to make one batch of cookie dough and your brother about 42 minutes to make one batch. How much time does it take you to make a batch of cookie dough together?

14. Your dad can clean the house in 2 hours and 10 minutes. Your mom can clean it in an hour and 45 minutes. How many hours does it take them to clean the house if they work together?

Solve each equation. Check your solutions. If there is no solution, write *no solution*.

15. $\dfrac{x-1}{x+2} + \dfrac{4x}{2x^2 - 2x - 12} = 2$

16. $\dfrac{t-1}{3t^2 - t - 2} - \dfrac{2t-3}{3t+2} = \dfrac{-4}{2t-2}$

17. $\dfrac{2-2p}{p^2 - 6p + 8} + \dfrac{3p}{p-4} = \dfrac{p}{p-2}$

18. $\dfrac{d-4}{d+4} = \dfrac{4+d}{d-2} - \dfrac{d+8}{d^2 + 2d - 8}$

11-5

Practice (continued)

Form G

Solving Rational Equations

19. It takes you 12 hours to paint a house, your brother 14 hours, and your sister 10 hours. If all three of you work together, how long will it take you to paint the house?

20. Maria, LaShawn, and Mike are all students. It takes Maria 8 hours to write half of her paper for history class. It takes LaShawn $2x$ hours to write one third of her paper, and Mike takes $(x - 2)$ hours to write half of his paper. If the teacher tells them they can work on the paper as a group, how long will it take them to complete it?

21. Error Analysis Edward solved the rational equation $\frac{3x(x - 2)}{x} - x\left(\frac{96}{3x}\right) = 3x\left(\frac{1}{3}\right)$ and got an answer of $x = -19$. What was his mistake?

22. Writing Write a rational equation that has $n = 10$ for the answer. Include at least 3 terms in your equation, one of which should be a quadratic equation or a perfect square.

23. A pool has 2 pipes, one to fill it and one to empty it. Ms. Simon wants to fill the pool, but she mistakenly turns on both pipes at the same time. The pipe that fills the pool can fill it in 6 hours and the one that drains it can do that job in 10 hours. How long will it take to fill the pool now that both pipes are filling and emptying it at the same time?

24. What is the LCD of the equation $\frac{t(t - 2)}{2t - 3} - 4\left(\frac{1}{t}\right) = 5t - \frac{3(t + 4)}{t + 1}$?

Solve each equation. Check your solutions.

25. $\frac{c}{c + 4} + \frac{3}{c - 3} = \frac{16}{c^2 + c - 12}$

26. $\frac{12}{y + 1} - \frac{(y + 4)(y - 4)}{y - 2} = -1$

11-5 Standardized Test Prep

Solving Rational Equations

Multiple Choice

For Exercises 1–4, choose the correct letter.

1. What is the excluded value of the equation $y = \dfrac{2}{x-1} + 1$?

   A. -1 **B.** 0 **C.** 1 **D.** 2

2. A bus trip along the coast takes one route going, for a total of 1024 miles, and another route returning, for a total of 896 miles. If the bus travels at a constant speed of 65 mi/h, how far did the bus travel per second on the return trip?

   F. 0.07 mi/s   **G.** 13.8 mi/s   **H.** 896 mi/s   **I.** 0.0181 mi/s

3. What is the LCD for the equation $\dfrac{6-x}{2x^2y} - \dfrac{2x}{3xy^2} = \dfrac{x}{x^2y^2}$?

   A. $6x^2y^2$ **B.** x^2y^2 **C.** $12x^2y^2$ **D.** $6xy$

4. What is the excluded value of the rational expression? Include all possible solutions.

$$y = \dfrac{1}{x^2 + 2x - 24}$$

   F. $0, 24$ **G.** $6, -4$ **H.** $4, 6$ **I.** $4, -6$

Short Response

5. Every morning Diane runs 6 miles in about an hour. What is her rate in feet per second? What equations would you use to solve? Explain and show your work.

11-6 Think About a Plan

Inverse Variation

Writing Explain how the variable y changes in each situation.
a. y varies directly with x. The value of x is doubled.
b. y varies inversely with x. The value of x is doubled.

Understanding the Problem

1. What is the formula for a direct variation involving the values x and y, and what is the constant of variation in that formula?

   _____

2. How does the value of y change when the value of x increases in a direct variation?

   _____

3. What is the formula for an inverse variation involving the values for x and y and what is the constant of variation?

   _____

4. How does the value of y change when the value of x increases in an inverse variation?

   _____

Planning the Solution

5. Choose a constant of variation and write the direct variation formula and the inverse variation formula using this constant of variation. Then find values of x and y that satisfy each equation. Be sure to double the values of x that you choose.

Getting an Answer

6. Explain how the variable y changes.
   a. For a direct variation, when x is doubled, y _____.

   b. For an inverse variation, when x is doubled, y _____.

11-6 Practice

Inverse Variation

Form G

Suppose y varies inversely with x. Write an equation for the inverse variation.

1. $y = 20$ when $x = 5$ **2.** $y = 16$ when $x = -2$ **3.** $y = \frac{3}{5}$ when $x = 15$

4. $y = 1.2$ when $x = -4$ **5.** $y = \frac{2}{3}$ when $x = \frac{4}{5}$ **6.** $y = -0.5$ when $x = -2.4$

7. If y varies inversely with x, and $y = 12$ when $x = 11$, find the constant of variation k.

8. If y varies inversely with x, solve for y if the constant of variation $k = 8$ and $x = \frac{2}{3}$.

Graph each inverse variation.

9. $y = \frac{12}{x}$ **10.** $xy = -6$ **11.** $xy = 30$ **12.** $y = \frac{-10}{x}$

13. Two fifth graders play on the seesaw. One fifth grader weighs 75 lb and the other weighs 90 lb. In order to balance the seesaw so both can ride, how far from the center pole does the 90 lb fifth grader have to be if the 75 lb fifth grader is 6 ft from the center? Weight and distance vary inversely.

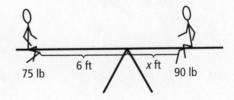

14. In Exercise 13, what if the 75 lb fifth grader and a friend of equal weight sit 4 ft from the center of the seesaw to balance the 90 lb fifth grader? How far from the center should the 90 lb fifth grader be?

15. Speed equals $\frac{\text{distance}}{\text{time}}$. If a car is traveling at a constant speed of 60 $\frac{\text{km}}{\text{h}}$, how many minutes does it take to go 20 km and then 40 km? Is this a direct variation or an inverse variation? How do you know?

16. In a given equation, C varies inversely with D. If C is 50 when $D = 11.5$, find C when D is 20.

11-6

Practice (continued)

Inverse Variation

17. Graph the equations $xy = 4$ and $xy = -4$. **18.** Graph $xy = \frac{1}{4}$. How is it like the graph How are the graphs of $xy = 4$ and of $xy = 4$? How is it different? $xy = -4$ alike? How are they different?

Do the data in each table represent a *direct variation* or an *inverse variation*? Write an equation to model the data in each table.

19.

x	y
−2	−6
3	4
6	2

20.

x	y
−2	−6
3	9
6	18

21.

x	y
−8	6
−2	24
12	−4

Tell whether each situation represents a *direct variation* or an *inverse variation*.

22. You buy strawberries for $2.99/pt.

23. You earn $7.25/hour.

24. A 10-in. cake is shared equally by your study group.

Tell whether each table represents a *direct variation* or an *inverse variation*. Write an equation to model the data. Then complete each table.

25.

x	y
−24	−2
	1
36	3

26.

x	y
−72	8
36	−4
63	

27.

x	y
−5	−5
1	25
	50

11-6 Standardized Test Prep

Inverse Variation

Gridded Response

Solve each exercise and enter your answer on the grid provided.

1. Suppose y varies inversely with x, and $y = 16$ when $x = 4$. What is the constant of variation k?

2. If 9 students sharpen 18 pencils in 2 minutes, how many students will it take to sharpen 18 pencils in 1 minute?

3. If y varies inversely with x, and $y = -16$ when $x = -64$, what is the constant of variation?

4. The pair of points $(3, 8)$ and $(x, 6)$ are on the graph of an inverse variation. What is the missing value?

5. The weight needed to balance a lever varies inversely with the distance from the fulcrum to the weight. A 120-lb weight is placed on a lever, 5 ft from the fulcrum. What amount of weight, in pounds, should be placed 8 ft from the fulcrum to balance the lever?

1.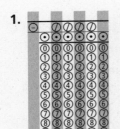
2.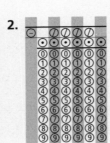
3.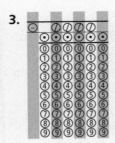
4.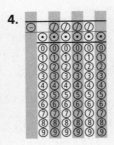
5.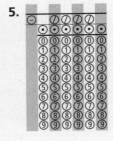

11-7 Think About a Plan

Graphing Rational Functions

Physics As radio signals move away from a transmitter, they become weaker. The function $s = \dfrac{1600}{d^2}$ gives the strength s of a signal at a distance of d miles from a transmitter.

   a. Graphing Calculator Graph the function. For what distances is $s \leq 1$?

   b. Find the signal strength at 10 mi, 1 mi, and 0.1 mi.

   c. Reasoning Suppose you drive by the transmitter for one radio station while your car radio is tuned to a second station. The signal from the transmitter can interfere and come through your radio. Use your results from part (b) to explain why.

Understanding the Problem

   1. What kind of equation is $s = \dfrac{1600}{d^2}$? _____

   2. What is s? What is d? _____

   3. As d gets bigger, what happens to s? As d gets smaller what happens to s? Can $d \leq 0$? _____

Planning the Solution

   4. For part (a): Before graphing in the graphing calculator, set $s = 1$ and solve the equation by hand. What does d equal ? _____

   5. For part (b): Now that you have found where $s = 1$, what does s equal when $d = 0$? How does the graph of s change between $d = 0$ and $d = 1$? _____

Getting an Answer

   6. For part (a): Use the graphing calculator to graph.

   7. For part (b): Solve by hand. Insert 10 mi, 1 mi, and 0.1 mi into the equation for d. What does s equal at each value? _____

   8. For part (c): Use the values of s at 10 mi, 1 mi, and 0.1 mi from part (b) to answer part (c). What is the pattern? Why is this important to answer part (c)? _____

_____

11-7 Practice   *Form G*

Graphing Rational Functions

Identify the excluded value of each rational function.

1. $y = \frac{2}{x}$

2. $f(x) = \frac{-3}{x + 1}$

3. $y = \frac{10}{2x + 2}$

4. $f(x) = \frac{-4}{x + 6}$

5. $y = \frac{9}{x}$

6. $y = \frac{x}{4x + 8}$

Identify the asymptotes of the graph of each function. Then graph the function.

7. $y = \frac{2.5}{x}$

8. $f(x) = \frac{4}{3 + x}$

9. Find the domain for x in the equation $xy = 1$.

10. Graph the equation $xy = 1$. What happens to the values of y as x approaches 0 from the left and from the right?

11. Identify the horizontal asymptote for the graph of the equation $y = \frac{-2.5}{x + 17} + 3$. How many units has the graph of $y = \frac{-2.5}{x}$ been vertically translated?

12. Identify the horizontal and vertical asymptotes of $y = \frac{1}{x} + 1$ without graphing or making a table. Explain how you figured out what they were.

Describe how the graph of each function is a translation of the graph of $y = \frac{-1}{x}$.

13. $y = \frac{-1}{x + 4} + 3$

14. $y = \frac{-1}{x - 4} + 3$

15. $y = \frac{-1}{x + 4} - 3$

11-7 **Practice** (continued)   *Form G*

Graphing Rational Functions

Describe the graph of each function.

16. $y = 5x$

17. $f(x) = 2^x$

18. $f(x) = |x - 3|$

19. $y = \sqrt{x + 5}$

20. $g(x) = \dfrac{4x + 1}{2}$

21. $y = -x + 6$

22. $y = x^2 - 16$

23. $g(x) = \dfrac{2}{x + 7} - 3$

24. Graphing Calculator Maria invites 14 friends over to eat a cake she baked that contains 3000 calories. Every friend also has a glass of milk worth 100 calories each, but two friends do not eat the cake. Write an equation for how many calories each person who has cake consumes. Solve the equation. Then use your graphing calculator to graph it. Find the number of calories each person would consume if only 8 people showed up.

25. Open-Ended Write an example of a rational function with a vertical asymptote at $x = 1$ and a horizontal asymptote at $y = -5$.

26. Graph and describe the similarities and differences between each of these functions.

    a. $f(x) = \dfrac{1}{x}$
    b. $f(x) = \dfrac{1}{x - 1}$
    c. $f(x) = \dfrac{1}{x + 1} + 5$

11-7 Standardized Test Prep

Graphing Rational Functions

Multiple Choice

For Exercises 1–4, choose the correct letter.

1. A philanthropist gives $50,000 to students who have helped the community. The money is divided equally among these students. There is no limit to the number of students x. All students with good community projects will get a share of the money. In addition, these students will get $2000 up front from a separate fund. What equation shows the amount of money each student receives?

   A. $y = \dfrac{50,000}{x + 2000}$ **B.** $y = \dfrac{50,000}{x} + 2000$ **C.** $y = \dfrac{50,000}{x - 2000}$ **D.** $y = \dfrac{50,000}{x} - 2000$

2. You have $1200 in a bank account. The simple annual interest rate is 4%. How much interest is added to the account after 9 months?

   F. $48 **G.** $96 **H.** $30 **I.** $36

3. A trip from Ohio to New York is 529 mi. What equation shows the time, t, it takes to go by car if r is the average speed during the trip?

   A. $t = \dfrac{529}{r}$ **B.** $t = 529r$ **C.** $r = 529t$ **D.** $t = \dfrac{r}{529}$

4. What is an equation for the graph that passes through points $\left(2, 2\frac{1}{4}\right)$ and $\left(-2, 1\frac{3}{4}\right)$?

   F. $y = \dfrac{-1}{4x} + 4$ **G.** $y = \dfrac{1}{2x} + 2$ **H.** $y = \dfrac{1}{4x} + 2$ **I.** $y = \dfrac{1}{2x} + 4$

Short Response

5. Tracey wants to buy a house. She needs a salary of $3600 a month to qualify for the mortgage. Tracey works at a bank for $20/h for 160 hours each month. After work, she has a second job at the mall and makes $16/h. How many hours would she have to work at the mall in order to make enough money to qualify for the mortgage? Show your work.

12-1 Think About a Plan

Organizing Data Using Matrices

Politics The results of an election for mayor are shown below. The town will hold a runoff election between the top two candidates if no one receives more than 50% of the votes. Should the town hold a runoff? If so, which candidates should be in the runoff? Explain your reasoning.

Votes by Precinct

Candidate	Precinct			
	1	2	3	4
Greene	373	285	479	415
Jackson	941	871	114	97
Voigt	146	183	728	682

Understanding the Problem

1. What does each column in the table represent?

2. What does each row in the table represent?

Planning the Solution

3. How will you find how many total votes each candidate received?

4. How will you find how many total votes were cast?

5. How will you find the percentage of votes for each candidate?

Getting an Answer

6. How many votes did each candidate receive?

7. What percent of the votes did each candidate receive?

8. Did any candidate receive more than 50% of the total votes?

9. Who are the top two candidates?

10. Should the town hold a runoff between the top two candidates?

12-1 **Practice**   *Form G*

Organizing Data Using Matrices

Find each sum or difference.

1. $\begin{bmatrix} 2 & 3 \\ -2 & -3 \end{bmatrix} + \begin{bmatrix} 1 & -5 \\ 3 & 2 \end{bmatrix}$ **2.** $\begin{bmatrix} 0 & 4 \\ 5 & -2 \end{bmatrix} + \begin{bmatrix} -2 & 2 \\ -6 & 1 \end{bmatrix}$ **3.** $\begin{bmatrix} 3 & -5 \\ 0 & -2 \end{bmatrix} - \begin{bmatrix} -2 & -1 \\ 3 & 3 \end{bmatrix}$

4. $\begin{bmatrix} 9 & 2 \\ -4 & 3 \\ 0 & -5 \end{bmatrix} - \begin{bmatrix} -3 & 1 \\ -1 & 0 \\ 6 & 5 \end{bmatrix}$ **5.** $\begin{bmatrix} 1 & 9 \\ -1 & 0 \\ -3 & 3.5 \end{bmatrix} - \begin{bmatrix} 1.3 & -2 \\ 1 & -3 \\ 4 & 2 \end{bmatrix}$ **6.** $\begin{bmatrix} 2.1 & 4 \\ 3.5 & 3 \\ 0 & 6.7 \end{bmatrix} + \begin{bmatrix} 3.4 & -8 \\ -3 & 2.2 \\ -4.1 & -0.7 \end{bmatrix}$

7. $\begin{bmatrix} 0.1 & -3 & 2.3 \\ 0 & 1.2 & -1 \\ 3 & 3.5 & -2.6 \end{bmatrix} + \begin{bmatrix} 3.2 & 0 & -2 \\ 4.7 & 8 & -8 \\ 3.4 & -2 & 6.1 \end{bmatrix}$ **8.** $\begin{bmatrix} 0.1 & -3 & 2.3 \\ 0 & 1.2 & -1 \\ 3 & 3.5 & -2.6 \end{bmatrix} - \begin{bmatrix} 3.2 & 0 & -2 \\ 4.7 & 8 & -8 \\ 3.4 & -2 & 6.1 \end{bmatrix}$

9. $\begin{bmatrix} -2 & 1.3 & 4.4 \\ 0 & 1.2 & -2 \\ 4 & 2 & -2.6 \end{bmatrix} - \begin{bmatrix} 3.4 & 0 & -0.5 \\ 5.2 & 8 & -1.2 \\ 2.3 & -2 & 1 \end{bmatrix}$ **10.** $\begin{bmatrix} 5 & -1.5 & 3.1 \\ 8 & 1.2 & -1 \\ 6 & 5.4 & -2.6 \end{bmatrix} + \begin{bmatrix} 3.2 & 0 & -2 \\ -4.9 & -3.5 & 1.9 \\ 0.5 & -2.4 & 2.6 \end{bmatrix}$

Find each product.

11. $3 \begin{bmatrix} 2 & -1 \\ 6 & 0 \end{bmatrix}$ **12.** $-5 \begin{bmatrix} -1 & 3 \\ 2 & -2 \end{bmatrix}$ **13.** $6 \begin{bmatrix} 0.5 & 1.2 & -2 \\ 3.2 & -0.4 & 0 \end{bmatrix}$

14. $4 \begin{bmatrix} 8 & -2 \\ 0 & 4 \end{bmatrix}$ **15.** $0 \begin{bmatrix} -2 & 7 \\ -5 & 3 \end{bmatrix}$ **16.** $-3 \begin{bmatrix} 0.4 & 6.6 & -5 \\ 2.7 & -0.3 & 0 \end{bmatrix}$

17. $-1 \begin{bmatrix} 4 & 9 \\ -3 & -6 \end{bmatrix}$ **18.** $3 \begin{bmatrix} 7 & -5 \\ 3 & 1 \end{bmatrix}$ **19.** $-4 \begin{bmatrix} 1.2 & -3.4 & -2 \\ 3.1 & -0.7 & 3 \end{bmatrix}$

12-1 **Practice** (continued)

Form G

Organizing Data Using Matrices

20. Seasonal rainfall, in inches, for four cities is shown below. Which city had the greatest increase in summer rainfall between 2006 and 2010? Find the answer using matrices.

Rainfall in 2006

	Spring	Summer
Franklin	6.32	7.21
Eugene	4.19	6.97
Millerville	1.24	5.46
Lafayette	5.51	7.19

Rainfall in 2010

	Spring	Summer
Franklin	6.41	7.52
Eugene	4.18	7.02
Millerville	1.67	4.24
Lafayette	6.01	7.94

21. Race times, in seconds, for four members of the track team are shown below. For each distance run, which runner showed the greatest improvement, in seconds, from the preliminary race to the final race? Find the answers using matrices.

Preliminary race

	200m	400m
Haddock	24.69	57.02
Romano	25.53	61.16
Chandra	25.56	59.67
Moore	24.81	58.11

Final race

	200m	400m
Haddock	24.61	58.08
Romano	25.52	60.38
Chandra	25.63	57.72
Moore	24.72	58.52

Simplify each expression. (*Hint*: Multiply before adding or subtracting.)

22. $\begin{bmatrix} 1 & -2 \\ 1 & 2 \end{bmatrix} + 6\begin{bmatrix} 0 & 3 \\ -1 & 1 \end{bmatrix}$ **23.** $-3\begin{bmatrix} 2 & -2 \\ 6 & 4 \end{bmatrix} - \begin{bmatrix} 0 & 1 \\ -4 & -5 \end{bmatrix}$ **24.** $\begin{bmatrix} -8 & 3 \\ 1 & 4 \end{bmatrix} + 1.5\begin{bmatrix} -6 & 4 \\ 6 & 0 \end{bmatrix}$

25. $\begin{bmatrix} 0 & -3 \\ 3 & 5 \end{bmatrix} - 2\begin{bmatrix} -1 & 4 \\ 3 & 0 \end{bmatrix}$ **26.** $-4\begin{bmatrix} 3 & 0 \\ -2 & 0.5 \end{bmatrix} - \begin{bmatrix} 11 & -5 \\ -6 & -2 \end{bmatrix}$ **27.** $\begin{bmatrix} 0 & 5 \\ 1.2 & 3 \end{bmatrix} + 0.5\begin{bmatrix} -8 & 6 \\ 1.2 & 8 \end{bmatrix}$

28. $3\begin{bmatrix} 5 & 2 \\ -3 & 2 \\ -1 & 1 \end{bmatrix} - 2\begin{bmatrix} 5 & 0 \\ 2 & 4 \\ -2 & 3 \end{bmatrix}$ **29.** $2\begin{bmatrix} -1 & -1 & 3 \\ 4 & 6 & 1.5 \\ 0 & -2 & 2.5 \end{bmatrix} + (-0.1)\begin{bmatrix} 2.2 & -4 & 10 \\ -1.6 & 3 & -1 \\ 0 & 4 & 6.6 \end{bmatrix}$

12-1

Standardized Test Prep
Organizing Data Using Matrices

Multiple Choice

For Exercises 1–5, choose the correct letter.

1. What is the sum: $\begin{bmatrix} 3 & -2 \\ 4 & -3 \end{bmatrix} + \begin{bmatrix} -5 & -4 \\ 3 & -2 \end{bmatrix}$?

   A. $\begin{bmatrix} -8 & 2 \\ 1 & 6 \end{bmatrix}$　　　**B.** $\begin{bmatrix} -2 & 2 \\ 7 & -1 \end{bmatrix}$　　　**C.** $\begin{bmatrix} 2 & 6 \\ -7 & 5 \end{bmatrix}$　　　**D.** $\begin{bmatrix} -2 & -6 \\ 7 & -5 \end{bmatrix}$

2. What is the difference: $\begin{bmatrix} 3 & -2 \\ 4 & -3 \end{bmatrix} - \begin{bmatrix} 2 & -5 \\ 7 & 12 \end{bmatrix}$?

   F. $\begin{bmatrix} -3 & 3 \\ -1 & 7 \end{bmatrix}$　　　**G.** $\begin{bmatrix} 1 & 3 \\ -3 & -15 \end{bmatrix}$　　　**H.** $\begin{bmatrix} -3 & -3 \\ 3 & 15 \end{bmatrix}$　　　**I.** $\begin{bmatrix} -1 & 3 \\ 3 & -15 \end{bmatrix}$

3. Which matrix is equal to $-6\begin{bmatrix} 2 & -7 \\ -3 & 4 \end{bmatrix}$?

   A. $\begin{bmatrix} -4 & -13 \\ -9 & -2 \end{bmatrix}$　　　**B.** $\begin{bmatrix} -8 & 1 \\ -3 & -10 \end{bmatrix}$　　　**C.** $\begin{bmatrix} -12 & 42 \\ 18 & -24 \end{bmatrix}$　　　**D.** $\begin{bmatrix} 12 & -42 \\ -18 & 24 \end{bmatrix}$

4. What is the value of x in the equation $2\begin{bmatrix} -6 & 9 \\ -3 & 1 \end{bmatrix} - \begin{bmatrix} -4 & -6 \\ -5 & 3 \end{bmatrix} = \begin{bmatrix} -8 & x \\ -1 & -1 \end{bmatrix}$?

   F. -24　　　　**G.** -12　　　　**H.** 12　　　　**I.** 24

5. What is the value of x in the equation $-x\begin{bmatrix} 5 & 12 \\ -2 & -3 \end{bmatrix} = \begin{bmatrix} -35 & -84 \\ 14 & 21 \end{bmatrix}$?

   A. -40　　　　**B.** -7　　　　**C.** 7　　　　**D.** 16

Short Response

6. The table at the right shows the sales of cell phones and televisions at an electronics store on Fridays, Saturdays, and Sundays of June and July. On which day did the store sell the most televisions during these two months? Find the answer using matrices.

June	Cell Phones	TVs
Fri	127	114
Sat	138	146
Sun	98	106

July	Cell Phones	TVs
Fri	112	117
Sat	122	152
Sun	101	92

12-2 Think About a Plan

Frequency and Histograms

Error Analysis A student made the frequency table at the right using the data below. Describe and correct the error.

40 21 28 53 24 48 50 55 42 29 22 52 43 26 44

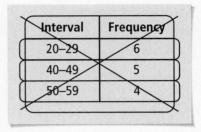

Interval	Frequency
20–29	6
40–49	5
50–59	4

Understanding the Problem

1. What does the first column represent? What errors might someone make in the first column?

2. What does the second column represent? What errors might someone make in the second column?

Planning the Solution

3. What is the minimum data value? What is the maximum?

4. What size interval would you choose to check the student's work?

5. How many intervals of that size are needed?

Getting an Answer

6. What error did the student make?

7. What change will you make to correct the student's frequency table?

12-2 Practice

Form G

Frequency and Histograms

Use the data to make a frequency table.

1. runs per game: 5 4 3 6 1 9 3 4 2 2 0 7 5 1 6

2. weight (lb): 10 12 6 15 21 11 12 9 11 8 8 13 10 17

Use the data to make a histogram.

3. number of pages: 452 409 355 378 390 367 375 514 389 438 311 411 376

4. price per yard: $9 $5 $6 $4 $8 $9 $12 $7 $10 $4 $5 $6 $6 $7

Tell whether each histogram is *uniform, symmetric,* or *skewed*.

5.
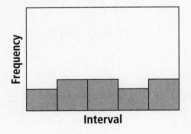

6.
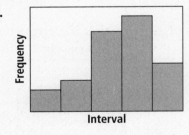

7.
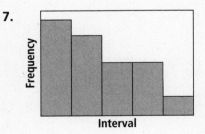

8.
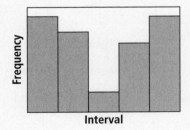

343

12-2

Practice (continued)

Frequency and Histograms

Form G

Use the data to make a cumulative frequency table.

9. call length (min):   3 5 12 39 12 3 15 23 124 2 1 1 7 19 11 6

10. package weight (kg): 1.25 3.78 2.2 12.78 3.15 4.98 3.45 9.1 1.39

Use the snowfall amounts, in inches, below.

   10 2.5 1.5 3 6 8.5 9 12 2 0.5 1 3.25 5 6.5 10.5 4.5 8 8.5

11. What is a histogram of the data that uses intervals of 2?

12. What is a histogram of the data that uses intervals of 4?

The amount of gasoline that 80 drivers bought to fill their cars' gas tanks is shown.

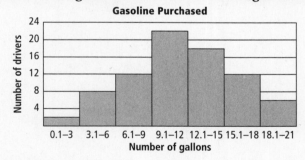

13. Which interval represents the greatest number of drivers?

14. How many drivers bought more than 12 gallons?

15. How many drivers bought 9 gallons or less?

12-2 Standardized Test Prep

Frequency and Histograms

Multiple Choice

For Exercises 1–2, choose the correct letter.

1. What is the shape of the histogram at the right?
   - **A.** symmetric
   - **B.** proportional
   - **C.** skewed
   - **D.** uniform

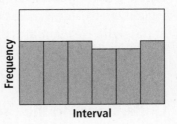

2. A student rolled two 6-sided number cubes several times. The numbers below are the sums of the numbers she rolled. Which histogram represents the data?

   7 11 2 6 7 9 12 3 7 4 8 3 5 10 7 8 11 5 4 12

   F.
   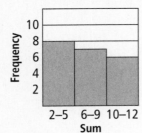

   H.
   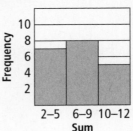

   G.
   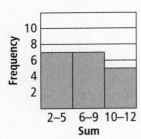

   I.
   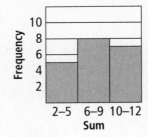

Short Response

3. The number of emails a friend received each day over the last 20 days is shown below. Create a cumulative frequency table that represents the data. For how many days did she receive 19 or fewer emails?

   15 22 18 9 32 35 14 10 34 45 21 25 6 12 7 14 16 20 5 37

12-3

Think About a Plan

Measures of Central Tendency and Dispersion

Wildlife Management A wildlife manager measured and tagged twelve adult male crocodiles. The data he collected are at the right. He estimates the crocodiles will grow 0.1 m each year. What will be the mean, median, mode, and range of the crocodiles' lengths after 4 yr?

Crocodile Lengths (m)			
2.4	2.5	2.5	2.3
2.8	2.4	2.3	2.4
2.1	2.2	2.5	2.7

Understanding the Problem

1. What do the data in the table represent?

2. How would you estimate the crocodiles' lengths after 1 year?

3. How would you estimate the crocodiles' lengths after 4 years?

Planning the Solution

4. How will the mean be changed by the crocodiles' growth?

5. How will the median be changed by the crocodiles' growth?

6. How will the mode be changed by the crocodiles' growth?

7. How will the range be changed by the crocodiles' growth?

Getting an Answer

8. What is the mean of the crocodiles' lengths after 4 years?

9. What is the median of the crocodiles' lengths after 4 years?

10. What is the mode of the crocodiles' lengths after 4 years?

11. What is the range of the crocodiles' lengths after 4 years?

12-3 Practice

Form G

Measures of Central Tendency and Dispersion

Find the mean, median, and mode of each data set. Explain which measure of central tendency best describes the data.

1. touchdowns scored:
1 3 4 4 3

2. distance from school (mi):
0.5 3.9 4.1 5 3

3. average speed (mi/hr):
36 59 47 56 67

4. price per pound:
$30 $8 $2 $5 $6

5. daily high temperature (°F):
74 69 78 80 92

6. number of volunteers:
24 22 35 19 35

Find the value of x such that the data set has the given mean.

7. 11, 12, 5, 3, x; mean 7.4

8. 55, 60, 35, 90, x; mean 51

9. 6.5, 4.3, 9.8, 2.2, x; mean 4.8

10. 100, 112, 98, 235, x; mean 127

11. 1.2, 3.4, 6.7, 5.9, x; mean 4.0

12. 34, 56, 45, 29, x; mean 40

13. One golfer's scores for the season are 88, 90, 86, 89, 96, and 85. Another golfer's scores are 91, 86, 88, 84, 90, and 83. What are the range and mean of each golfer's scores? Use your results to compare the golfers' skills.

Find the range and mean of each data set. Use your results to compare the two data sets.

14. Set A: 5 4 7 2 8
Set B: 3 8 9 2 0

15. Set C: 1.2 6.4 2.1 10 11.3
Set D: 8.2 0 3.1 6.2 9

16. Set E: 12 12 0 8
Set F: 1 15 10 2

17. Set G: 22.4 20 33.5 21.3
Set H: 6.2 15 50.4 28

18. The heights of a painter's ladders are 12 ft, 8 ft, 4 ft, 3 ft, and 6 ft. What are the mean, median, mode, and range of the ladder heights?

12-3 Practice (continued)   Form G

Measures of Central Tendency and Dispersion

Find the mean, median, mode, and range of each data set after you perform the given operation on each data value.

19. 4, 7, 5, 9, 5, 6; add 1

20. 23, 21, 17, 15, 12, 11; subtract 3

21. 1.1, 2.6, 5.6, 5, 6.7, 6; add 4.1

22. 5, 2, 8, 6, 11, 1; divide by 2

23. 12.1, 13.6, 10, 9.7, 13.2, 14; divide by 0.5

24. 3.2, 4.4, 6, 7.8, 3, 2; subtract −4

25. The lengths of Ana's last six phone calls were 3 min, 19 min, 2 min, 44 min, 120 min, and 4 min. Greg's last six phone calls were 5 min, 12 min, 4 min, 80 min, 76 min, and 15 min. Find the mean, median, mode, and range of Ana's calls and Greg's calls. Use your results to compare each person's phone call habits.

26. The table shows a basketball player's scores in five games. How many points must the basketball player score in the next game to achieve an average of 13 points per game?

Game	Points
Westlake	10
Davis	14
Mason	8
Leeberg	18
Warren	11

27. You and a friend weigh your loaded backpack every day for a week. The results are shown in the table. Find the mean, median, mode, and range of the weights of your backpack and your friend's backpack. Use your results to compare the backpack weights.

Day	Weight (lbs)	
	Yours	Friend
Monday	13.5	12.6
Tuesday	12.2	13
Wednesday	13.2	12.8
Thursday	11.6	11.6
Friday	10.5	12.5

28. Over six months, a family's electric bills averaged $55 per month. The bills for the first five months were $57.60, $60, $53.25, $50.75, and $54.05. What was the electric bill in the sixth month? Find the median, mode, and range of the six electric bills.

12-3 Standardized Test Prep

Measures of Central Tendency and Dispersion

Multiple Choice

For Exercises 1–5, choose the correct letter.

1. What is the mean of the data set 23, 36, 42, 33, 27, 32, 42, 28, 18, and 39?

   A. 23   **B.** 32   **C.** 35   **D.** 42

2. Six line segments were drawn at equal intervals across a sketch of Jackson Pond. Using the lengths of the line segments, what is the mean width of Jackson Pond?

   F. 190 ft   **H.** 301.67 ft

   G. 300 ft   **I.** 375 ft

325 ft
300 ft
375 ft
375 ft
250 ft
185 ft

3. What is the range of the data set 125, 236, 185, 125, 201, and 155?

   A. 62.5   **B.** 111   **C.** 125   **D.** 171.17

4. A world-class sprinter is the coach of a high school track team. There are 52 members of the track team. The coach times everyone on the team, including himself, running the 100-meter race. Which measure will be the most greatly affected by the inclusion of the coach's time?

   F. mean   **G.** median   **H.** mode   **I.** range

5. What is the mode of the data set 87, 78, 42, 97, 78, 92, 78, 48, 87, 94, and 59?

   A. 55   **B.** 76.36   **C.** 78   **D.** 87

Short Response

6. The table at the right shows the number of wins a baseball team had in its first five seasons. What is the mean number of wins the team had per season? What is the median number of wins the team had per season?

Season	Wins
1	68
2	89
3	76
4	59
5	93

12-4

Think About a Plan

Box-and-Whisker Plots

Basketball The heights of the players on a basketball team are 74 in., 79 in., 71.5 in., 81 in., 73 in., 76 in., 78 in., 71 in., 72 in., and 73.5 in. When the 76-in.-tall player is replaced, the percentile rank of the 73.5-in.-tall player becomes 60. Write an inequality that represents the possible heights of the replacement player.

1. How many players are there?

2. Before the replacement is made, how many players are less than or equal to 73.5 in. tall?

3. Before the replacement is made, what is the percentile rank of the 73.5-inch player? Show your work.

4. If the 76-inch player is replaced with a player less than or equal to 73.5 in. tall, how does that affect the percentile rank of the 73.5-inch tall player?

   _____

   _____

   _____

5. If the 76-inch player is replaced with a player greater than 73.5 in. tall, how does that affect the percentile rank of the 73.5-inch tall player?

   _____

   _____

   _____

6. Write an inequality that represents the height of the replacement player if the percentile rank of the 73.5-inch player becomes 60.

12-4 Practice

Form G

Box-and-Whisker Plots

Find the minimum, first quartile, median, third quartile, and maximum of each data set.

1. 220 150 200 180 320 330 300

2. 14 18 12 17 14 19 18

3. 33.2 45.1 22.3 76.7 41.9 39 32.2

4. 5 8 9 7 11 4 9 4

5. 1.4 0.2 2.3 1.0 0.8 2.4 0.9 2.1

6. 90 47 88 53 59 72 68 62 79

Make a box-and-whisker plot to represent each set of data.

7. snack prices: $0.99 $0.85 $1.05 $3.25 $1.49 $1.35 $2.79 $1.99

8. ticket buyers: 220 102 88 98 178 67 42 191 89

9. marathon race finishers: 3,869 3,981 3,764 3,786 4,310 3,993 3,258

10. winning times (min): 148 148 158 149 164 163 149 156

11. ticket prices: $25.50 $45 $24 $32.50 $32 $20 $38.50 $50 $45

12. head circumference (cm): 60.5 54.5 55 57.5 59 58.5 58.5 57 56.75 57

12-4 Practice (continued) Form G

Box-and-Whisker Plots

13. Use the box-and-whisker plot below. What does it tell you about the test scores in each class? Explain.

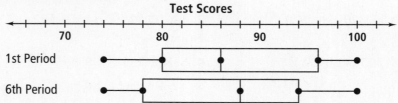

Test Scores

14. Of 200 golf scores during a city tournament, 32 are less than or equal to 90. What is the percentile rank of a score of 90?

15. Of 25 dogs, 15 weigh more than 35 pounds. What is the percentile rank of a dog that weighs 35 pounds?

16. The table shows how many votes each student who ran for class president received. What is Li's percentile rank?

Student	Votes
Brooke	112
Li	100
Suman	118
Greg	98
Grace	98

17. Ten students earned the following scores on a test: 89, 90, 76, 78, 83, 88, 91, 93, 96, and 90. Which score has a percentile rank of 90? Which score has a percentile rank of 10?

Make box-and-whisker plots to compare the data sets.

18. Test scores:
Andrew's: 79 80 87 87 99 94 77 86
Dipak's: 93 79 78 82 91 87 80 99

19. Monthly sales:
Kiera's: 17 50 26 39 6 49 62 40 8
Paul's: 18 47 32 28 12 49 60 28 15

12-4 Standardized Test Prep

Box-and-Whisker Plots

Gridded Response

Solve each exercise and enter your answer on the grid provided.

1. During the eight-game regular season, a running back ran the football for 125, 82, 105, 155, 98, 68, 111, and 95 yards. What is the third quartile of the data set?

2. During the last two weeks of work, a salesperson has sold 14, 22, 31, 7, 14, 15, 34, 42, 10, and 17 items each day. What is the first quartile of the data set?

3. This year, a toy drive for a charity lasted 15 days. The charity received 55, 63, 44, 110, 99, 67, 88, 75, 53, 47, 64, 76, 92, 56, and 110 toys on the days of the drive. What is the median of the data?

4. Using the box-and-whisker plot shown below, what is the interquartile range of the data?

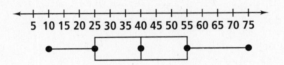

5. Of the 32 students in the class, 12 stand 5 feet 5 inches or are shorter. What is the percentile rank of a student who is 5 feet 5 inches tall?

1. 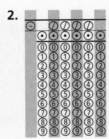 2. 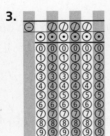 3. 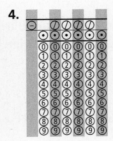 4.   5.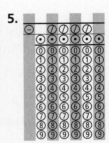

12-5   **Think About a Plan**

Samples and Surveys

Travel A travel agent wants to determine whether a trip to France is a popular vacation for young adults. How could each factor described below cause bias in the survey results?

    a. The agent interviews people at an international airport.
    b. The agent asks, "Would you prefer to vacation in France or Italy?"
    c. Of the people interviewed, 86% took a French class in high school.

1. What reasons might a person have for being at an international airport? How might those reasons cause bias in the survey results?

2. Name three locations for the agent's survey that are less likely to cause bias in the survey results.

3. How many different answers can the agent expect to his question, "Would you prefer to vacation in France or Italy?" How might the set of potential answers cause bias in the survey results?

4. Write three questions for the agent's survey that are less likely to cause bias in the survey results.

5. How might someone's familiarity with a foreign language create bias in a survey about travel to a foreign country?

6. How could the travel agent reduce bias caused by the potential customers' familiarity with French?

12-5

Practice

Samples and Surveys

Form G

Determine whether each data set is *qualitative* or *quantitative*.

1. price of cell phones

2. video game sales

3. favorite clothing brand

4. age at graduation

5. ounces per package

6. birthday month

Determine whether each data set is *univariate* or *bivariate*.

7. ages and gender of your neighbors

8. weights of your friends' pets

9. how many TV shows your friends watch

10. distances ran

11. number of games played

12. width and depth of lakes

Determine whether the sampling method is *random*, *systematic*, or *stratified*. Tell whether the method will produce a good sample.

13. A bottle manufacturer checks the quality of every third bottle it makes.

14. A pollster phones every fourth registered Republican in the state to find out which candidate for Senator the person prefers.

15. Every student whose driver's license ends in an odd number is asked to complete a survey on safe driving habits.

16. You ask 15 of the residents on your street whether they support the local bond issue to build a community center across town.

Determine whether each question is biased. Explain your answer.

17. What is your favorite television show?

18. Would you rather go to a boring museum or an exciting amusement park?

12-5

Practice (continued)   *Form G*

Samples and Surveys

19. You want to find out how much families in your community spend on entertainment each month. You ask every tenth person at the local movie theater. How might this cause a bias in your results?

20. You want to find out how much time students in your school spend doing math homework each week. You ask every fourth student in your math class. How might this cause a bias in your results?

21. An ice cream store owner wants to determine whether a new flavor, café mocha, would be popular with his customers. How could each factor below cause bias in the survey results?
    a. The owner interviews customers outside a local coffee shop.

    b. The owner interviews his adult customers.

    c. The owner asks, "Which flavor would you prefer: café mocha or chocolate?"

In each situation, identify the population and sample. Tell whether each sample is a *random*, *systematic*, or *stratified* sample.

22. At an online store, every tenth purchaser is asked to complete an online survey.

23. You text all of the people in your cell phone's contact list and ask them what their favorite website is.

Classify the data as *qualitative* or *quantitative*, and as *univariate* or *bivariate*.

24. age of movie goers at the Tuesday afternoon showing of a popular film

25. names of U.S. Senators and how many terms they have served

26. length and weight of fish caught in fishing contest

27. hours of daylight per day in Anchorage, Alaska

28. number of jellybeans for each color in a five-gallon jar

29. names of baseball players and their batting averages over three seasons

12-5

Standardized Test Prep

Samples and Surveys

Multiple Choice

For Exercises 1–6, choose the correct letter.

1. When statisticians collect information to find characteristics of a large group of people, they survey part of the group. What is the part of the group called?
   A. specimen **B.** part **C.** population **D.** sample

2. You want to find out what the favorite hot lunch in the school cafeteria is among the high school students. At an assembly for the whole school, you decide to survey all students who are sitting on the end of their rows in the auditorium. What type of survey are you conducting?
   F. biased **G.** random **H.** systematic **I.** stratified

3. A survey is being conducted to determine the favorite movies for various ages. Which of the following best describes this survey?
   A. qualitative and univariate **C.** quantitative and univariate
   B. qualitative and bivariate **D.** quantitative and bivariate

4. A town wants to know the number of cell phones in each household. The town divides the population up by neighborhood and surveys a random number of households in each. What type of survey is this?
   F. biased **G.** random **H.** systematic **I.** stratified

5. In order to find out what the best restaurant in town is, you call 25 of your friends at random. What type of survey is this?
   A. stratified **B.** systematic **C.** biased **D.** unbiased

6. A store would like to understand what is important to their customers. They randomly select every 50th customer to survey. What type of survey is this?
   F. biased **G.** random **H.** systematic **I.** stratified

Short Response

7. A pollster is trying to determine who the people in the state think will be the best candidate for senate. Her staff calls 1000 people in the 4 major cities of the state. Will this plan give a good sample? Explain.

Name _____ Class _____ Date _____

12-6 | Think About a Plan

Permutations and Combinations

Media The call signs of radio and television stations in the United States generally begin with the letter W east of the Mississippi River and the letter K west of the Mississippi. Repetition of letters is allowed.

    a. How many different call signs are possible if each station uses a W or K followed by 3 letters?

    b. How many different call signs are possible if each station uses a W or K followed by 4 letters?

1. How many different call signs are possible if a station uses a W followed by 3 letters? Use the formula for permutations.

2. How many different call signs are possible if a station uses K followed by 3 letters? Compare this answer to the one above.

3. How would you combine your answers above to determine how many different call signs are possible if each station uses a W or K followed by 3 letters?

4. How many different call signs are possible if each station uses a W or K followed by 3 letters?

5. How many different call signs are possible if a station uses a W followed by 4 letters? Use the formula for permutations.

6. How many different call signs are possible if each station uses a W or K followed by 4 letters?

12-6 Practice

Permutations and Combinations

Form G

1. A six-character license plate number can begin with any two letters and end with four one-digit numbers.
   a. How many possible choices are there for the first two characters? For the last four characters?
   b. How many different six-character license plate numbers are possible?

2. Use the map at the right and the Multiplication Counting Principle to find each of the following:
   a. the number of routes from Piketon to Dublin
   b. the number of routes from Piketon to Blaise
   c. the number of routes from Blaise to Piketon

3. Six runners are available for the 400-meter relay. Four runners are needed to run 100 m a piece, in a specified order. How many different runner lineups can the coach consider for the relay with one of each?

4. A restaurant's menu offers 8 different sandwiches and 5 side dishes. How many lunch combinations can you order?

Find the value of each expression.

5. $_5P_2$

6. $_4P_3$

7. $_9P_3$

8. $_{10}P_3$

9. $_9P_4$

10. $_6P_3$

11. $_5P_3$

12. $_{11}P_2$

13. $_8P_5$

14. $_5P_4$

15. $_6P_5$

16. $_{100}P_2$

17. There are 100 songs on your music player. In how many different ways can you arrange 20 songs to listen to while exercising?

Find the value of each expression.

18. $_5C_2$

19. $_{10}C_8$

20. $_5C_4$

21. $_9C_4$

22. $_6C_3$

23. $_7C_5$

24. $_4C_3$

25. $_8C_4$

26. $_6C_5$

27. $_5C_4$

28. $_7C_3$

29. $_{10}C_3$

12-6 Practice (continued)   Form G
Permutations and Combinations

30. There are 15 slips of paper in a jar. Each slip has a different name on it. How many ways can you draw 5 names from the jar?

Find the number of combinations of numbers taken four at a time can be formed from each set of cards.

31. [23] [24] [25] [26] [27]   **32.** [10] [11] [12] [13] [14] [15]

33. [9] [11] [13] [15] [17] [19]   **34.** [5] [6] [7] [8]

Explain whether each situation is a combination problem or a permutation problem.

35. Your friends rented 6 different video games. In how many different orders can you play the 6 games?

36. There are 20 games to choose from at the local game store. How many different sets of 4 games could you choose to rent?

37. The Aluru family has a garage door that opens with a 4-digit PIN. They decide to base the code on Mrs. Aluru's birthday: 01/24/63. How many PINs are there that use four of the digits in Mrs. Aluru's birthday?

38. You have 10 photographs to choose from. How many different ways can you arrange 5 of the photographs in a single row above the sofa?

39. There are 6 class periods in the school day. There are 10 subjects to choose from. How many different class schedules are possible?

Determine which value is greater.

40. $_9P_6$ or $_6P_3$ **41.** $_9C_6$ or $_9C_5$ **42.** $_{10}C_4$ or $_{10}C_6$ **43.** $_{10}P_4$ or $_6P_6$

12-6 Standardized Test Prep

Permutations and Combinations

Multiple Choice

For Exercises 1–7, choose the correct letter.

1. What is the value of $_5P_3$?

   A. 20 **B.** 40 **C.** 60 **D.** 120

2. What is the value of $_{10}C_6$?

   F. 210 **G.** 5040 **H.** 151,200 **I.** 3,628,800

3. There are 12 people on the basketball team. How many different 5-person starting lineups can be chosen?

   A. 120 **B.** 792 **C.** 95,040 **D.** 3,991,680

4. The manager of a baseball team has 15 players to choose from for his 9-person batting order. How many different ways can he arrange the players in the lineup?

   F. 5005 **G.** 362,880 **H.** 3,603,600 **I.** 1,816,214,400

5. For a road trip, a friend is going to place 5 CDs into her CD player. She has 9 CDs to choose from. How many different selections of CDs can she make?

   A. 126 **B.** 3024 **C.** 15,120 **D.** 362,880

6. There are 8 students on the ballot who are running for student council. Four students will be selected for the council. How many different groups of students can be selected for the council?

   F. 24 **G.** 70 **H.** 1680 **I.** 40,320

7. A website requires a 4-digit numerical password in which the digits cannot repeat. How many possible passwords are there?

   A. 24 **B.** 5040 **C.** 151,200 **D.** 3,628,800

Short Response

8. A restaurant serves 4 different sandwiches, 3 different sides, and 3 different beverages for lunch. How many possible meals are there? Show your work.

12-7 Think About a Plan

Theoretical and Experimental Probability

Transportation Out of 80 workers surveyed at a company, 17 walk to work.

a. What is the experimental probability that a randomly selected worker at that company walks to work?

b. Predict about how many of the 3600 workers at the company walk to work.

Understanding the Problem

1. Write a fraction that represents the probability that a randomly selected worker at the company walks to work.

$$P(\text{walks to work}) = \frac{\text{number surveyed who walk to work}}{\text{total number surveyed}} = \frac{\Box}{\Box}$$

Planning the Solution

2. Let w represent the number of workers who walk to work. Write an equation that could be used to predict the total number of workers who walk to work.

$$w = \frac{\Box}{\Box} \times \boxed{}$$

Getting an Answer

3. Solve the equation.

4. Is your answer reasonable? Explain.

_____

_____

5. The experimental probability is _____, and I predict that approximately _____ workers walk to work.

12-7 Practice

Form G

Theoretical and Experimental Probability

You spin a spinner that has 15 equal-sized sections numbered 1 to 15. Find the theoretical probability of landing on the given section(s) of the spinner.

1. $P(15)$

2. $P(\text{odd number})$

3. $P(\text{even number})$

4. $P(\text{not } 5)$

5. $P(\text{less than } 5)$

6. $P(\text{greater than } 8)$

7. $P(\text{multiple of } 5)$

8. $P(\text{less than } 16)$

9. $P(\text{prime number})$

10. You roll a number cube. What is the probability that you will roll a number less than 5?

11. The probability that a spinner will land on a red section is $\frac{1}{6}$. What is the probability that the spinner will not land on a red section?

You choose a marble at random from a bag containing 2 red marbles, 4 green marbles, and 3 blue marbles. Find the odds.

12. odds in favor of red

13. odds in favor of blue

14. odds against green

15. odds against red

16. odds in favor of green

17. odds against blue

18. You roll a number cube. What are the odds that you will roll an even number?

12-7 Practice (continued) Form G

Theoretical and Experimental Probability

One hundred twenty randomly selected students at Roosevelt High School were asked to name their favorite sport. The results are shown in the table. Find the experimental probability that a student selected at random makes the given response.

Favorite Sport Survey	
Sport	Number of Responses
Basketball	30
Baseball	22
Football	34
Soccer	20
Other	14

19. P(basketball)

20. P(soccer)

21. P(baseball)

22. P(football)

23. A meteorologist says that the probability of rain today is 35%. What is the probability that it will not rain?

24. Hank usually makes 11 out of every 20 of his free throws. What is the probability that he will miss his next free throw?

25. There are 250 freshmen at Central High School. You survey 50 randomly selected freshmen and find that 35 plan to go to the school party on Friday. How many freshmen are likely to be at the party?

26. The Widget Company randomly selects its widgets and checks for defects. If 5 of the 300 selected widgets are defective, how many defective widgets would you expect in the 1500 widgets manufactured today?

12-7 Standardized Test Prep

Theoretical and Experimental Probability

Multiple Choice

For Exercises 1–5, choose the correct letter.

1. A letter from the word *MISSISSIPPI* is selected at random. What is the probability that the letter is *I*?

   A. $\frac{2}{11}$ **B.** $\frac{1}{5}$ **C.** $\frac{4}{11}$ **D.** $\frac{2}{5}$

2. You spin a spinner that has 8 equal-sized sections numbered 1 to 8. Which event is least likely to occur?
   F. The number is even.   **H.** The number is less than 3.
   G. The number is greater than 3.   **I.** The number is a multiple of 5.

3. You toss a number cube. What are the odds against getting a number less than 3?
   A. $2:1$ **B.** $1:2$ **C.** $3:1$ **D.** $1:3$

4. A meteorologist says that the probability of snow today is 45%. What is the probability that it will *not* snow?
   F. $\frac{2}{11}$ **G.** $\frac{9}{20}$ **H.** $\frac{11}{20}$ **I.** $\frac{9}{11}$

5. What is the probability that a number picked from the set $\{-4, -3, -2, -1, 0, 1, 2, 3, 4, 5\}$ will be a solution of $2x + 5 > 1$?
   A. 20%   **B.** 30%   **C.** 70%   **D.** 80%

Short Response

6. A pizza restaurant is having a contest. The restaurant advertises that one out of every 25 customers will win a small pizza.
   a. What is the probability that a customer will win?
   b. If the restaurant has 275 customers on Monday, how many winners would you expect?

12-8

Think About a Plan

Probability of Compound Events

Phone Poll A pollster conducts a survey by phone. The probability that a call does not result in a person taking this survey is 85%. What is the probability that a pollster makes 4 calls and none result in a person taking the survey?

Understanding the Problem

1. What is the probability that the first call results in the person not taking the survey?

2. What is the probability that the second call results in the person not taking the survey?

3. Are the first and second calls *independent* or *dependent* events?

4. How could you find the probability that the first two calls result in neither person taking the survey?

Planning the Solution

5. Write an expression for the probability that none of the 4 calls result in a person taking the survey.

Getting an Answer

6. Evaluate the expression you wrote in Exercise 5.

7. Explain whether it is more likely that the 4 calls result in no one taking the survey or that at least one person takes the survey.

12-8 **Practice**

Probability of Compound Events

Form G

You spin a spinner that has 12 equal-sized sections numbered 1 to 12. Find each probability.

1. $P(3 \text{ or } 4)$

2. $P(\text{even or } 7)$

3. $P(\text{even or odd})$

4. $P(\text{multiple of } 3 \text{ or odd})$

5. $P(\text{odd or multiple of } 5)$

6. $P(\text{less than } 5 \text{ or greater than } 9)$

7. $P(\text{even or less than } 8)$

8. $P(\text{multiple of } 2 \text{ or multiple of } 3)$

9. $P(\text{odd or greater than } 4)$

10. $P(\text{multiple of } 5 \text{ or multiple of } 2)$

11. Reasoning Why can you use $P(A \text{ or } B) = P(A) + P(B) - P(A \text{ and } B)$ for both mutually exclusive events and overlapping events?

You roll a red number cube and a blue number cube. Find each probability.

12. $P(\text{red } 2 \text{ and blue } 2)$

13. $P(\text{red odd and blue even})$

14. $P(\text{red greater than } 2 \text{ and blue } 4)$

15. $P(\text{red odd and blue less than } 4)$

16. $P(\text{red } 1 \text{ or } 2 \text{ and blue } 5 \text{ or } 6)$

17. $P(\text{red } 6 \text{ and blue even})$

18. $P(\text{red greater than } 4 \text{ and blue greater than } 3)$

12-8 Practice (continued)   Form G
Probability of Compound Events

19. The probability that Bob will make a free throw is $\frac{2}{5}$. What is the probability that Bob will make his next two free throws?

You choose a marble at random from a bag containing 3 blue marbles, 5 red marbles, and 2 green marbles. You replace the marble and then choose again. Find each probability.

20. P(both blue)   **21.** P(both red)

22. P(blue then green)   **23.** P(red then blue)

24. P(green then red)   **25.** P(both green)

You choose a tile at random from a bag containing 2 tiles with X, 6 tiles with Y, and 4 tiles with Z. You pick a second tile without replacing the first. Find each probability.

26. P(X then Y)   **27.** P(both Y)

28. P(Y then X)   **29.** P(Z then X)

30. P(both Z)   **31.** P(Y then Z)

32. There are 12 girls and 14 boys in math class. The teacher puts the names of the students in a hat and randomly picks one name. Then the teacher picks another name without replacing the first. What is the probability that both students picked are boys?

12-8 Standardized Test Prep

Probability of Compound Events

Multiple Choice

For Exercises 1–5, choose the correct letter.

1. You spin a spinner that has 10 equal-sized sections numbered 1 to 10. Which compound event is most likely to occur?

   A. a 2 or a 3
   B. a 1 or a number greater than 8
   C. an odd number or a 7
   D. an even number or a 5

2. What type of compound event is represented by the roll of two number cubes?

   F. dependent events
   G. overlapping events
   H. independent events
   I. mutually exclusive events

3. You choose a marble at random from a bag containing 3 orange marbles, 4 green marbles, and 3 yellow marbles. You replace the marble and then pick a second marble. What is the probability that you will pick a green marble both times?

   A. $\frac{6}{50}$
   B. $\frac{2}{15}$
   C. $\frac{4}{25}$
   D. $\frac{8}{45}$

4. Seven of 28 domino tiles show the same number of dots on each side. These tiles are called *doubles*. You pick a domino tile at random. Then you pick another tile without replacing the first. What is the probability that both tiles are doubles?

   F. $\frac{3}{56}$
   G. $\frac{1}{18}$
   H. $\frac{1}{16}$
   I. $\frac{7}{648}$

5. There are 8 jellybeans in a bag. The probability of randomly picking two orange jellybeans without replacement is $\frac{3}{14}$. How many orange jellybeans are in the bag?

   A. 3 orange jellybeans
   B. 4 orange jellybeans
   C. 5 orange jellybeans
   D. 6 orange jellybeans

Extended Response

6. There are 20 marbles in a bag. The probability that you pick one red marble at random is $\frac{1}{5}$. What is the probability that you will pick two red marbles in a row if you do not replace the first? Explain.